Ritual, Myth,
and the Modernist Text

This book is part of a series. The publisher will accept continuation orders which may be cancelled at any time and which provide for automatic billing and shipping of each title in the series upon publication. Please write for details.

Ritual, Myth, and the Modernist Text

The Influence of Jane Ellen Harrison on Joyce, Eliot, and Woolf

Martha C. Carpentier

Seton Hall University
South Orange, New Jersey, USA

Gordon and Breach Publishers

Australia Canada China France Germany India
Japan Luxembourg Malaysia The Netherlands
Russia Singapore Switzerland

Amsteldijk 166
1st Floor
1079 LH Amsterdam
The Netherlands

Opening chapter illustrations and selected excerpts printed with permission of Cambridge University Press, New York.

Chapter 1 epigraph originally appeared in *Ancient Art and Ritual*, Jane Ellen Harrison, Greenwood Press: Westport, Connecticut, 1969.
Copyright © 1951 Oxford University Press: United Kingdom. Reprinted with permission of Oxford University Press.

Cover art by Ralph Carpentier.

British Library Cataloguing in Publication Data

Carpentier, Martha C.
    Ritual, myth, and the modernist text : the influence of
    Jane Ellen Harrison on Joyce, Eliot, and Woolf. – (The
    library of anthropology. Anthropology and literature ; v. 12 –
    ISSN   0141-1012)
    1. Harrison, Jane Ellen, 1850–1928 – Influence 2. Mythology
    in literature
    I. Title
    301

ISBN   90-5700-517-4

For Dennis Burns

Contents

Introduction to the Series

The Library of Anthropology now encompasses both a classical orientation and current directions in the field. It seeks to promote an awareness of new developments and changing orientations, while continuing to stress its long-term interest in traditional anthropological fields.

The section Physical Anthropology and Archaeology continues to address the substantive and theoretical issues of biological and cultural evolution. Ethnographic Studies and Theory remains a major focus. The range of interest is global in terms of contemporary cultures and ethnic populations, and ethnohistorical in terms of past cultures and societies. Three new sections augment the more traditional four-fields approach to anthropology.

Volumes in the section Anthropology and Language address issues in linguistic anthropology broadly conceived: studies of the communicative means people use to accomplish social ends—from political oratory to storytelling, from joking to sermonizing, and from gossiping to testifying. Anthropological studies that explore the interrelation of language and political economy are especially encouraged.

Works in Anthropology and Literature examine and attempt to define the areas in which these two disciplines come together and blend the personal, poetic and scientific. Cultural or ethnic studies, literature as ethnography, literary theory in anthropological studies, and anthropological theory in cultural (ethnic) studies are topics for consideration.

Volumes in Anthropology and Religion explore the practice of religion and attendant notions of ritual, identity and world view from a variety of theoretical and methodological perspectives in a number of settings and contexts.

Anthony L. LaRuffa

Joel S. Savishinsky

Acknowledgments

I would like to thank Philip Sicker for his encouragement and guidance from the beginning and Rose DeAngelis for the opportunity to complete this project.

I would also like to thank my mother Sallie Blake for invaluable indexing and copy editing expertise; my father Ralph Carpentier for the cover art; and my husband Donald Sherblom for his unstinting support of me and my work.

1 : INTRODUCTION

In 1923 two important essays appeared, charting the immense changes taking place in fiction: T.S. Eliot's review "*Ulysses*, Order and Myth," and Virginia Woolf's "Mr. Bennett and Mrs. Brown." What were some of these changes? Eliot and Woolf agree that literature must grow out of the writer's direct, concrete, emotional experience of life, not out of an abstract, conceptual or moral construct imposed on life. In this sense they both saw their generation, the "Georgian" to use Woolf's nomenclature, as radically opposed to the past, specifically to Victorian and Edwardian attitudes and literary conventions.

Eliot posed himself against Richard Aldington: both were "agreed as to what we want in principle, and agreed to call it classicism," but they disagreed as to how classicism should be achieved and "as to what contemporary writing exhibits a tendency in that direction." Eliot then defined a contrast, crucial in its ramifications, between the old orientation toward classicism in literature and the new:

> One can be 'classical', in a sense, by turning away from nine-tenths of the material which lies at hand and selecting only mummified stuff from a museum. ... Or one can be classical in tendency by doing the best one can with the material at hand. ... And in this material I include the emotions and feelings of the writer himself, which, for that writer, are simply material which he must accept — not virtues to be enlarged or vices to be diminished. (176–7)

Here Eliot voiced the modernist's conviction that writing should derive from life itself, "the material at hand," "the emotions and feelings of the writer," not from abstractions imposed on life by the writer, such as moral preconceptions — "virtues to be enlarged or vices to be diminished." Note, however, that Eliot termed this new orientation to life and art "classicism," thus suggesting that this literary innovation rose out of an equally radical reevaluation of classical literature and myth. No longer did modern writers consider the classics divorced from life, "mummified stuff from a museum;" rather, classical myth had become "living material."

In his review of *Ulysses*, Eliot praised Joyce's method of "manipulating a continuous parallel between contemporaneity and antiquity," and advocated the substitution of this "mythical method" for traditional "narrative method" as a strategy others should "pursue", as indeed he himself had done in *The Waste Land*. But he did not perceive of myth as an artificial construct or frame for the writer to pin his or her experience on. Far beyond merely a fictional strategy, for Eliot, the mythic method provided "a way of controlling, of ordering, of giving a shape and a significance to the immense panorma of futility and anarchy which is contemporary history" (177–8). Myth did not merely supply allegories for modern experience; rather myth, as felt and lived by the modern writer, could provide an antidote to the sterility of modern life.

Eliot attributed this new conception of myth to science. Not only did Joyce's paralleling with the *Odyssey* have the "importance of a scientific discovery," as Eliot noted, but it was made possible by scientific discoveries. Eliot concluded that "psychology ... ethnology and *The Golden Bough* have concurred to make possible what was impossible even a few years ago." However, these were culminations of earlier scientific innovations and discoveries, announced to the world largely in the year 1871, when Darwin published *The Descent of Man*, firmly linking his theory of evolution and natural selection to man. The slow triumph of Darwinian evolutionism had made a connection apparent between "primitive" and "civilized" humanity where none had been thought to exist, validating the study of primitive peoples in the new science of anthropology. Anthropology in turn radically altered myth interpretation. Also in 1871, E.B. Tylor published one of the first and most influential handbooks of anthropology, *Primitive Culture*, opening, along with Robertson Smith and others, the whole world of primitive religion for discussion and study.

Ironically, the evolutionists whom Yeats "detested" for depriving him "of the simple-minded religion of [his] childhood" ("TV" 142–3) opened to his generation a whole new world of religious meaning more suited to their needs than Christianity: the world of primitive folktale, myth, and ritual. The steps by which anthropology became this source of spiritual renewal and potent symbolism were gradual and need to be traced more searchingly than they have been. Overemphasis on the contribution of Sir James Frazer has obscured the subtle progression and the communal nature of this change, and important contributions made by Frazer's contemporaries have been too long ignored.

Virginia Woolf, like Eliot, felt strongly that her generation must write out of the "living material" of the individual's subjective experience.

In "Mr. Bennett and Mrs. Brown," she objected to the Edwardian writers because they attempted to create character through "artificial" "literary conventions," moral visions of what the world ought to be, not what it is (115). For Woolf and the "Georgian writers," among whom she included Forster, Lawrence, Strachey, Joyce, and Eliot, the purpose of literature was not abstract or moral, but emotional and experiential: "not to preach doctrines, sing songs, or celebrate the glories of the British empire," but to look at Mrs. Brown "as she is," sitting "in the corner of the carriage," and to communicate "human nature," "life" itself (102, 110). Woolf suggested one reason for this change in literary values: "All human relations have shifted — those between masters and servants, husbands and wives, parents and children. And when human relations change there is at the same time a change in religion, conduct, politics, and literature" (96).

Woolf's feminism is implicit here: traditional hierarchies have broken down particularly between men and women, either "husbands and wives" or "masters and servants." This idea is expressed in her metaphors and examples, which all focus on women. The compelling Mrs. Brown is an instance of woman — "very small, very tenacious; at once very frail and very heroic" — demanding to be looked at and understood. To illustrate social change Woolf chose the "character of one's cook," at once an example of the breakdown of social hierarchy and of women's emerging financial independence: "The Victorian cook lived like a leviathan in the lower depths, formidible, silent, obscure, inscrutible; the Georgian cook is a creature of sunshine and fresh air; in and out of the drawing-room, now to borrow the *Daily Herald*, now to ask advice about a hat." For an example of the changing roles of husband and wife she chose "the married life of the Carlyles" and asked her readers to "bewail the waste, the futility, for him and for her, of the horrible domestic tradition which made it seemly for a woman of genius to spend her time chasing beetles, scouring saucepans, instead of writing books" (96). To Woolf it was a hallmark of her generation that a wife need no longer sublimate her own "genius" to further her husband's; she might, like Woolf herself, write her own books.

How was this incipient feminism encouraged by the Georgian generation's new "classicism"? Woolf offers an enigmatic and revealing clue: "Read the *Agamemnon*, and see whether, in process of time, your sympathies are not almost entirely with Clytemnestra" (96). The classical literature most revitalized in the Georgian generation was Greek drama, largely due to the translations of Gilbert Murray. From 1904, when his translation of Euripides' *Hippolytus* became a box office hit, through the early 30s, one Murray translation after another was staged, with great critical and popular success. Murray's reinterpretation of Greek drama had been inspired by the new anthropology, largely through the influence of Jane Ellen Harrison, Frazer's contemporary. Again, for the origins of this movement which resulted in a generation able to reappraise Clytemnestra — a female archetype of primitive violence, sexuality, and power — we must return to the crucial source-year, 1871, when Nietzsche published *The Birth of Tragedy*.

No classicist, philologist, archeologist, or anthropologist could view Greek drama or myth in the same way after Nietzsche's startling un-earthing of the dark "Dionysian" side of Greek religion. Contrary to common 19th-century idealizations of Hellenism as "clear light and truth and reason and order and symmetry and the harmony of the heavenly bodies and all the supposed Greek virtues" (Harrison, *T* 395), Nietzsche theorized that the Olympian or "Apollinian" theocracy, sym-bolized principally by the rationalist Apollo, represented only half the Hellenic ethos; the other half was expressed through the more primi-tive, often violent worship of Dionysus. For Nietzsche the Dionysian Greek was no rationalist, but passionately "intoxicated" by religion, in its earliest form comprised of "festivals centered in extravagant sexual licentiousness ..., [a] horrible mixture of sensuality and cruelty which has always seemed to me to be the real 'witches' brew ..." (Nietzsche 33, 39). Later, after "reconciliation" between the two cults, "dually-minded revelers" expressed themselves in "song and pantomime ... and the Dionysian *music* [that] in particular incited awe and terror" (40).

Nietzsche termed the ancient festivals a "witches' brew" with more accuracy than he realized, since archaeological research had not yet established the primacy of matriarchal goddesses behind Dionysian fertility rituals. He could see that in the "Dionysian orgies of the Greeks," "nature for the first time attains her artistic jubilee," but for Nietzsche both the Apollinian and Dionysian principles were domi-nated by male archetypes; no goddesses or heroines figure in his con-ception of Hellenic religion. Briefly, this attitude is revealed by his strange prejudice against Euripides, whose plays are dominated by powerful female archetypes. This prejudice is especially odd since Euripides' *Bacchae* had always been the primary source for informa-tion about Dionysian rites. Further, Nietzsche did not discuss Aeschylus' Oresteian trilogy in the *Birth*, again odd because these plays, begin-ning with Clytemnestra's murder of Agamemnon and culminating in the matriarchal Eumenides' demand for revenge, tell the story of the penultimate confrontation between the old Dionysian religion and the new Olympian or Apollinian religion. Nietzsche focused instead on Aeschylus' *Prometheus*, since Prometheus was his ideal Dionysian hero, presenting a view of early Greek religion as dominated by male archetype as the later.

It remained for a later generation to discover that "the Great Mother is prior to the masculine divinities," that even Dionysus was a later cult fused with earlier mysteries and rituals dominated by goddess-worship (Harrison, *T* ix). The power of matriarchal goddesses in pre-Olympian Greek religion — Artemis, Demeter, Persephone and others — began to emerge in Frazer's *Golden Bough*, primarily in Part V, "Spirits of the Corn and of the Wild," vols. i and ii. However, Frazer did not consciously pursue the status of women in early Greek religion; rather his pursuit of the male archetype, the "Dying God," led him to discover that at the basis of ritual sacrifice lay fertility cults, and at the basis of fertility cults stood powerful primitive mother-goddesses, which he then delineated as his purposes required.

The study of Hellenic matriarchal goddesses was pursued more vigorously by Jane Ellen Harrison, an archaeologist and classicist who once described herself as a "disciple of Nietzsche," but who researched Dionysian ritual with a scientific exactitude undreamt of by him (*T* viii). In her first major work, the *Prolegomena to the Study of Greek Religion* (1903) — which, according to Gilbert Murray, "transformed the whole approach to the study of Greek religion" (*JEH* 11) — Harrison explained the differences between "chthonic" matriarchal rituals and Homeric patriarchal rituals, then explored the meaning of matriarchal rituals at seasonal festivals, and described "The Making of a Goddess," the genesis of Hellenic female archetypes of witch, mother and maid, and tripartite goddesses such as the Erinyes and the Charites. On Crete, the cradle of Greek religion, Harrison explored exciting new archaeological discoveries which revealed to her the primacy of Dionysian worship, "the ancient ritual of the Mother and the Son which long preceded the worship of the Olympians" (*R* 71). In *Themis* (1912), her second major work, Harrison linked Dionysian rituals — "dromenon" or "things done" — and the Dionysian dithyramb or song and pantomime, with the beginnings of Greek drama, forming the "ritual theory" with Gilbert Murray. As she wrote in her slim volume of *Reminiscences*, "Art in some sense springs out of Religion; and ... between them is a connecting link, a bridge, and that bridge is ritual.

On that bridge, emotionally, I halt" (84). Her scholarship provided a new understanding of the powerful female archetypes so prevalent in primitive Greek ritual and drama, leading to a younger generation of writers whose "sympathies" could be "almost entirely with Clytemnestra" — mother, lover, powerful queen, and vengeful witch.

The prominence of women in modernist literature is extraordinary. Think merely of Mrs. Wilcox, Margaret and Helen in Forster's *Howards End*, Gudrun and Ursula in Lawrence's *Women in Love*, Mrs. Ramsay and Lily in *To the Lighthouse*, and Molly in *Ulysses*, to name only the most obvious. I do not think it is too rash to assert that female archetypes assume a force in the writing of the Georgian generation that they have rarely known at any time before or since. By "female archetypes" I mean women rendered as symbols of power, both creative and destructive. And, since archetypal images are universal and unchanging, female archetypes appearing in these modern works bear many of the qualities and functions of the three traditional archetypal female forms found in myth: Earth-mother, witch, and virgin (or, more precisely, maiden). Through a greater understanding of their qualities and functions in Greek myth and drama, we can better understand their qualities and functions in modernist literature. For writers like Joyce and Eliot, who consciously employed the "mythic method," the comparative methodology of myth criticism is the best way to fully appreciate the meaning of these archetypal figures.

At the same time that female archetypes began to loom large in the literary imagery of this period, the female ethos or principle they represent began to permeate many works with a sense of renewal and hope. As feminist cultural critiques from Simone DeBeauvoir to Hélène Cixous have made clear, the female principle in Western culture has been traditionally embodied in Nature, the male principle in God; the female in Earth, the male in Heaven, in a hierarchical relation that has long devalued women: "This opposition to woman cuts endlessly across all the oppositions that order culture. It's the classic opposition, dualist and hierarchical. Man/Woman automatically means great/small, superior/inferior ... means high or low, means Nature/History, means transformation/inertia" (Cixous, 44). The manifold series of oppositions that this gender dichotomy has traditionally ratified can be found in "every theory of culture, every theory of society, the whole conglomeration of symbolic systems ... everything that's organized as discourse, art, religion, the family, language," but it is particularly dominant in Western culture because of the binaristic Platonic origins of Christian theology, reflected in all Western cultural artifacts until very recently (44). The female principle is material, the male abstract; the female emotional and sexual, the male rational; the female experiential, the male cognitive; the female mutable, the male eternal; the female amoral, the male moral; the female collective, the male individualistic; the female undifferentiating, the male hierarchical, etc. Nature, the ultimate female principle, is indifferent; she creates and destroys regardless of the moral behavior of the individual. For the female principle to dominate in the Judeo-Christian world vision meant utter disaster: the domination of chaos, the dissolution of order, the invalidation of morality, the alienation of man from God, an existence rendered meaningless because physical life, without the spiritual promise of eternity, ends only in death.

In the creative vision of the Georgian writers, however, the dominance of the female principle — the "'amoral fertilisable untrustworthy engaging shrewd limited prudent indifferent *Weib*,'" to use Joyce's words — does not represent disaster but salvation (Ellmann 517). The world of primitive myth and ritual opened to the modernists through anthropology showed that, contrary to Christianity, eternity in primitive matriarchal religion was envisioned through regeneration, through sexuality. Suddenly, Earth could provide a fruitful alternative to Heaven, with its now vitiated patriarchal vision of eternity through the salvation of individual souls, and through moral rectitude. For Georgian writers, particularly Forster, Joyce, Lawrence and Woolf, life gains meaning through physical realities that recur eternally, year after year, which they appropriately symbolized in the female archetype. Such fecundity is embodied, for instance, in Mrs. Ramsay, and vividly contrasted with the desiccation of her husband, the Apollinian philosopher who needs her life desperately when his abstractions leave him lost and empty:

> It was sympathy he wanted, to be assured of his genius, first of all, and then to be taken within the circle of life, warmed and soothed, to have his senses restored to him, his barrenness made fertile, and all the rooms of the house made full of life — the drawing-room; behind the drawing-room the kitchen; above the kitchen the bedrooms; and beyond them the nurseries; they must be furnished, they must be filled with life. (59)

Mrs. Ramsay dies, yet she lives on eternally in her children, who may be said to include every other character in the book, even the old house itself. Her role as life-giver is clearly symbolized when she calms her daughter's fear of death by wrapping a green shawl around the ox skull hanging on the wall, where it stays long after her own death. Similarly, Forster's Mrs. Wilcox, though dead, hovers over the characters as a living immanent spirit of the female principle — regeneration through the material "realities" of house, tree, field, child that transmit the human spirit from generation to generation. As Margaret tells Helen:

> "Except Mrs. Wilcox, dearest, no one understands our little movements."
> "Because in death — I agree."
> "Not quite. I feel that you and I and Henry are only fragments of that woman's mind. She knows everything. She is everything. She is the house, and the tree that leans over it. ... I cannot believe that such knowledge as hers will perish with knowledge such as mine. She knew about realities." (313)

The process of change toward female archetypes began with Darwin, whose theory of adaptation — natural selection brought on by the struggle for survival — re-throned Nature over God as the pre-eminent force in humanity's survival and development. Darwinian evolution projects a world that is not static, as in the biblical version of order brought out of chaos by divine will at a certain point in time. Rather, it is a dynamic, anarchic process, Nature's "blind-law," with "death the constant penalty for a species' lack of successful adaptation" (Ruse 167). And, natural selection works through sexual regeneration. While Darwin did not understand Mendelian genetics, he did perceive that "sexual selection has played an important part in differentiating the races of man," and Part II of *The Descent of Man* is devoted to examining secondary sexual characteristics and sexual selection (5). Thus, material survival and sexuality begin to replace spirituality and morality as the forces through which humanity ensures eternal life. Even human intelligence, for so long regarded as our link to ethereal angels and distinction from beasts, was in Darwin's theory naturally evolved and sexually transferred.

Darwin was able to break the "great chain of being" because he was unusually free from the hierarchical thinking that characterizes patriarchal religions, particularly Christianity. Thoroughly devoted to the phenomenal world, he had no metaphysical need to view humanity as specially beloved by God, intellectually higher or morally superior, and his observations of animals and the natives of Tierra del Fuego convinced him that, "there is no fundamental difference" between "the highest men of the highest races and the lowest savages," nor are human mental powers "of a wholly different nature from those of the lower animals" (34–5). Many of Darwin's contemporaries had already relinquished the Judeo-Christian God of revealed religion, but they still clung to human intellectual superiority as a product of divine design. Darwin, however, remained undisturbed by his deflated image of humanity and the existential chaos released by his conception of its fortuitous place in nature. He did not feel that the universe was rendered meaningless when deprived of God's divine purpose, because he did not see the universe as evolving specifically *for* humanity; he did not see humanity as the "crown of creation": " 'People talk of the wonderful event of intellectual man appearing. The appearance of insects with other senses is more wonderful' " (qtd. in Ruse 181).

Thus, Darwin's view of nature began leveling many of the variables essential to the male principle: hierarchy, individuality, morality, and spirituality. Darwin posited a primarily physical view of humanity, since any superior mental traits evolved out of the species' physical struggle to survive. Darwin's world view was also, like that of the female principle, amoral and collective. For Darwin, morality is not an objective, unchanging right and wrong laid down by religion. Rather, law is based on social need — changeable, fluid, dynamic. Whatever helps the group to prosper will eventually be perceived as moral behavior: "If, for instance, to take an extreme case, men were reared under precisely the same conditions as hive-bees, there can hardly be a doubt that our unmarried females would, like the worker-bees, think it a sacred duty to kill their brothers, and mothers would strive to kill their fertile daughters; and no one would think of interfering" (Darwin 73). Law is part of the social entity's will to survive and prosper, just as matriarchal "blood-law" is portrayed in Aeschylus' *Oresteia* as not based on justice or mercy, but on retribution in order to protect family structure, particularly ties to the mother.

However much Darwin's world view may have undermined the cultural dominance of the male principle, he would have been shocked to learn that it did so. It is amazing, in fact, how little these discoveries of innate human primitivism shook the confidence of 19th-century scientists such as Darwin, Tylor, and Huxley, in rational, progressive development. At the same time as he forced the scholarly world to accept complicity with lower forms of life as well as with "savages,"

Darwin expressed relief that human reason had become more highly evolved, and confidence that it would continue to do so. Many "savage" "superstitions and customs" were "terrible to think of" for Darwin and, he wrote, "it is well occasionally to reflect on these superstitions, for they shew us what an infinite debt of gratitude we owe to the improvement of our reason, to science, and our accumulated knowledge" (68–9). Neither did later anthropologists and folklorists, such as Andrew Lang and Frazer, abandon patriarchal values, far from it. As rationalists and progressivists, they still saw humanity's highest achievements as intellectual, but the rational mind became the way to study the material world through science, rather than a spiritual link to an abstract God.

Thus, they managed to straddle a remarkable divide: while enthroning rationalism, they were materialists; while discovering more and more similarities between "civilised" cultures and "savages," their confidence in the wall of intellectual achievement separating "higher" and "lower" peoples remained unshaken. Nevertheless, Darwinian evolution was the first step toward reassertion of the female principle because it chipped away at three crucial props to the male principle: hierarchy, morality, and the abstract spirituality of revealed religion. Darwin's imagination could envision the life of bees as on a par with the human life, just as later scholars such as Jane Harrison could perceive "savage" rituals as valid religious experiences, although they had long been condemned or rationalized because of their radical difference from the Judeo-Christian concept of what is religious. In her seminal essay "Darwinism and Religion," Harrison wrote that the study of primitive religions "has been made possible, and even inevitable, by the theory of Evolution," since it freed humanity from the "presupposition that the essence of religion is dogma." Instead of a static world Darwinism postulates endless mutability, "the continuity of life, the absence of breaks," the "'acquirement of each mental capacity [even religion] by gradation.' " "With these memorable words," Harrison wrote, "the door closes on the old and opens on the new horizon. The mental focus henceforth is not on the maintaining or refuting of an orthodoxy, but on the genesis and evolution of a capacity, not on perfection, but on process" — in other words, not on the male principle, but the female (*AO* 143–150). As primitive spirituality became increasingly understood through the researches of comparative anthropology, 19th-century "horror" at its "savagery" gave way first to nostalgia and finally to longing, not for the bloody side of primitive ritual, but for its "intense vitalism," to use Jane Harrison's words: "Through the examination of primitive ritual we have at last got one tangible, substantial factor in religion, a real, live experience" (169).

Revitalized female archetypes and the female principle they represent bear a special creative significance for the artist in modernist literature. Characters representing the young artist, such as Lily Briscoe in *To the Lighthouse*, Stephen in *Ulysses*, and Harry in *The Family Reunion* are portrayed as experiencing ritual union with the female archetypes who dominate these works, before they are fully able to create. It is as if they must draw the final strength and vision necessary for their craft from a deep symbolic understanding of the ultimate creatrix. This ritual is usually violently purgative before it is visionary or renewing, just as primitive Greek rituals often began in bloody, frightening purgative acts before resulting in the visionary consolation of life eternal. We have, in our own day, sentimentalized the "Earth-mother" archetype until she is no more than an overweight nurturing cliché. However, the Georgian writers knew, perhaps because of their revitalized understanding of ancient myth, that the Earth-mother and the witch are two masks of the same goddess, just as creation and destruction are two sides of a single process. So Stephen must past through the violence of "Circe" before Bloom takes him to 7 Eccles Street where he perceives the "visible splendid sign" of Molly; so Harry suffers, persecuted by vengeful Erinýes, until Agatha's understandin shows him that he is "chosen/To resolve the enchantment under which we suffer"; so Lily cries out for Mrs. Ramsay in "anguish," before she experiences "mysteriously, a sense of some one there, of Mrs. Ramsay ... staying lightly by her side and then (for this was Mrs. Ramsay in all her beauty) raising to her forehead a wreath of white flowers with which she went."

This vision of the artist reborn as creator through a deepened, often symbolic or ritualistic, understanding of the female principle, marks the final step in the radical shift of values begun in 1871. My purpose is to trace in detail precisely how the female principle, for so many centuries perceived as a threat to human spiritual well-being, became in the span of approximately 50 years a source of spiritual reaffirmation for a generation of writers who found in the "mythic method" an answer to the "futility and anarchy" of their world.

2: THE "ANTHROPOLOGICAL METHOD" OF MYTH INTERPRETATION: E. B. TYLOR AND ANDREW LANG

"Science has given us back something strangely like our World-Soul, and art is beginning to feel she must utter our emotion towards it."

— Jane Ellen Harrison, *AAR* 246

In *The Descent of Man*, Darwin began dismantling the hierarchical supremacy of civilized European man over the animal kingdom, but his theories also opened the way for his contemporary Edward Burnett Tylor, the first cultural anthropologist, to find cultural, religious, and even psychological similarities between "savages" and "civilised" humanity. No longer could humanity's "mental powers" be construed as godlike, for in the *Descent*, Darwin catalogued the "faculties" long held to be particular to humans — "Attention," "Memories," "Imagination" (dreaming), "Reason," "Morality," "Language," "Self-consciousness or Individuality," "Sense of Beauty," even "Belief in God" — and demonstrated that they share these attributes with dogs, cats, horses, monkeys, bees, and other creatures, by piling up multiple instances of observed evidence (36–46). According to the traditional hierarchical "chain of being", comparison between classifications is anathema, but Darwin's leveling of creation suddenly made comparison an enormously fruitful methodology. Instead of looking everywhere for humanity's special differences from the rest of creation, scientists now became fascinated with finding similarities.

According to Darwinian evolution, all creation is deeply similar, driven by the same needs and instincts for survival. An equally revolutionary corollary, that humanity is everywhere similar, from the Australian aborigine, to the ancient Greek poet, to the contemporary English villager, provided the *raison d'etre* for anthropology. In *The Descent* Darwin also popularized the "comparative method", a prose style necessitated by such a collective vision of creation. While employed occasionally in the 18th century, not until Darwin did "the comparative method begin to take on a truly scientific and philosophical importance" (Irving 545). It is simple, and deadening, if read for any length of time, consisting of general postulates proven by citing example after example after example, culled from diverse sources throughout the natural world. Tylor's enormously influential two-volume study, *Primitive Culture*, established the comparative method as the prose style of anthropology, and it culminated in Frazer's massive 12-volume compilation of comparative data. But beyond drawing comparisons, scholars realized that the comparative method "was also a method of *explanation* by comparisons" (546). Therefore, it was fundamental to the radical reinterpretation of classical myth some 30 years after Tylor, as knowledge of the tribal rituals of contemporary aborigines garnered by anthropology was compared with, and finally provided a reasonable explanation for, the baffling "savagery" often found in classical myth and literature.

Like Darwin, Tylor was unusually free from orthodoxy; he bypassed a "classical" education since his "Quaker faith prevented him from entering universities like Oxford or Cambridge" (*PC* I, x), and also similar to Darwin, his theories derived from direct scientific observation through field work in South America. From Darwin Tylor adopted evolutionary development and the comparative method, applying them both solely to the study of humanity, and virtually creating the science of anthropology. However, Tylor went much further than Darwin in breaking down the barriers of traditional Eurocentric thinking. For him, a "general likeness in human nature on the one hand and a general likeness in the circumstances of life on the other" established the basic similarity of humanity everywhere, not only cross-culturally, but throughout time, despite the evolutionary march forward. In justifying his use of the comparative method, Tylor wrote: "Little respect need be had in such comparisons for date in history or for place on the map; the ancient Swiss lake-dweller may be set aside the mediaeval Aztec, and the Ojibwa of North America beside the Zulu of South Africa" (I, 6).

Tylor continually lessened the gap between primitive and contemporary humanity: "Even when it comes to comparing barbarous hordes with civilized nations, the consideration thrusts itself upon our minds, how far item after item of the life of the lower races passes into analogous proceedings of the higher, in forms not too far changed to be recognized, and sometimes hardly changed at all ... [thus] we may draw a picture where there shall be scarce a hand's breadth difference between an English ploughman and a negro of Central Africa" (I, 6–7). Tylor's wording, "thrusts itself upon our minds" is interesting here, implying that however difficult such widespread leveling of hierarchical barriers might be for the upper-class educated Englishman to accept, an impartial scientist could no longer ignore the evidence. For, while it was fairly palatable for an English gentleman to accept similarities between an "English *ploughman*" and an African native, Tylor's comparative data often ran the gamut from Australian aborigines to Swedenborg or Tennyson (34). Every paragraph of Tylor's work tightened the bond between "primitive" and "civilized" humanity through his use of the comparative method, providing examples from both "high" and "low" culture to prove his general points. For example, one typical paragraph cites evidence from a 16th-century Catholic mystic, an Australian witch doctor, a Khond priest, a Greenland "angekok," a Turanian shaman, a Norse chief, Pliny and Lucian, "our own folklore", and A.R. Wallace, a contemporary British scientist (II, 23–24).

Out of his conviction that humanity is linked across the barrier of time came Tylor's key concept of "survivals", so essential to the later reinterpretation of classical literature. For much of what had been perceived in myth as inexplicably brutal or immoral, such as Zeus's castration of his father Kronos, became comprehensible when seen as a ritualistic "survival" from a more primitive time cropping up in the literature of a later, more developed culture. Tylor introduced survivals as "processes, customs, opinions, and so forth, which have been carried on by force of habit into a new state of society different from that in which they had their original home, and they thus remain as proofs and examples of an older condition of culture out of which a newer has evolved" (I, 16). Tylor was fascinated with customs such as peasant holidays, proverbs and riddles, children's games and toys, folk-tales and superstitions, which his researches among native peoples convinced him were survivals of more primitive times, still existing in his own day, in modern "civilized" England. He strove to reform the sanctimonious superiority felt by most of his contemporaries toward "savages" and their beliefs into tolerance and acceptance, not only of modern humanity's direct descent from primitives, but also of its enduring "connexion" with primitivism through survivals. Tylor saw the ancient past very much alive in the present: "It needs but a glance into the trivial details of our own daily life to set us thinking how far we are really its originators, and how far but the transmitters and modifiers of results of long past ages" (17). Thus the seeds of Eliot's mythic method and Joyce's "paralleling of contemporaneity and antiquity" may be seen in Tylor's thought. Moreover, Tylor was ahead of his time in foreshadowing psychology's use of primitive myth as a means of self-examination: "they who wish to understand their own lives ought to know the stages through which their opinions and habits have become what they are" (19).

Tylor first made primitive spirituality accessible and comprehensible to moderns through his doctrine of "animism": a "minimum definition of Religion {as] the belief in Spiritual Beings," and through his explanation of magic as an expression of natives' entirely subjective perception of phenomena (II, 8). Overemphasis on Tylor's rationalism has since obscured his important contribution to the modernist (early 20th century) understanding of primitive mysticism. Tylor is condemned as a rationalist because he perceived primitive religion as "devised by human reason without supernatural aid or revelation," that is, as natural religion (11). By the early 1900s "it became something of a dogma to ascribe to Tylor a purely intellectualistic approach" (II, xi), a prejudice that persists today, for example, in the myth critic Stanley Edgar Hyman who blithely dismisses Tylor: "like many rationalists before him, Tylor believed that [myths] had been consciously devised as explanations" (47). Not quite. A more accurate evaluation of Tylor's thought might be that his rationalism opened his mind to a more impartial view of religion and a sympathetic understanding of "savages ... living in the myth-making stage of the human mind"; thus, he was among the first to propose that "savages" had any culture to study at all (I, 283).

Tylor's theory of animism is rationalistic in that he thought primitive people's belief in spiritual beings rose out of their desire to explain two aspects of natural phenomena: death and dreams. However, it is important to remember that Tylor was battling against the pervasive assumption that people who did not believe in one omnipotent Creator, as Christians do, had no religion at all. As Radin points out in his introduction to the 1958 edition of *Primitive Culture*, Tylor was "protesting against those who could see religious evolution only in terms of the dogmas ... of revealed religion" (xi). Tylor castigated the explorers and missionaries who frequently declared natives to "have nothing whatever of the character of religion, or of religious observance, to distinguish them from the beasts that perish," at the very same time as they recorded what were obviously, to an impartial eye, religious practices. In exasperation, Tylor cited many authors "to whom ethnology owes much valuable knowledge of the tribes they visited, but [who] seem hardly to have recognized anything short of the organized and established theology of the higher races as being religion at all" (3). Thus animism, Tylor's "rudimentary definition of religion," as rationalistic as it may seem, was actually an attempt to expand his contemporaries' understanding of what is religious (8). By 1900, primitive spirituality had become so popular that even greater mystical forces such as "*mana*" were eagerly attributed to it, so that Tylor's simple doctrine was considered too rational and outdated. There is no reason to perpetrate the misconception today, however.

In his introduction to volume II of *Primitive Culture*, Radin notes that Tylor's rationalism "included all forms of religious experience. To a person brought up in the Quaker tradition, reason and a mystical experience could be easily combined" (xi). These two strands run comfortably side by side throughout Tylor's work. Tylorian anthropology by definition rested on a confidence in the observed data of objective reality, but at the same time it drew attention to the importance of extremely subjective psychological states, states shared by the dreamer, the native, and the child. Like Darwin, Tylor was confident that modern scientific objectivism was evidence of man's evolutionary progress: "even in healthy waking life, the savage or barbarian has never learnt to make that rigid distinction between subjective and objective, between imagination and reality, to enforce which is one of the main results of scientific education" (II, 28). Yet, at the same time he encouraged his pragmatic audience to understand visionary experience by couching it in the empirical language they could accept: "Everyone who has seen visions while lightheaded in fever, everyone who has ever dreamt a dream, has seen the phantoms of objects as well as of persons. How can we charge the savage with far-fetched absurdity for taking into his philosophy and religion an opinion which rests on the very evidence of his senses?" (62).

The above passage shows Tylor's rationalism clearly: in encouraging his readers to approach "savages" more openmindedly, he argued that primitive humanity's "personifying stage of thought," which endowed the entire universe with soul, spirit, intelligence, was not a "far-fetched absurdity," but a rational conclusion based upon the evidence of the senses: "Men to whom the cries of beasts and birds seem like human language, and their actions guided as it were by human thought, logically enough allow the existence of souls to beasts, birds, reptiles, as to men." But, while the rationalist in Tylor tried to argue that primitive animism was rooted in logic, and the scientist in Tylor clearly felt it was "lower," less highly evolved than "the sense of absolute psychical distinction between man and beast, so prevalent in the civilized world," the mystic in Tylor (a quality entirely absent from Darwin's work) almost envied primitive people's childlike subjectivity (as he saw it), able to perceive life even in "stocks and stones, weapons, boats, food, clothes, ornaments, and other objects which to us are not merely soulless but lifeless" (II, 53–61). Fifty years before *Totem and Taboo*, Tylor foreshadowed Freud's connection between the psychology of the child and of the primitive: "He who recollects when there was still personality to him in posts and sticks, chairs, and toys, may well understand how the infant philosophy of mankind could extend the notion of vitality to what modern science only recognises as lifeless things" (II, 62). Despite his progressivist faith in science, this passage hints at Tylor's regret that empiricism had robbed humanity of its spiritual vitality, a nostalgia he shared with Jane Ellen Harrison and W.B. Yeats, among others of the *fin-de-siecle* generation.[1]

Tylor's explanation of magic rested on the theory he called "association of ideas," defined as primitive people's inability to distinguish between subjective thought and objective reality (I, 116). It was another extremely influential concept, establishing the basis for later anthropological discussions of magic, including Frazer's and Harrison's. Man, "in a low intellectual condition" believes that objects associated in his thought must also be associated in reality; he thus mistakes "an ideal for a real connexion." For the primitive, according to Tylor, symbolism and analogy are not subjective, but as real as the actual occurance they denote: thus "the Zulu may be seen chewing a bit of wood, in order, by this symbolic act, to soften the heart of the ... woman he wants for a wife" (118). Because the Zulu connects the wood with the woman's heart in his mind, a connection must exist in reality also, so that he actually influences his beloved by affecting the wood.

Jane Ellen Harrison acknowledged her debt to Tylor when she described magic as man's gloriously "egocentric" effort to impose his will on the universe (*AO* 162–72). Primitive man "does not pray, he *wills*" she wrote, and "instead of asking a god to do what he wants done, he does it, or tries to do it himself; instead of prayers he utters spells." Thus, he "recognizes no limits to his own power" because he does not divide his subjective mind from objective reality. Like Tylor, Harrison saw this primitive quality as childlike: "A child's mind is, indeed, throughout the best clue to the understanding of savage magic. A young and vital child knows no limit to his own will, and it is the only reality to him." Like Tylor, Harrison envied such a state of mind in which "the limitations of personality fall away." She disavowed Tylor's rationalism, however. To explain primitive man's spirit world, his animism, as a result of "seek[ing] to account" for natural phenomena, is to attribute a "quite alien quality of rationality" to his mind: "Man is at first too busy *living* to have any time for disinterested *thinking*. He dreams a dream, and it is real for him. He does not seek to account for it anymore than for his hands and feet." For Harrison magic was entirely "emotional, pre-intellectual," and experiential: "The real savage is more actively engaged ... he is busy practising magic, and, above all, he is strenuously engaged in dancing magical dances."

With all the fervor of the 19th-century rationalist and progressivist Tylor called magic "one of the most pernicious delusions that ever vexed mankind," rightfully condemned "as a contemptible superstition" by "the modern educated world" (113). However, when applying his understanding of the subjectivity of the primitive mind to mythology and from there to poetry, Tylor's attitude was precisely opposite — nostalgia and even longing for the childlike, mystical states modern humanity can no longer experience. He longed to free "the mythology of classic Europe, once so true to nature and so quick with her ceaseless life" from its fallen state "among the commentators ...

plastered with allegory or euhemerized into dull sham history" (280). Far from being a rationalist here, Tylor rejected "the old systems of rationalizing myth," insisting that we must not interpret myth according to our own standards, either as a rational explanation of natural phenomena or as metaphor or allegory. Rather, we must attempt to regain a pre-rational state, to "admit that in our childhood we dwelt at the very gates of the realm of myth," to achieve "a lively sense of the state of men's minds in the mythologic period" (284, 305). Indeed, the most unfortunate effect of Tylor's lingering reputation as a rationalist has been to bury his significant contribution to modernist myth interpretation.

Tylor's nostalgia for the "myth-making stage of the human mind" is apparent in a particularly lyrical passage in which he insisted that myth is not allegoric but experiential. It represents one of the first comprehensive expressions of the new modernist perception of myth:

> Analogies which are but fancy to us were to men of past ages reality. They could see the flame licking its yet undevoured prey with tongues of fire, or the serpent gliding along the waving sword from hilt to point; they could feel a live creature gnawing within their bodies in the pangs of hunger; they heard the voices of the hill-dwarfs answering in echo, and the chariot of the Heaven-god rattling in thunder over the solid firmament. Men to whom these were living thoughts had no need of the schoolmaster and his rules of composition, his injunctions to use metaphor cautiously, and to take continual care to make all similes consistent. The similes of the old bards and orators were consistent, because they seemed to see and hear and feel them: what we call poetry was to them real life, not as to the modern versemaker a masquerade of gods and heroes, shepherds and shepherdesses, stage heroines and philosophic savages in paint and feathers. ... The civilized European may contrast his own stiff orderly prosaic thought with the wild shifting poetry and legend of the old mythmaker, and may say of him that everything he saw gave birth to fancy. Wanting the power of transporting himself into this imaginative atmosphere, the student occupied with the analysis of the mythic world may fail so pitiably in conceiving its depth and intensity of meaning, as to convert it into stupid fiction. Those can see more justly who have the poet's gift of throwing their minds back into the world's older life. ...   (I 297, 305)

We can see in these lines the seeds of Eliot's mythic method, of Woolf's insistence that art must come out of experience, not knowledge, of Joyce's thorough identification of myth with modern life.

Tylor, however, perceived himself as a prosaic, imagination-impoverished scientist, so how did he define his role in resurrecting the fantastic world of myth? "Such of us as share but very little in this rare gift, may make shift to let evidence in some measure stand in its stead. ... and if the moderns cannot feel myth as their forefathers did, at least they can analyse it" (305, 317). Again, Tylor saw as little contradiction in the phrase "scientific myth-interpretation" (280) as Harrison later did in her phrase "the scientific study of religion." In fact, only science can rescue myth from the "masses of commentators' rubbish" by applying the comparative method of anthropology to it. By gathering and comparing "similar myths from different regions," repeated patterns become apparent; thus, myths that had long seemed bizarre and inexplicable when isolated, are suddenly comprehensible when shown in "their place among the well-marked and consistent structures of the human mind" (280). Another benefit of such a method would be "to determine the general relation of myths of savage tribes to the myths of civilized nations" (283), a phrase that illustrates again Tylor's willingness, unusual in his generation, to close the gap between "savage" and "civilized" cultures. Both of Tylor's proposals were carried out by later scholars and the results were just as he predicted: by 1922 when Eliot published *The Waste Land*, Frazer's "Dying God" symbolized a universal human experience, and myths and legends of European cultures (as in Jesse Weston's *From Ritual to Romance*) were being reinterpreted based on anthropological studies of aboriginal mythologies. Tylor rightly called the anthropological approach to myth an "intellectual frontier," one that he more than any other scholar opened to future explorers (317).

Andrew Lang was a man with a mission: to prove the validity of the anthropological interpretation of myth. Lang was a prolific writer with a lively, quick-witted, often vituperative style. A poet, folklorist, classicist, translator, historian, biographer, and novelist, he also contributed significantly to the debates stimulated by anthropology. Between 1884 and 1907 he published six books on the subject, thereafter turning his attention solely to Homeric studies. His prose translations of Homer with S.H. Butcher were extremely popular, and Joyce used their edition of the *Odyssey* as his source for *Ulysses*.

Lang saw himself as a "revolutionary mythologist" and enjoyed the scholarly fray. His cause — to apply the discoveries of cultural anthropology to a new interpretation of classical myth — opposed the long-established, predominantly German method of philological interpretation, as he announced with relish: "Philological comparative mythology seemed securely seated for a generation. Her throne is tottering" (*MM* xxiii). His first work, *Custom and Myth* (1884), heralded "The Method of Folklore," a name he devised to distinguish the anthropological method from " 'comparative mythology,' " the name "claimed exclusively by the philological interpreters." By his second, and most important work, *Myth, Ritual and Religion* (1887), he was able to drop this nomenclature since "comparative mythology" had by then come to mean the application of comparative anthropology to myth. His third work, *Modern Mythology* (1897), answered the criticisms of philologists, particularly "Mr. Max Muller ... the learned author [who] keeps up an irregular fire at the ideas and methods of the anthropological school of mythologists," and succinctly summarizes the progress of the movement since 1884.

Like others, Lang attributed the anthropological interpretation of myth originally to Darwin: "Our system is but one aspect of the theory of evolution, or is but the application of that theory to the topic of mythology" (*MM* vii). His mentor was E.B. Tylor; *Custom and Myth* is dedicated to Tylor, and his theory is based entirely on Tylor's concept of survivals. For Lang, archaeologists study "material 'survivals' — ancient arms, implements, and ornaments. ... fossil relics of an early social and political condition," and the "anthropological method in mythology is the same," the study of "immaterial relics of old races, the surviving superstitions and stories, the ideas which are in our time but not of it":

> In civilised religion and myth we find rudimentary survivals, fossils of rite and creed, ideas absolutely incongruous with the environing morality, philosophy and science of Greece. ... Parallels to these things, so out of keeping with civilisation, we recognise in the creeds and rites of the lower races, even of cannibals, but *there* the creeds and rites are *not* incongruous with their environment of knowledge and culture. There they are as natural and inevitable as the flint-headed spear or marriage by capture. We argue, therefore, that religions and mythical faiths and rituals, which, among Greeks are inexplicably

incongruous, have lived on from an age in which they were natural and inevitable, an age of savagery. (*MM* viii; *CM* 11)

It may hard for us, in the post-Freudian era, to understand how "inexplicably incongruous" much of classical myth was to previous generations. We are so used to accepting elements in myth such as Zeus' castration of his father as symbolic of universal psychological states that we no longer realize how "revolting," "obscene" (*MM* xv), "wild," "unspeakable," "childish and disgusting," "cruel and loathsome," "grotesque," "puerile" (*MRR*, 13–15), "'utterly unintelligible, absurd, strange'" (Muller, *MM* 5) such elements were to past mythologists. To 19th-century Christians, for whom, however agnostic, religion by definition meant "high" moral and spiritual ideals, as well as to classicists who saw the equally lofty Socratic and Platonic ideals as the basis of Greek civilization, such "absurdities and horrors" (Tylor II, 5) as human sacrifice, "Greeks dancing serpent-dances or bear-dances like Red Indians, or swimming with sacred pigs, or leaping about in imitation of wolves, or holding a dog-feast and offering dog's flesh to the gods" were simply anathema (Lang, *CM* 12). These comprise the "fossils of rite and creed" Lang noted, so "incongruous with the environing morality, philosophy, and science" of the classical Greeks, "so out of keeping with civilisation." In *Modern Mythology* he summarized the crux of most classicists' discomfort: "The ugly scars were the problem! A civilised fancy is not puzzled for a moment by a beautiful beneficent Sun-god, or even by his beholding the daughters of men that they are fair. But a civilised fancy *is* puzzled when the beautiful Sun-god makes love in the shape of a dog" (4–5).

The "civilised fancy," in short, was not puzzled by gods who echoed his own conception of what religion should be: patriarchal, anthropomorphic, celestial, rational, moral. Classicists like Lang no longer denied evidence that primitives had a kind of religious experience, however strange: matriarchal, zoomorphic, sexual, chthonic, anarchic, based on religious acts such as ritual dances and sacrifices, rather than on religious knowledge, the word of God. Yet to go one step further and accept that the rational, civilized Greeks worshiped according to such values — that was too much! Crudities in Greek myth and religion *had* to be explained as survivals from a more primitive time. This is the frame of mind to recapture if one is to understand the tremendous boon offered by cultural anthropology to myth interpretation. For anthropology uncovered "horrors and absurdities" in the myths of native peoples from all over the world, identical to those found in classical myth. Therefore, these elements in the classics had to be survivals from an earlier age when Hellenic civilization was as "primitive" as Australian aboriginal tribes. At last, the disturbing "ugly scars" could be explained, through the comparative method, as survivals:

> That Greeks should dance about in their mysteries with harm-less serpents in their hands looks quite unintelligible. When a wild tribe of Red Indians does the same thing, as a trial of courage, with real rattlesnakes, we understand the Red Man's motives, and may conjecture that similar motives once existed among the ancestors of the Greeks. Our method, then, is *to compare* the seemingly meaningless customs or manners of civil-ised races with the similar customs and manners which exist among the uncivilised and still retain their meaning. It is not necessary for comparison of this sort that the uncivilised and the civilised race should be of the same stock, nor need we prove that they were ever in contact with each other. Similar conditions of mind produce similar practices, apart from the iden-tity of race, or borrowing of ideas and manners.   (*CM* 21–2, my ital.)

Lang's concluding sentences show how thoroughly this new inter-pretation of myth was based on the Tylorian concept that humanity is universally similar. Moreover, in this concept lay the essential differ-ence between Lang's comparative "method of folklore" and the more limited "comparative mythology" of his adversaries, the philologists. Their approach was based on figuring out the etymological deriva-tions of the proper names of gods and heroes. Myths grew up around names through a process philologists called the "disease of language," whereby names became metaphorical as succeeding generations lost their original meaning and resorted to creating "absurd" stories to explain them (*CM* 1). Once the original derivation of the god's name could be found, his or her myth could be correctly interpreted. Muller explained the often offensive oddities in myth as distortions resulting from man's "perpetual misconceptions of the meaning of old words in his own language" and his confused attempts to explain them (*MM* xv). But philological nit-picking over derivations gave rise to as many interpretations of the meaning of a god's name as there were philolo-gists: "where one scholar decides that the name is originally Sanskrit, another holds that it is purely Greek, and a third, perhaps, is all for an

Accadian etymology, or a Semitic derivation" (*CM* 2). Thus, according to Lang, "very little ingenuity is needed to make [a name] indicate one or other aspect of Dawn or Night, or Lightening or Storm, just as the philologist pleases" (*MM* xvii). Lang gleefully pilloried such "discrepancies of interpretation" by listing philologists' contradictory interpretations, for instance, of Kronos as Time, Sun, Midnight sky, Harvest, or Storm, or of Demeter as Storm-cloud, Sun Goddess, Earth and Moon Goddess, Night (*MM* 35, 53). "The analysis of names, on which the whole ediface of philological 'comparative mythology' rests," he concluded, "is a foundation of shifting sand ... discredited by the disputes of its adherents" (*CM* 2).

Because it was based solely on language, philological theory could only compare myths from the same linguistic family, the Aryan, and it could only explain similarities in myths of different cultures as the result of borrowing between peoples who came into actual contact with one another. For Lang, however, "the amazing similarity of myths" could never be explained by "that in which all races formally differ — their language — but that in which all early races are astonishingly the same — their ideas, fancies, habits, desires" (*MM* xvi). With each new report from the field, anthropology revealed more striking similarities in the myths and rituals of races that never could have come into contact, and that spoke entirely different languages. "Like other inquiring undergraduates in the sixties" (*MM* 3) Lang had been indoctrinated into the philological approach, but he became "more and more impressed with a sense of the inadequacy of the prevalent method of comparative mythology" (*CM* 1). Whereas the philologists explained Greek myths by "etymologies of words in the Aryan languages, chiefly Greek, Latin, Slavonic, and Sanskrit, I kept finding myths very closely resembling those of Greece among Red Indians, Kaffirs, Eskimo, Samoyeds, Kamilaroi, Maoris, and Cahrocs" (*MM* 4). How could one explain the ubiquity of a harvest goddess made of corn sheaves known as the "kernababy" to contemporary Scottish peasants, as the "Mama Cora" to Peruvian Indians, and as Demeter of the threshing floor to the ancient Greeks? How could one explain that the "Ovahereroes in South Africa appease with a black sheep the spirits of the departed" just as Odysseus did? How could one explain the "bull-roarer," a "toy familiar to English country lads," used in "religious mysteries in New Mexico, in Australia, in New Zealand, in the Dionysiac mysteries of ancient Greece, and in Africa?" (*CM* 18–20, 32) Lang found the philological theory that these remote peoples must be "akin by blood, ...

or at some forgotten time, they met, and borrowed each other's superstitions" woefully inadequate. The more valid explanation lay in the
similarity everywhere of the "myth-making stage of the human mind,"
to use Tylor's terms, or to use Lang's, of early man's "mythopoeic
faculty," the "mental stage" at which he produces myth (*CM* 23; *MRR*
8). Lang relied on the Tylorian concept that "similar conditions of
mind produce similar practices," but he went further than Tylor in
frequently describing mythic images and rites as "universal" (20, 51).
Thus Jung's theory of the communicability of archetypes through a
"collective unconscious" had been essentially established 50 years earlier in the work of Tylor and Lang, who discovered "the universality of
the mythopoeic mental condition" (*MRR* 8).

   Andrew Lang's battle with the philologists helped shift myth interpretation from Heaven to Earth, just as Darwin gave Nature preemin-
ence over God. Embued in Judeo-Christian tradition, philological interpretation assumed that that "all mythology is a terrestrial reflection of
celestial phenomena" (*MM* 53). Thus, Lang wrote in derision, "even
the story of the Earth Goddess, the Harvest Goddess, Demeter, was
usually explained as a reflection in myth of one or another celestial
phenomenon — dawn, storm-cloud, or something else according to
taste" (2). Lang's insistence that anthropology provided a truer understanding of myth than philology enabled him to perceive that even in
the myths of classical Greece, primitive people often did not look to
Heaven for their gods, but to Earth. However, although Lang acknowledged the presence of primitive chthonic survivals in classical
myth, he did not feel comfortable with them. In fact, it would not be
too extreme to say that their presence in the classics caused him
considerable anguish. Lang felt no Tylorian nostalgia for the childlike, primitive myth-making state of mind. The "ugly scars" continued to plague him; he returned again and again to the dichotomy he
saw between the "high" spiritual elements of Greek myth and the
"low" physical elements. While he refused to ignore barbaric ritual
survivals in myth, his traditionally hierarchical and moral conception
of spirituality kept him from perceiving their vital role in Greek religion, other than as survivals from a more primitive epoch.

   This is nowhere more apparent than in his major work, *Myth, Ritual
and Religion*, where he continued to develop the disparity he perceived
in Greek religion, now under the nomenclature, significantly, of "rational" vs. "irrational." In this work he attempted to go beyond his mentor, Tylor. Dissatisfied with Tylor's rationalistic definition of religion as

simply "the belief in spiritual beings" resulting from the need to explain natural phenomena, he wanted to credit primitives with metaphysical yearnings closer to those of moderns. This desire rose out of his greater knowledge of primitive Greek religion, where the metaphysical element is clearly evident in close context with rituals that appeared to him as bizarre, crude survivals. Unfortunately, Lang could only view metaphysics according to traditional patriarchal values; thus, his definition of religion became "the belief in a primal being, a Maker, undying, usually moral" (*MRR* 2–3). Such a definition led him to see an "essential conflict between religion and myth," where there really was none. He realized that while this "Maker" might be mythic, "however that may be, the attitude of awe, and of moral obedience, in the face of such a supposed being, is religious in the sense of the Christian religion, whereas the fabrication of fanciful, humorous, and wildly irrational fables about that being, or others, is essentially mythical" (*MRR* 4). Thus, for Lang, the spiritual and ethical elements of faith comprised religion, while the physical belonged to myth. In *Myth, Ritual and Religion* Lang renamed his "ugly scars" the "*chronique scandaleuse,*" suitably putting in French, the language in which illicit "amours" were permissible for Englishmen, all the powerful sexuality of myth:

> Now the whole crux and puzzle of mythology is, "Why, having attained (in whatever way) to a belief in an undying guardian, "Master of Life," did mankind set to work to evolve a *chronique scandaleuse* about *Him*? And why is that *chronique* the elaborately absurd set of legends which we find in all mythologies? ... Among the lowest known tribes we usually find, just as in ancient Greece, the belief in a deathless "Father," "Master," "Maker," and also the crowd of humorous, obscene, fanciful myths which are in flagrant contradiction with the religious character of that belief. That belief is what we call rational, and even elevated. The myths, on the other hand, are what we call irrational and debasing.   (*MRR* 4)

Lang's "puzzle" here was not solely the result of Victorian prudery, nor of his immersion in a Christian ethos that denied physicality. It was not just mythic sexuality that appalled, but the suspicion that sexuality or physicality could be *sacred*, could be the vehicle for metaphysical consolation. That the female principle could be as *religious* as the male was incomprehensible, for how could it lead to anything but anarchy?: "The dead and the living, men, beasts and gods, trees and stars, and rivers, and sun, and moon, dance through the region of myths in a burlesque *ballet* of Priapus, where everything may be anything, where nature has no laws and imagination no limits" (*MRR* 13). Not only was such a spiritual experience incomprehensible to the 19th-century mind, but Lang perceived it as incomprehensible to the Greeks themselves: "The pious remonstrances and the forced constructions of early thinkers like Xenophanes, of poets like Pindar, of all ancient Homeric scholars and Pagan apologists ... are so many proofs that to Greece, as soon as she had a reflective literature, the myths of Greece seemed impious and *irrational*" (*MRR* 6–7); "The Greeks themselves, from almost the earliest historical ages, were deeply concerned either to veil or explain away the blasphemous horrors of their own 'sacred chapters,' poetic traditions and temple legends" (*MRR* 248).

The actual evidence Lang provided of this "explaining away" is unconvincing (his perception of Socrates is particularly equivocal, see *CM* 48 and *MRR* 14–18); further, what was one to do about Pindar, Sophocles, Euripides, even Aristophanes, Plutarch, Cicero and others who attested to the metaphysical vision of eternity experienced during the ritual worship of Demeter at Eleusis? Again Lang was a curious mixture of openmindedness and limitation. He condemned earlier efforts like those of the German mythologist Lobeck, to "minimise the evidence." We cannot be so "cavalier" as to "dismiss" the proof of these "ancient witnesses" that there was "something sacred in Greek mysteries, something purifying, ennobling, consoling." Nevertheless Lang was unable to reconcile these "high ideas" with the "low myths," "scenes of debauchery," and "buffoonery" also recorded as part of the Eleusinian mysteries. What *could* "Sophocles see, after taking a swim with his pig? Many things far from edifying, yet the sacred element of religious hope and faith was also represented." Lang's answer was that Pindar and Sophocles must have overlooked such porcine "buffooneries" as survivals. They did not let such "mummeries" and other "stupid indecencies" destroy the "sacred value," the "precepts" and "moral and religious teaching" also imparted there. Yet there is no evidence of teaching or preaching at Eleusis; therefore Lang could only guess that "religious consolations" were "represented" or "somehow conveyed." That these two elements could have been one, that religious hope or faith could be experienced through ritual actions, even through swimming with a pig, was incomprehensible to Lang and many others (*MRR* xviii; 270, 277–9). Not until Frazer's emphasis on fertility in ancient religion, and Jane Harrison's feminist dicussions of chthonic ritual and matriarchal goddesses, was pre-Olympian Greek religion finally understood to be experiential and physical, not cognitive and abstract, but nonetheless sacred.

Anthropology's discovery of the survival of primitive rituals in myths and classical literature led to an interesting reassessment of Homer. In a lecture delivered at Oxford in 1908, "Homer and Anthropology," Lang discussed the curious fact that there is no mention in Homer whatsoever of the "primaeval devices," the "savage" rituals of Greek religion:

> Now, as far as these primaeval devices go, Homer has wonderfully little to tell us. Though he is by far the most ancient Greek author extant, it is in all the literature that follows after him that we find most survivals of the barbarian and the savage. ... The tragedians, the lyric poets, and the rest, all allude to vices which Homer never mentions — to amours of the gods in bestial forms ... to a revolting rite of sanguinary purification from the guilt of homicide [blood-law], and to many other distressing vestiges of savagery and barbarism in the society of ancient Greece. We do not find these things in the *Iliad* and the *Odyssey*. (Marett 44)

Again, Lang's strong aversion to the "female" side of Western binaristic values is evident, but it is true that the rites, myths, and principles of matriarchal religion, so potent in Greek drama, are entirely absent from the epic. As the "Homeric question" raged, many theories were proposed. Those who felt that the Homeric epics were compilations suggested that later Greeks "expurgated" them for "educational purposes." But, Lang asked the cogent question, "why was Hesiod not Bowdlerized? Hesiod certainly entered into public knowledge no less than Homer ... [and] Homer must have been familiar with the savage cosmogonic legends [such as paternal castration] which Hesiod does not scruple to state openly; but about such things Homer is silent." Finally, he argued, "if the taste of the seventh and sixth centuries were so pure and austere, why were the poets of the seventh and sixth centuries so rich in matters which the *Iliad* and *Odyssey* omit? In no Greek literature of any age do we find the clean austerity of Homer" (48). This was particularly baffling to Lang, who could only accept these mythic "vices" as survivals from a more primitive time; therefore why were they entirely lacking from the work of the earliest Greek poet, while figuring prominently in the literature of his successors?

Lang's answer was characteristic. First, on the Homeric question Lang felt that the harmony of the epics, poetically as well as archaeologically, argued single authorship in a single age. The poet, Homer, he then took to be a man much like himself, "embarrassed" by the "savage survivals" he found in the "legendary materials on which his works are based." Homer, "unlike Hesiod does not love to speak of what the gods did 'in the morning of time', things derived from a remote past of savage mythology; the incest, the amours in animal form, the cannibalism, the outrage of Kronos on his father, the swallowing of Zeus. ... The mythological survivals are, to Homer, inevitable, but distasteful" (62). So, Homer represented for Lang one of the earliest "attempts to shake off the burden of religious horror at mythical impiety ... by way of silent omission" (*MRR* 14) and instead Homer celebrated and immortalized the new race of rational gods, the Olympians:

> If we look at Greek religious tradition, we observe the coexistence of the *rational* and the apparently *irrational* elements. The *rational* are those which represent the gods as beautiful and wise beings. The Artemis of the *Odyssey* "taking her pastime in the chase of boars and swift deer, while with her the wild woodnymphs disport them, and high over them all she rears her brow, and is easily to be known where all are fair," is a perfectly *rational* mythic representation of a divine being. We feel, even now, that the conception of a "queen and goddess, chaste and fair," the abbess, as Paul de Saint-Victor calls her, of the woodlands, is a beautiful and natural fancy, which requires no explanation. On the other hand, the Artemis of Arcadia, who is ... said to have become a she-bear, and later a star; and the Brauronian Artemis, whose maiden ministers danced a bear-dance, are goddesses whose legend seems unnatural, and needs to be made intelligible. (*MRR* 10–11)

This passage illustrates how different the perception of women was in the Homeric Olympian theogony from the powerfully sexual matriarchs of religion and myth prior to Homer, prefigurations of the volatile queens of Greek drama. According to Harrison, Homeric goddesses had been remade to suit the increasing dominance of patriarchal ideology — chaste, anthropomorphic, rational — and it is no wonder Lang felt more comfortable with them. Moreover, nothing shows more clearly the radically changing perception of female archetypes in the early 20th century than contrasting Lang's perception of the Homeric Artemis with Frazer's interpretation of the pre-Olympic, matriarchal "Ephesian" Artemis, derived from his view of fertility as the primary life-force:

> No notion could well be further from truth ... [than] the popular modern notion of Diana or Artemis as the pattern of a straight-laced maiden lady with a taste for hunting. To the ancients, on the contrary, she was the ideal and embodiment of the wild life of nature — the life of plants, of animals, and of men — in all its exuberant fertility and profusion. ... At Ephesus, the most celebrated of all the seats of her worship, her universal motherhood was set forth unmistakably in her sacred images ... [which] represent the goddess with a multitude of protruding breasts; the heads of animals of many kinds, both wild and tame, spring from the front of her body in a series of bands that extend from the breasts to the feet; ... her bosom is festooned with a wreath of blossoms, and she wears a necklace of acorns. ... It would be hard to devise a more expressive symbol of exuberant fertility, of prolific maternity, than these remarkable images. (*GB* I, 35–8)

Unlike Lang, Frazer saw the chthonic matriarch as far from unnatural, nor did her legends "need to be made intelligible." Like Lang, however, Frazer saw her reformation as chaste huntress in Homer's epics as the effort of a later, more "ethical" age to tame the exuberant excesses of an earlier, pre-ethical age: "With the growth of a purer morality among men a stricter code of ethics is imposed by them upon their gods; the stories of the cruelty, deceit and lust of these divine beings are glossed lightly over or flatly rejected as blasphemies, and the old ruffians are set to guard the laws which before they broke" (I, 36). Frazer's language here — "a purer morality," "cruelty, deceit and lust," "the old ruffians" — reveals his roots, firmly planted in rationalist soil. Like other rationalists he felt that the advent of morality according to patriarchal, Eurocentric values was a step forward for humanity. Yet apparent also in the passage is Frazer's somewhat greater impartiality; he began to see that perhaps female sexuality had been "glossed lightly over or flatly rejected" unfairly, since these goddesses had once been "divine beings" of immense importance for human survival.

Where Frazer was impartial, Jane Harrison was fervent, and therefore even more strikingly opposed to Lang's point of view. Lang perceived a split between religion and myth because he saw myths as the "*chronique scandaleuse*," whereas religion must be based upon morality. For Harrison the "confusion of religion with morality" was not only "pernicious" but "a sad limitation." Truer to the spirit of Darwinism, Harrison saw morality merely as the result of social needs: "Morality is social, due to the reaction of man on man; it is human. But religion is our reaction to the whole, the unbounded whole." Religion, for Harrison, was limited by being reduced to "a moral obligation, a thing you seek to impose." In its purest form, it was a "reaction," an experience of "the terror and emptiness of the Absolute." Harrison's feminism caused her to attempt to reverse the hierarchal relation of gender binarism here; for her, religion was identified with the traditionally "female" — experiential, emotional, physical, amoral, anarchic. Religious experience was sadly "limited" by being confined to the moral, rationalistic precepts of patriarchal theology: "We have confused theology — a rational thing that can be intellectually defined, though it must never be morally imposed — with religion, an external reaction towards the unknown, the hidden spring of our physical, spiritual life. ... the god of theology is simply an intellectual attempt to define the indefinable; it is not a thing lived, experienced" (*AO* 199–205). To Lang, whose concept of religion was essentially patriarchal and based on theology, rituals such as "dancing serpent-dances or bear-dances like Red Indians, or swimming with sacred pigs, or leaping about in imitation of wolves" could not possibly be religious (*CM* 12). To Harrison, ritual, especially dancing and chanting, was the essence of religion since religion can only be experienced, not known.

Lang's dichotomy between the "rational" and "irrational" elements in Greek religion became, in Harrison's conception, the "eikonic" as opposed to the "aneikonic," with an exactly reversed valuing of the two. If we recall the gender traditionally attributed to these two qualities, male/rational and female/irrational, the overt feminism of Harrison's scholarship becomes more clear. No wonder Lang's reviews of her books were barely charitable (*R* 62). He had found in Homer's

Olympians a great civilizing step forward, whereas Harrison deprecated the Homeric "rationalization" of religious experience into the
worship of "eikons," such as the Olympians, made in man's image.
"Eikonism takes the vague, unknown, fearful thing, and tries to
picture it as known, as distinct, definite — something man can think
about and understand; something that will think about and understand him; something as far rationalized as man himself" (*AO* 202).
For Harrison the "aneikonic" cults of Demeter and Dionysus represented "the supreme golden moment achieved by the Greek" because they
were irrational, "the outcome rather of emotion than of intellect."
Aneikonic gods are not safely anthropomorphic but "vague *daemones*,"
"life principles within the whole of Nature," "always imaginatively
more awful than eikonism." Aneikonic ritual "aims at union;" it is the
"sacramental, mystical" experience of a force beyond human comprehension, of Nature (198–205).

Contrary to Lang, Harrison felt that "the greatest advance made in
the study of Greek religion of late has been to show that the Greek
gods, Zeus, Apollo and the rest, are a temporary phase," not even
religious, but "an outcome of particular social activities and social structure" (198). She realized that her "own deep inward dissatisfaction
with Olympian religion rose from the fact that, while developing and
expressing to the full the eikonic element, it disallowed the aneikonic"
(201). She referred to the Olympian patriarch Zeus as an "impostor"
and her "lifelong antipathy" to Homer's Olympians was "a standing
joke" between herself and her young friend Gilbert Murray (Stewart
31). In all of this her rebellion against a patriarchal power that "disallowed" the expression of the female and "imposed" a "moral obligation" upon "the hidden spring of our physical, spiritual life" can be
seen. To "define the undefinable," to bind the "unbounded Whole" is
for Harrison, the imposition of patriarchal law over female experience. Her elevation of "aneikonism" — "vague, unknown, fearful" —
is an attempt, in Lacanian terms, to reassert the primacy of preoedipal
"sacramental, mystical" "union" with a maternal "Absolute" over the
intervention of the "nom du père," the law of the father.

She took plenty of criticism from her "friends" in the patriarchal
scholarly community for her "lack of reverence for the Olympian gods"
(*AO* 200). She attempts, in *Alpha and Omega*, to "justify my lawless
instincts" by "submit[ting] some reasoned *apologia pro haeresi mea*" in
answer to the charge that "I prefer savage disorders, Dionysiac orgies,
the tearing of wild bulls, to the ordered and stately ceremonial of

Panathenaic processions" (201). But finally her "heresy" cannot be explained in reasonable terms because it is not rational, it is emotional. Remaining true to herself she can only reveal her enthusiasm: "the mystery gods, their shapes and ritual, Demeter, Dionysus, the cosmic Eros, drew and drew me. ... The mystery gods are ... life-spirits barely held; they shift and change. Aeschylus, arch-mystic, changes his Erinyes into Eumenides, and is charged with impiety. Dionysus is a human youth, lovely, with curled hair, but in a moment he is a Wild Bull and a Burning Flame. The beauty and the thrill of it!" (204–5)

Harrison's "deep conviction" that religion must be experiential led her to form the "ritual theory," connecting the aneikonic religious impulse with drama: "It is this childlike power of utter impersonation, of *being* the thing we act or even see acted, this extension and intensification of our own personality, that lives deep down in all of us, and is the very seat and secret of our joy in the drama" (166). Her use of the first person plural pronoun in this passage shows that, in her work, all the hierarchical barriers between "low" and "high," "savage" and "civilized," "primitive" and "modern" — barriers which persist in the work of all her contemporaries, even Frazer — have been broken down. Primitive experience, both religious and creative, has become one and the same as modern experience. Eliot's new classicism, emotional and experiential, Joyce's "continuous parallel between contemporaneity and antiquity" were fully formulated in the work of Jane Harrison. Furthermore, since the 17th century the classical form that dominated England's literary imagination had been the Homeric epic, eikonic, rational, heroic, male. Because of Jane Harrison, and through her enormous influence on Gilbert Murray and Francis Cornford, Greek drama — aneikonic, full of the rites, myths and archetypes of the female principle — spoke anew to the literary imagination of the modernist generation.

In 1907 Andrew Lang withdrew from the field of anthropological mythology, preferring the "clean austerity" of Homeric scholarship. The child he had done so much to create had become an adolescent, too hot to handle. Yet we certainly cannot blame Lang for his limitations. He saw himself, correctly, as a "revolutionary mythologist." By insisting on the validity of the anthropological approach even to classical myth, he wrested myth interpretation out of the arid, abstract etymological ponderings of the philologists and plunked it firmly into life: "The old mythologists worked at ... myths dried and pressed in thoroughly literary books, Greek and Latin. But we now study ... mythology *in situ* — in savages and peasants still in the mythopoeic stage of thought" (*MM* xix). One of Lang's chapter headings in *Myth, Ritual and Religion* reads, "Object of inquiry: to find condition of human intellect in which marvels of myth are parts of practical everyday belief." Although Lang and many others of his generation maintained a strict line between the primitive "condition of human intellect" and their own "civilised" intelligence, anthropology had shown them that the "marvels of myth" could be experienced in contemporary life, a vital part of "everyday belief," albeit only as survivals amongst the peasant class. It remained for Harrison and the younger generation of scholars and writers, to take the further step of finding this vital experiential spirituality in their own vision of life and to communicate it through the universal images and archetypes of myth in their art.

3: MYTH AND MAGIC: FRAZER, HARRISON, AND THE "RITUAL THEORY"

*Our age is in a sense anti-rational. If your writings are rational-
ist in tone, your youngest reviewer is sure to crush you nowadays
with the epithet, "Early Victorian," and say you are "out of touch"
with vitalism. The present age is concerned with affirming life as
a whole, not Reason as the Lord over Life.*

— Jane Ellen Harrison, *AO* 137

It is clear that Jane Harrison played a much larger role in the modernist understanding of myth and ritual and their relation to classical
literature than has hitherto been recognized. One reason Harrison's
contribution has been de-emphasized is that scholars have consistently overemphasized Frazer's, particularly John B. Vickery in his
important and influential 1973 study, *The Literary Impact of the Golden
Bough*. Some have perceived the value of Harrison's work, for instance
Stanley Edgar Hyman, Robert Allen Ackerman, and Harry
C. Payne.[1] Feminist literary critics such as Jane Marcus and Bonnie
Scott Kime are beginning to acknowledge Harrison's profound influence as an accomplished scholar and role model for women writers of

the modernist generation, particularly Virginia Woolf. However, none of their essays and comments can compare in scope with Vickery's book, and studies of Frazer's influence continue to proliferate, while Harrison's considerable oeuvre remains largely neglected.

Vickery's contention that without Frazer "the literary concern with myth and related matters would have been substantially different, if indeed it had existed at all" vastly overstates the case (6). As I have shown, the groundwork for a literary concern with myth had already been laid in Tylor's *Primitive Culture* and further developed by Frazer's contemporaries Andrew Lang and Jane Harrison, both of whom were personally, even passionately, committed to revolutionizing outmoded concepts of myth and ritual. Vickery minimizes the importance of both Tylor and Lang, for instance, when he asserts that Lang's studies "reflect in varying degrees the opinions and basic attitudes of *The Golden Bough*" (83). If Andrew Lang thought that anyone would ever attribute his work to "the opinions and basic attitudes of *The Golden Bough*," he would breathe fire. He considered Frazer's work "unscientific," based far too much on "undemonstrated conjectures" and too little on "the known facts" (*FR* 242, 244), an opinion shared by several of Frazer's colleagues, such as the Cambridge classicist and Harrison's professor, William Ridgeway (Stewart 17). Lang's review of the second edition of *The Golden Bough* (1900) in the *Fortnightly Review* was devastating:

> To reach Mr. Frazer's solution — that the ghastly priest was an incarnate spirit of vegetation, slain, after the plucking of mistletoe, in order that he might be succeeded by a stronger soul, more apt to increase the life of vegetation, — we have to cross at least six "light bridges" of hypothesis, "built to connect isolated facts" (i.xv.). To me these hypotheses seem more like the apparently solid spots in a peat-bog, on which whoso alights is let into the morass.   (241–2)

Clearly Frazer's contemporaries did not view him as a god among men but rather as a colleague whose contribution was often weak and open to criticism. Harrison's assessment of Frazer in her *Reminiscences* reveals her skepticism of his exalted position among other more scientific and innovative scholars of her generation:

> Classics were turning in their long sleep ... I had just left Cambridge when Schliemann began to dig at Troy. Among my own contemporaries was J.G. Frazer, who was soon to light the dark

wood of savage superstition with a gleam from *The Golden Bough*. The happy title of that book — Sir James Frazer has a veritable genius for titles — made it arrest the attention of scholars. They saw in comparative anthropology a serious subject actually capable of elucidating a Greek or Latin text. Tylor had written and spoken; Robertson Smith, exiled for heresy, had seen the Star in the East; in vain ... but at the mere sound of the magical words "Golden Bough" the scales fell.   (82)

This passage also suggests a reason for the enduring popularity of Frazer's work — his "genius for titles," that is, for vivid imagery and lush Ruskinian phrasing: "the fleeting beauty of the damask rose, the transient glory of the golden corn, the passing splendour of the purple grapes," etc. (Part V, vol. i, 2). Indeed, Frazer indicated in his prefaces on more than one occasion that, given the choice between strict scientific veracity and artistic effect, he often chose the latter. For example, when he had been informed by a critic that "the church-bells of Rome cannot be heard, even in the stillest weather, on the shores of the Lake of Nemi," Frazer chose to leave the "blunder" "uncorrected," consciously modeling himself on Scott, in the interest of the artistic effect of the chiming bells: "I make bold to say that by the Lake of Nemi I love to hear, if it be only in imagination, the distant chiming of the bells of Rome, and I would fain believe that their airy music may ring in the ears of my readers after it has ceased to vibrate in my own" (preface to 2nd ed. vol I, xxvii; preface to 1st ed., viii).

Vickery also portrays Frazer as singlehandedly responsible for the demise of the philological school (90), but as we have already seen, Lang waged a vociferous battle against the philological interpretation of myth from as early as 1884 through 1897, when he devoted an entire volume to the subject (*MM*). Frazer certainly did not agree with the philologists' approach (he wrote in a footnote, for instance, that "etymology is at the best a very slippery ground on which to rear mythological theories" Part V, vol. i, 41), but he never challenged them as Lang did. Nor did he affect Harrison's liberation from the "school that thought it was far more important to parse a word than to understand it" (*R* 58). Rather, she learned the importance of empirical data over the obscure etymologies of the philological school straight from Sir Francis Darwin, who was thoroughly imbued with his father's methodology from years of assisting the aged Darwin in botanical research:

One scientific friend, Francis Darwin, had lasting influence on me. Classics he regarded with a suspicious eye, but he was kind to me. One day he found me busy writing an article on the "Mystica vannus Iacchi" ... "What is a *vannus?*" he asked. "Oh, a 'fan'," I said; "it was a mystical object used in ceremonies of initiation." "Yes, but Virgil says it is an agricultural implement. Have you ever seen one?" "No," I confessed. *"And you are writing about a thing you have never seen,"* groaned my friend. "Oh, you classical people!" It did not end there. He interviewed farmers — no result; he wrote to agricultural institutes abroad, and, finally, in remote provincial France, unearthed a mystic "fan" still in use, and had it despatched to Cambridge. ... On his lawn were to be seen a gathering of learned scholars trying, and failing, to winnow with the *vannus.* ... Three months later I despatched a paper to the *Hellenic Journal* on what I *had* seen and *did* understand. It was a lifelong lesson to me. (58)

This passage reveals how much more empirically oriented Harrison was than Frazer. Vickery admits that Frazer "himself had never been on a field trip and indeed was the leader of the armchair, or as Andrew Lang christened it, Covent Garden school of anthropology" (83). Harrison, however, traveled yearly to museums and archaeological excavations across Europe — Athens, Crete, Delphi, Olympia, Eleusis, Sicily, Etruria, and Berlin — studying with the great turn-of-the-century archaeologists, such as Wilhelm Doerpfeld, Ernst Curtius, and M. Homolles. All her work is filled with concrete evidence gleaned from archaeological ruins, artifacts, bas-reliefs, sculpture, vases, in addition to the compendious literary and scholiastic references necessary to the classicist. Both Doerpfeld and Homolles relied upon her to write up and announce their findings to England (Stewart 11–15, 19).

In fact, Frazer greatly admired Harrison's article on the "Mystica Vannus Iacchi" and relied upon it in his own discussion of Dionysus: "The literary and monumental evidence as to the winnowing-fan in the myth and ritual of Dionysus has been collected and admirably interpreted by Miss J. E. Harrison in her article "Mystica Vannus Iacchi"...[and] her *Prolegomena to the Study of Greek Religion*" (5). Frazer cites these and other works by Harrison seven times in his chapter on Dionysus, three times in discussing the rituals at Eleusis, and wherever he focuses specifically on Greek rituals. He did not make the monumental claims for his influence that Vickery and others have subsequently made for him. As he wrote in a preface to the *Golden Bough*, E.B. Tylor's *Primitive Culture* "opened up a mental vista undreamed of by me before," while "the central idea of my essay — the conception of the slain god — is derived directly, I believe, from my friend ... Robertson Smith" (xiv).

Frazer was but one member of a group of scholars with an enormous sense of community and shared knowledge. Furthermore, the exciting discoveries of anthropology and their application to myth and classical literature was a progressive movement through three generations of teachers, mentors, students, collaborators, and friends. If we examine the dedications and prefaces of the seminal works by the major contributors to this movement, we find that they do not reveal the overwhelming influence of any one figure (or if they do, that figure is not Frazer); rather, they clearly reflect this sense of community and generational progression. Frazer dedicated *The Golden Bough* (1890) to William Robertson Smith, citing Tylor and Mannhardt in the preface as his other two important influences, while Lang dedicated *Custom and Myth* (1884) to Tylor and *Modern Mythology* (1897) to J. F. McLennan. In the preface to *Prolegomena* (1903) Harrison acknowledged her debt to the Cambridge classicists Jebb, Ridgeway and Verrall, to Frazer, Francis Darwin, and A.B. Cook, and especially a "deep and frequent debt" to F. M. Cornford, while she dedicated *Themis* (1912) to Gilbert Murray. F. M. Cornford dedicated his *Thucydides Mythistoricus* (1907) to Harrison, and his *Origin of Attic Comedy* (1914) to Gilbert Murray, while acknowledging the help of "two friends," A.B. Cook and Jane Harrison: "Miss Harrison has let me draw upon stores of learning far greater than my own. My theory, moreover, like Professor Murray's, rests upon conceptions which she has done much to elucidate" (viii). Gilbert Murray paid tribute to Jane Harrison "above all" in the preface to *The Rise of the Greek Epic* (1907) and to *The Four Stages of Greek Religion* (1912): "I cannot adequately describe the advantage I have derived from many years of frequent discussion and comparison of results with a Hellenist whose learning and originality of mind are only equalled by her vivid generosity towards her fellow-workers" (xii).

These dedications reveal a generational progression. The first generation, including Tylor, McLennan, Smith, and Mannhardt, was primarily scientific and not literary. They developed a handful of key anthropological concepts that figure prominently in every discussion in the field thereafter. We have already seen the importance of Tylor's survivals, animism, and his theory of magic. J. F. McLennan explored "totemism", a societal structure based on clans, each having its own sacred emblem or "totem" animal; Robertson Smith was the first to propose that animal and human sacrifice could have religious significance, leading to the concept of a "scapegoat" sacrificed to purify the community; and Mannhardt established the importance of vegetation and fertility rites among contemporary European peasantry. Although Lang and Frazer were both Tylorians, Lang adopted McLennan's totemism while Frazer leaned toward Mannhardt's "corn-spirits" as the primary basis for primitive ritual. As Lang teasingly noted about *The Golden Bough*: "The corn-spirit starts up in most unexpected places," but he later conceded that Frazer's view "holds its ground better than my totemistic suggestion" (*MM* xxii, 86). We can see that the second generation of scholars, primarily Lang, Frazer and Harrison, but including others of lesser importance, debated, narrowed, and further developed these basic concepts introduced by their professors and mentors. They exchanged ideas, edited each other's manuscripts, cited each other's findings and criticized each other's work freely.

The third generation, primarily Murray, Cornford, and Cook, came to be known as the "Cambridge Anthropologists," but they were all classicists. They applied the theories derived from comparative anthropology to a reassessment of Hellenic religion, philosophy, and particularly, drama. In this they followed the lead of Jane Harrison. Vickery commits an understandable error in describing Frazer as one of "the four major figures in what came to be called the Cambridge School of Anthropology," since Frazer was known as an anthropologist of sorts and lectured at Cambridge. But a contemporary, T.S. Eliot, in a 1920 review of Murray's translation of *Medea*, did not mention Frazer as part of the "philosophy [that] arose at Cambridge" or as one of the "scientists" who "have sensibly affected our attitude toward the Classics," although he paid tribute to him four years later as "most eminent" in the science of "folklore" (*AL* 38; *VF* 29). Rather, in 1920, Eliot noted that, "Few books are more fascinating than those of Miss Harrison, Mr. Cornford, or Mr. Cooke [*sic*], when they burrow in the origins of Greek myths and rites" (*AL* 38). Today anthropologists and literary critics, when refering to this group, preface the name "Cambridge School" with the adjective "so-called" because it is a complete misnomer. Only three of the members resided at Cambridge and none were anthropologists. Joseph Fontenrose cites the four members of "the so-called Cambridge School" as "Jane Harrison, Gilbert Murray,

Francis Cornford, and A.B. Cook" (1), as does Haskell M. Block (130). These four comprise the group that formulated and popularized the "ritual theory" or "ritual approach" to classical literature upon the foundation built by the new anthropological understanding of primitive myth and ritual.

Since Frazer contributed greatly to this new anthropology he certainly influenced the "Cambridge School," but again scholars have vastly overestimated his influence and marginalized Harrison, who was demonstrably the matriarch of the group. Haskell M. Block notes, "the meticulous and fascinating investigations of Sir James Frazer into almost every area of primitive rite were followed by the studies of Jane Harrison, F. M. Cornford, A. B. Cook, and Gilbert Murray, all applying the findings of comparative anthropology to the origins of Greek drama," completely ignoring Harrison's equally meticulous analyses of artifacts and archaeological remains, and perpetuating the misconception that Frazer's work was "followed by" Harrison's, when in fact their major works were contemporaneous (130). Fontenrose too credits Frazer's Dying God or "King of the Woods" as being the "springboard ... from which the whole ritual school ultimately takes off" (36) as does Vickery when he claims, for instance, that the "Excursis" contributed by Murray to Harrison's *Themis* "develops in detail Frazer's point about the intimate connection of rites with myths or stories," or that F. M. Cornford's "indebtedness to Frazer's orientation is seen" in *Thucydides Mythistoricus*.

By making Frazer appear responsible for inspiring the entire ritual movement from its birth in anthropology all the way to its flowering in revisionist classicism, these scholars consistently ignore the many dedications and prefaces that establish Harrison, not Frazer, as the link between the anthropology of the older generation and the classicism of the younger. Murray wrote of his *Five Stages of Greek Religion*: "In the first essay my debt to Miss Harrison is great and obvious ... in the main I follow her lead," while F. M. Cornford wrote in the preface to *Thucydides Mythistoricus*: "Any element of value there may be in the mythological chapters is due, directly or indirectly, to her" (xii). While these writers occasionally cite Frazer in a footnote, on more than one occasion Murray wrote that he considered Harrison's *Prolegomena* "a work of genius" and "a book which, in the current phrase, made an epoch" (*JEH* 11–12; Stewart 3). Cornford, too, regarded Harrison's work as "'the intuition of a genius backed by knowledge greater than my own'" (Stewart 87).

Furthermore, Harrison's personal friendships with both Murray and Cornford are well-documented, a closeness none of them had with Frazer. Jessie Stewart, Harrison's student and close friend of the Murrays, wrote that the "triad" of Harrison, Murray, and Cornford "must be studied as a group of which Jane was the forerunner in age and inspiration" (83). Harrison's letters reveal how much she relied on Murray's translations, opinions and advice during the composition of both *Prolegomena to the Study of Greek Religion* and *Themis*, and show as well her intimacy with both Murray and his wife Lady Mary Murray, stretching over two decades. In 1902 Murray joined her on an expedition to Naples, to help decipher several Orphic tablets which she needed for her discussion of Orphism in *Prolegomena*. His involvement in translating Euripides changed her focus in the *Prolegomena* more and more to Dionysus; thus he turned her attention to drama, just as she turned his to ritual (25). She also relied on Murray's translation of the fragmentary *Hymn of the Kouretes to Zeus*, recently discovered in Crete as the basis of her argument in *Themis*, working out her interpretation of it with his help. Of her fertile friendship with Murray she wrote, "We had better not talk of debts. My cup of gratitude brims over. It was a good God that sent us into the world in the same century" (36). Likewise, Murray's memorial tribute to Harrison addressed to Newnham College on October 27th, 1928, is an eloquent expression of her importance in his life, both as a scholar and a friend.

Yet Murray was at Oxford, while F.M. Cornford, like Harrison, was at Cambridge. Her relationship with Cornford was a day-to-day sharing of ideas, whether "over the black brew of tea we both found needful to resume the powers of thought" or during their daily bicycle rides: "for eleven years, the most fruitful of her life and in many ways of his, they continued closely together" (20, 104). They pooled their money and traveled together to Crete, to Athens, and in 1904 to Cornwall where, influenced by Victor Bérard, they both studied Cuneiform and Phoenician. Twenty years her junior, Cornford regarded Harrison as his friend, mentor, even "Aunt", and although she fostered his eventual marriage to Frances Darwin, Charles Darwin's granddaughter, she experienced a breakdown after their marriage, suggesting the depth of her emotional dependence on Cornford.

Harrison saw herself, Murray, and Cornford as a "triad" of scholars who shared the same approach — that early ritual and religion (dubbed "*origines*" by Harrison) lay behind much of Greek literature, as she wrote to Murray: "You see there are only two people who are scholars and with literary minds who understand that ... mythology and *ori-gines* ... are at the back of everything — F.M.C. here for Cambridge and I hope you for Oxford" (85). She saw herself as responsible for exploring Greek religion from the ritual approach, while "the philosophical investigation belonged to Francis Cornford [and] the delicate literary task she assigned to Gilbert Murray," and she insisted that her friends both contribute to *Themis*, Cornford a chapter (VII) on "The Origin of the Olympic Games" and Murray an "Excursis on the Ritual Forms Preserved in Greek Tragedy" (84). A.B. Cook, the fourth member of the "Cambridge School" became "perhaps the most erudite and fertile of her helpers" (102). While she was ill he, along with Cornford, helped correct proofs of *Themis*, just as she read and critiqued in turn "the bulk" of Cook's proofs of *Zeus* (see his prefaces, I, xiv; II, iv). When she left for Paris in 1922, she bequeathed to Cook "her whole assemblage of photographs representing Greek votive reliefs and other religious monuments" (iv), an extensive collection since she had been one of the first to use slides and photographs in her lectures on Greek art as early as the 1880s (Stewart 10, 14).

Harrison was Frazer's contemporary, yet she had an affinity with the younger generation that he never did. She commented on the importance of remaining connected to young people in her essay, "Crabbed Age and Youth," and Gilbert Murray sensitively analyzed her preference for "the society of the young, because they were less likely to have fixed views and established orthodoxies, and therefore, less likely to be critical of her or displeased with her" (*JEH* 19–20). Harrison actively sought the intimacy of younger people and she dreaded "becoming like many old people whom she had known long ago, still able to repeat formulae but no longer able to think" (Stewart 187). Harrison alone of her generation rejected the rationalism that dominated the thinking of her contemporaries. For her alone among the scholars of her generation, primitivism became not only a valid, but a superior, way of life because it was not rational, but emotional and wholly experiential. She alone anticipated modernism in her sense that the "immense panorama of futility and anarchy" of the modern world, to use Eliot's phrase, could not be answered by the 19th-century rationalist's naive faith in man's intellect, "because we are beginning to know what knowledge is, and what are its limitations" (*AO* 207). Thus, not only did she pursue friendships with young people, but she herself felt and expressed the need of the younger Georgian generation to find meaning in sensory experience, in life, rather than in rational constructs. And she paid a price for her rebellion, as Murray states: "with all her fame and influence, she never became an accepted orthodox authority. She was always frowned upon by a fair number of important persons: she was always in spirit a little against the government, against orthodoxy. And, thus, since orthodoxy is the belief of the established authorities, she never went over, as most successful writers do, from the ranks of the young to those of the old" (*JEH* 20).

Orthodoxy obviously still frowns upon Jane Harrison, minimizing her role as senior member of the Cambridge Anthropologists, slighting the monumental and often radical achievement of her scholarship, missing completely her formulation of the ritual theory, as well as ignoring her influence, both direct and indirect through Gilbert Murray and F. M. Cornford, on modernism. Harrison knew comparative anthropology from Tylor to Robertson Smith to Mannhardt to Frazer to Lang to Codrington to Marett and more; however, she was also profoundly influenced by the French sociologist Émile Durkheim and the philosopher Henri Bergson, as well as by Freud. Her interests grew from archaeology and art to primitive rituals to "the religious impulse in human psychology and in modern life," and her books became increasingly theoretical, moving from "the monuments and mythology of Greece, and thence to the things that have lain and still lie implicit in all forms of religion and beneath the tide of temporal change" (Murray, *JEH* 15–16). The ritual theory evolved throughout her oeuvre from its simplest expression, common to all the comparative anthropologists, that rituals preceded myths or that myths originated to "explain" anachronistic rituals, to her connection of the communal, religious expression of primitive ritual with the universal human motivation for all artistic creation. In addition, her works express a powerful feminist critique of the "superimposition" of patriarchal Olympian theology over ancient matriarchal cults, and the attempted erasure ever since of the earlier chthonic female-dominated faiths.

Harrison's first work, *Mythology and Monuments of Ancient Athens*, grew out of her archaeological training, but it reveals that the "primitive layer of deities [which] lay under the Olympian cult" was already "simmering in her mind" as early as 1890 (Stewart 12). By 1903, in *Prolegomena to the Study of Greek Religion* she had "clearly stated the priority of ritual over myth or theology," as well as the priority of early Greek matriarchal chthonic goddesses and gods over the patriarchal Olympians (Hyman 13). *Themis*, while still based on detailed evidence from Greek archaeology, art, and artifacts, was an even more theoretical work in which Harrison first elaborated on the ritual theory, connecting Dionysian rites with the birth of Greek drama, and went on to redefine religion itself in light of Bergsonian *durée* and Durkheim's ideas of collective consciousness. It was a "dangerous" book according to Murray: the narrow circle of Harrison's disciples and friends, the "Cambridge School," admired it, but it was "too full of new ideas, or rather of new lights which made all the material on which they fell look different" to be accepted by the "orthodox circles" of Verrall and Ridgeway, professors who had taught her so much (*JEH* 13–14).

Yet however daring, her work was always firmly grounded in the proof of her own observations, "what I *had* seen and *did* understand":

> a clay sealing which was a veritable little manual of primitive Cretan faith and ritual. I shall never forget the moment when Mr. Arthur Evans first showed it to me. ... It represented the Great Mother standing on her own mountain with her attendant lions, and before her a worshipper in ecstasy. ... The minotaur is none other than the human king — God wearing the mask of a bull [Dionysus]. Here was this ancient ritual of the Mother and the Son which long preceded the worship of the Olympians: here were the true Prolegomena.   (*R* 71–2)

This clay sealing revealed a strong connection to Harrison between the late Dionysian cult and earlier chthonic matriarchal rituals, and her conviction was strengthened on another trip to Crete in 1904. There the archaeologist R.C. Bosanquet showed her his latest discovery, a fragmentary "Hymn of the Kouretes found in the temple of Diktaean Zeus," more evidence to Harrison of "the magical rite of the Mother and the Son, the induction the Year-Spirit who long preceded the worship of the Father" that served as her inspiration for *Themis*.

Although resisted by the patriarchs of the academic establishment, Harrison's work was popular. Both she and Murray published volumes for "The Home University Library," Oxford's series designed to make classical scholarship more accessible to the general public. In her volume, *Ancient Art and Ritual* (1913), Harrison summarized her conclusions about the origins of Greek drama from *Themis*, simplifying the connection she saw between ritual and its evolution into art, so that F. M. Cornford declared, he "never understood *Themis* till he read *Art and Ritual* (Stewart 114). Thus, the ritual theory evolved throughout Harrison's oeuvre, which was widely read and, it is important to note, appeared concurrently with all three editions of *The Golden Bough*, not subsequently. There is no doubt that Frazer influenced Harrison, but early in the 1890s, while ritualism was a vague impulse as yet unformulated in her mind. She acknowledged her debt to Frazer in the introduction to *Prolegomena*: "To all workers in the field of primitive religion Dr Frazer's writings have become so part and parcel of their mental furniture that special acknowledgement has become almost superfluous" (xiv). It is obvious from this almost dismissively perfunctory tribute, that Frazer's influence on her was inchoate rather than specific: he affected her "mental furniture" rather than suggesting any specific theory *per se*. In *Prolegomena*, Harrison discussed many of the same annual Hellenic festivals and rituals that Frazer did in *The Golden Bough*, and her footnotes reveal their relationship as colleagues, sharing information and sources, sometimes agreeing and sometimes disagreeing in interpretation (111, 126–7, 132).

However, a postscript written to Lady Mary Murray from Rome reveals Harrison's disillusionment with the "great man" as early as 1901: "P. S. — Mrs. Frazer (your double!) has been sitting on my bed for two hours, telling me 'who not to know', i.e. who has not paid Mr. Frazer 'proper attention'! This is the price I pay for a few shy radiant moments under the Golden Bough — " (Stewart 37). It would appear that Harrison had already relegated Frazer's influence to "a few shy radiant moments," over by the publication of the second edition of *The Golden Bough*! Further, her reference to Mrs. Murray as Mrs. Frazer's "double" indicates that she already regarded Gilbert Murray as a scholar of equal stature with Frazer, even at the very beginning of their acquaintance. Finally, however much Frazer may have influenced her early on, Harrison saw *Themis*, the work in which she first seriously formulated the ritual theory, as a departure from Frazer's theory, not an outgrowth of it, as so many have assumed. She (among others, including Andrew Lang) seriously disagreed with his theory of magic, and this divergence over a concept so basic to her formulation of the ritual theory shows that, far from being "Frazer-generated," the theory in fact grew in opposition to him.

The relation between magic and religion had been vigorously debated from Tylor's basic definitions on, and even today the question remains unsettled. We have already seen that by the early 1900s Tylor's definitions of religion and magic were condemned as too rationalistic, largely due to the increasing popularity of Codrington's *The Melane-sians* (1891) and R.R. Marett's *The Threshold of Religion* (1909). For these anthropologists magic was not merely primitive peoples' effort to control the universe for practical purposes, i.e., to bring rain or to encourage fertility, but was rather the expression of a pre-intellectual "vitalism," a spiritual force inherent in nature and humanity. They cited evidence of this life force among the Melanesians, who called it *mana*, among the Iroquois, whose word for it was *orenda*, and others. Harrison adhered to this view, defining *orenda* as "the soul of magic ... your bodily life, your vigour, your passion, your power, the virtue that is in you to feel and do." This "power, actually experienced in person by the individual, and by him projected, extended into the rest of the world" not only informed magic for Harrison, but religion, ritual, and ultimately, art. All are "the projection of man's inner experience, vague and unanalyzed, into the outer world" (*AO* 167–9).

In contrast, Frazer's interpretation of magic reveals his rationalism and hierarchical thinking. Although based on Tylor's "association of ideas," his theory was far more rationalistic than Tylor's ever was. For Tylor, magic and animism (the early stirrings of religion), were closely related since both grew out of primitive peoples' inability to make "psy-chical distinctions" between subjective and objective, imagination and reality, themselves and nature (*PC* I, 116; II, 29, 53). For Frazer, magic and religion are not only unrelated, they are opposed. He saw a "funda-mental distinction and even opposition of principle between magic and religion" (*GB* intro to 2nd ed., xx), since the "fundamental conception" of magic is "identical with that of modern science" — "the faith, implicit but real and firm, in the order and uniformity of nature." Both magic and science comprise man's attempts to understand the "laws of na-ture" so that he may "turn the order of natural phenomena to his own advantage." The difference is that magic is a "misconception of the na-ture of the particular laws," while science is a true understanding; magic is "dross" while science is "golden." Religion Frazer then defined as "a propitiation or conciliation of powers superior to man which are be-lieved to direct and control the course of nature and of human life" (Part I, vol. i, 221–2). Only when the "inefficacy of magic" became apparent did "the shrewder intelligences" among men turn to religion, the perception of nature as resulting from God's law, beyond man's control except through prayer and placation of the deity (237).

For Frazer religion was rational and elevated because it resulted from abstract thought; magic was material and inferior because the result of practical experience. In a characteristically colorful passage he imagined the "practical savage" replying to "the subtleties ... of the philosophical radical": " 'Can anything be plainer,' he might say, 'than that I light my twopenny candle on earth and that the sun kindles his great fire in heaven? I should be glad to know whether, when I have put on my green robe in spring, the trees do not afterwards do the same? These are the facts patent to everybody, and on them I take my stand. I am a plain practical man, not one of your theorists and splitters of hairs and choppers of logic' " (243).

Frazer's view of magic as serving entirely practical purposes divests primitive humanity of any religious impulse whatsoever, and for that reason it disgusted Andrew Lang: "His position would be entirely that of scientific men, without God in the world. It is, apparently, taken for granted that man, in his primitive condition, with magic and without religion, has none but physical needs; has no spiritual, moral, or speculative needs, such as might impel him to seek after God" (*FR* 244). Frazer's materialist view of primitive culture often allowed him to interpret myth and ritual with greater impartiality than Lang, however. The "bestial buffooneries" of Demeter's rituals at Eleusis which so baffled Lang, for instance "making Proserpine out of a porker" (*HH* 65), were to Frazer entirely natural: in fertility rites the corn-spirit is often "conceived and represented in animal form," perhaps because "wild creatures are commonly penned by the advance of the reapers into the last patch of standing corn," which is "to the primitive mind, enough to identify him as the spirit of the corn escaping ... from his ruined home" (see Part V, vol. ii, 1, 16–19 and vol. i, 304). Typically, however, Frazer grasps at a rather far-fetched explanation in order to align this rite with his ubiquitous "corn-spirit." It is interesting to contrast both Lang and Frazer's views with Harrison's explanation as to why worshippers at Eleusis bathed with pigs: The pig was a "*pharmakos*" that conducted out evil through purification in the sea, and it "was the cheapest and commonist of sacrificial animals, one that each and every citizen could afford" (*PSGR* 153).

Frazer's rationalism supports his rigidly hierarchical conception of humanity. For, he explains, even animals possess the primitive mental capacity that produced magic, the association of ideas: "The very beasts associate the ideas of things that are like each other or that have been found together in their experience; and they could hardly survive for a day if they ceased to do so." But what animals have ever devised a

God, have ever believed in a "multitude of invisible animals or one enormous and prodigiously strong animal behind the scenes?" (234) Religion, the belief in spirits or in one omnipotent deity, is the result of "human reason" alone; thus it separates civilized humanity from "the merely animal intelligence" and marks a crucial departure in "the evolution of our race." "But this deepening sense of religion, this more perfect submission to the divine will in all things, affects only those higher intelligences who have breadth of view enough to comprehend the vastness of the universe and the littleness of man. Small minds cannot grasp great ideas; to their narrow comprehension, their purblind vision, nothing seems really great and important but themselves. Such minds hardly rise to religion at all" (240).

Thus Frazer, like so many of his 19th-century colleagues, straddled a remarkable divide between empathy with and contempt for primitives. Like Tylor, whose work wove strands of both rationalism and mysticism, and like Lang, who agonized over the contrast he perceived between "rational" religion and "irrational" myth, Frazer's work was often contradictory. On the one hand, his pragmatic materialism and his passionate love of nature infused his prose with lyrical imagery, and made many myths and rituals comprehensible for the first time; yet on the other hand, he could vent an astonishing disdain for the peasant class whose religious customs he analyzed so closely, i.e., "the muzzy mind of the Sicilian bumpkin who looked with blind devotion" to his gods and goddesses. For Frazer, "theological subtleties" belonged solely to "longer heads than are commonly to be found on bucolic shoulders" (V, i, 59). In fact, "such minds hardly rise to religion at all."

All her life Jane Harrison was drawn to the *act* and rejected the *word*. This is explicit in everything she wrote. Logos, i.e. "theology", she regarded as an imprisonment of the human soul: "Theology is the letter that killeth, religion the spirit that maketh alive" (*AO* 186). As discussed in Chapter 2, true religious experience for her was not rationalized "Omega, a full-blown theology" with its "eikonic" anthropomorphic gods, but rather "Alpha," "a thing lived, experienced" as in the aneikonic mysticism of the matriarchal cults of Dionysus and Demeter. She viewed the "more perfect submission to the divine will" exalted by Frazer as a degradation of the human spirit. She not only disagreed with such rationalistic, hierarchical thought, she reversed it. The so-called "higher intelligences" who rationalized religion and subjugated humanity to its gods in her view destroyed the glorious mysticism and "vitalism" of early pre-intellectual religious experience. For Harrison, neither magic nor the rituals of aneikonic religion derived from human reason nor the cognitive attempt to understand nature's laws, but were "the outcome rather of emotion than intellect, begotten probably in that early stage when thought and emotion were not segregate as now" (203; see also *T* 445–479). For Harrison, primitives were not "purblind" as for Frazer, but visionary; their religion was not based upon "great ideas", but upon "this personal experience, this exaltation, this sense of immediate, non-intellectual revelation" (175–6).

Also contrary to Frazer, she viewed magic, not religion, as the "borderline between man and beast," since magic was man's active effort to impose his will, his ego, on nature, something animals are incapable of. Magic in Harrison's interpretation, was the "spiritual protoplasm" which "gives rise to Religion and other 'civilized' things," including science and art. (Stewart 96, *AO* 162–3). Primitives were not cowed by the immensity of the universe and their own "littleness"; rather they participated in the gigantic forces of nature through "dancing magical dances." How different is this from Frazer, who saw the survival of magic "among the ignorant and superstitious classes ... who constitute, unfortunately, the vast majority of mankind" as a "standing menace to civilisation," that could only be saved by the continuing scientific education of the elite. And, like Lang, Frazer was torn. While he regarded anthropology as "one of the great achievements of the nineteenth century" because it ran "shafts down into this low mental stratum in many parts of the world, and thus discover[ed] its substantial identity everywhere," at the same time he sometimes portrayed man's "irrational" side, still evident in modern European peasants, as a threat: "We seem to move on a thin crust which may at any moment be rent by the subterranean forces slumbering below" (236). Of all these scholars, Harrison's theory alone seems unified, and only she seems wholly of the 20th century. Hers was not the vision of the 19th-century rationalist, but of the 20th-century social psychologist. To her the "subterranean forces slumbering below" did not represent a threat but a salvation, for it was "an essential of religious life," "a matter of deep conviction" to reject the "intellectual attempt to define the indefinable" (*AO* 205). Here lies the key to Harrison's affinity for the younger generation, for the young Georgian writers, who also rebeled against the rational, patriarchal certitudes of the Victorian generation, and sought spiritual meaning in "a thing lived, experienced."

Frazer announced his theory of magic and definition of religion in the second edition of *The Golden Bough* (1900), and it is thus no wonder that by 1901 Jane Harrison was writing to Lady Mary Murray that her "few shy radiant moments under the Golden Bough" were over. By 1908, while working on *Themis*, she wrote: "The question now stirring is the relation between Magic and Religion (Frazer is all wrong in thinking them utterly opposed)" (Stewart 96). Nor did she hesitate to state her divergence from Frazer more publicly. In her essay "Darwinism and Religion," written the same year for the Darwin Centenary volume, she aligned herself with R.R. Marett, criticizing "the view held by Dr. Frazer" that magic and religion "are at the outset diametrically opposed" (*AO* 173). In thinking out her own view of magic, so radically opposed to Frazer's, she credits the help of "Professor Gilbert Murray." Thus it is obvious that these two, who formulated the ritual theory together beginning with Jane Harrison's *Themis*, were far, far from viewing themselves as disciples of Frazer, as Vickery and everyone else except Stanley Hyman has since assumed. Harrison praised Frazer's "immense learning," his "burning devotion to truth," and "steadfast and unflinching scholarship," but she disagreed strenuously with "the author of *The Golden Bough*" that pagan religion "is mainly a delusion and a darkness, a savage thing, a snake hardly scotched" (*Spectator*, 303).

Part of the reason misconceptions have persisted is that contemporary restatements of the ritual theory have been too general. If one takes the ritual theory as simply the assertion that rituals preceded myths, then it is explicit throughout Frazer's work, indeed, throughout Tylor's and Lang's work, as well as that of any other comparative anthropologist of the period who reinterpreted the hitherto baffling elements of myths as survivals of customs and rituals. The theory of survivals grows quite naturally into the idea that rituals preceded myths, since that is what survivals are — relics in folklore, legends, and myths of acts once performed: "The religion which retained most of the myths ... keeps up acts of ritual that have lost their significance in their passage from a dark and dateless past" (Lang, *MRR* 186). *The Golden Bough* is based upon the assumption that myths derived as explanations of rituals, but Frazer hardly saw himself as proposing anything radical when he stated: "It needs no elaborate demonstration to convince us that the stories told to account for Diana's worship at Nemi are ... made up to explain the origin of a religious ritual" (Part I, vol. i, 21). He, as well as Lang, saw that the purpose of the *Homeric*

Hymn to Demeter was to "explain the origin of the Eleusinian mysteries": "It has been generally recognized, and indeed it seems scarcely
open to doubt, that the main theme which the poet set before himself
in composing this hymn was to describe the traditional foundation of
the Eleusinian mysteries by the goddess Demeter" (V, i, 37; see also
vol. ii, 19). And Frazer concluded, "Thus myth and ritual mutually
explain and confirm each other" (39). Just as Harrison asserts in
Prolegomena, "A rite frequently throws light on the myth made to explain it. Occasionally the rite itself is elucidated by the myth to which
it gave birth" (133). By 1903 this view was a commonplace.

For contemporary anthropologists the theory that rituals preceded
myths has long since become a "hen or the egg question" (Kluckhohn
37) and, according to Joseph Fontenrose, "the findings of field
anthropologists" now "point in one direction, to a conclusion that myths
are generally not ritual texts" (50–2). That modern anthropology has
refuted this definition of the ritual theory, while pertinent to the scientist, makes little difference to literary criticism, contrary to Fontenrose's
assumptions. Whether rituals preceded myths or precisely how the
two are entwined has never really been the important issue for writers
or literary critics: the important discovery was the connection between
ritual and *art*, that "they actually arise out of a common human impulse," and this connection was made solely by Jane Harrison with
the help of Gilbert Murray (*AAR* 18). While no one did more to popu-
larize a new understanding of myths as explanations of fertility rituals
than Frazer, he never came close to making the leap, or to use Harrison's
metaphor, crossing the "bridge" between ritual and art. As Harrison
wrote in her preface to *Ancient Art and Ritual*, her purpose was not to
give a "general summary" of ancient ritual (v). For a particular understanding of "Primitive Ritual" she in fact recommends Frazer's *Golden
Bough*, from which she took many ritual "instances" to illustrate her
ideas (253). Rather,

> the point of my title and the real gist of my argument lie perhaps
> in the word "*and*" — that is, in the intimate connection which I
> have tried to show exists between ritual and art. This connection
> has, I believe, an important bearing on questions vital today, as
> for example, the question of the place of art in our modern civi-
> lization, its relation to and its difference from religion and moral-
> ity; in a word, on the whole enquiry as to what the nature of art
> is and how it can help or hinder spiritual life.   (v)

It is clear from this quotation how consciously Harrison crossed the bridge not only between ritual and ancient art, but even to modern art. That Frazer never crossed such a bridge is seen upon examining his discussion of "the parallelism between the modern drama and the ancient worship" of Dionysus (Part V, vol. i, 24–34). But by "modern drama" Frazer does *not* mean Yeats' Cuchulain cycle! He means the peasant drama "annually performed at the Carnival in the villages round Viza, an old Thracian capital" by "mummers," and "masqueraders" dressed in goatskins. These public "ceremonies" included displaying an infant in the Dionysian "winnowing fan" (Harrison's "*Mystica Vannus Iacchi*"), wild dancing while "the gypsy man and wife enact an obscene pantomime on the straw-heap," a "simulation of plowing and sowing, accompanied by prayers for good crops," parading "the same coarse symbol of reproductive energy which characterized the ancient ritual of Dionysus," etc. Frazer was no different from Mannhardt, Tylor, or Lang, in his fascination with the survival of ancient rituals in modern peasant customs, nor was he any different from them in maintaining a strict division between the mentality of the contemporary European peasant, the "English yokel," and the enlightened, educated, English gentleman. For Frazer the link between "the high tragedy of the death and resurrection of Dionysus" and "a rustic mummers' play acted by ploughmen for the purpose of fertilising the brown earth" was perfectly clear, but he would never have dreamed of establishing a link between Dionysian ritual and himself. But for Jane Harrison, influenced by William James, Freud, Durkheim and Bergson, the "savage" is important not as a fascinating survival, but because "we want to understand his psychology, ... since we realize that our own behavior is based on instincts kindred to his" (*AAR* 29). Unlike Frazer, she wanted to "trace the secret motive springs that move the artist now as then" to a "common *emotional* factor ... that makes art and ritual in their beginnings well-nigh indistinguishable" (24–6).

Sir James Frazer's major accomplishment was that he explained countless rituals for the first time by relating them to fertility, both vegetative and human. His most important contribution to comparative anthropology was his understanding, apparent in every myth or ritual he interpreted, that spirituality and sexuality were united in the ancient world: "the sexual instinct has moulded the religious consciousness of our race" (V, i, vii). Certainly Frazer's primary interest was in the male archetype of Dying God, which could be said to be the unifying theme of the entire *Golden Bough*. But this male archetype is invariably in the service of a more powerful goddess; he is ritualistically slain in order to engender her fertility. Frazer painted a world dominated and made meaningful by powerfully sexual, generative mothers and their consorts, from Artemis/Hippolytus and Diana/Virbius of Part I, to Aphrodite/Adonis and Cybele/Attis of Part IV, to Demeter/Persephone/Dionysus of Part V. He vividly portrayed the dominance of female archetypes in primitive religion, but this was a natural outcome of his materialist, Darwinian world view. For Frazer magic, ritual, and religion all evolved out of the need to regulate the seasons and fertility so vital to the survival of the species:

> To them the principle of life and fertility, whether animal or vegetable, was one and indivisible. To live and to cause to live, to eat food and to beget children, these were the primary wants of men in the past, and they will be the primary wants of men in the future so long as the world lasts.   (IV, i, 4–5)

No myth or ritual was too violent or sexual for Frazer to interpret in an "objective" tone according to this view. Human or animal sacrifice in which victims were beaten, hung, dismembered, or torn apart while still alive represented "the violent destruction of the corn by man, who cuts it down on the field, stamps it to pieces on the threshing-floor, and grinds it to powder in the mill," with "fragments of their bodies" distributed "over the fields for the purpose of fertilising them" (IV, i, 232–3). Whether his interpretation was accurate or not is irrelevant; for the first time he made these "barbarisms" comprehensible. Sacred prostitution as well he described "not as an orgy of lust, but as a solemn religious duty performed in the service of that great Mother Goddess, the personification of all the reproductive energies of nature." Even Cybele's castration rites were rendered intelligible according to Frazer's interpretation: the initiates' "broken instruments of fertility were afterwards reverently wrapt up and buried in the earth or in subterranean chambers sacred to Cybele, where, like the offering of blood, they may have been deemed instrumental in recalling Attis to life and hastening the generative resurrection of nature" (268).

The cult of the mother obviously appealed to Frazer. He established the importance of the generative Earth-mother archetype as early as the first chapter of the first volume of *The Golden Bough* in his portrait of Artemis, and the first thing he established about the goddess was that, contrary to Homeric and modern opinion, she was not virginal, nor was her relationship with her consort Hippolytus one of platonic devotion. Neither virginity nor chastity had much appeal for Frazer: immaculate births in mythology, he explained, never arose "from that perverse and mischievous theory that virginity is more honourable than matrimony":

> The truth is, that the word *parthenos* applied to Artemis, which we commonly translate virgin, means no more than an unmarried woman, and in early days the two things were by no means the same. ... the Grecian divinity, like her Asiatic sister, was at bottom a personification of the teeming life of nature. (I, i, 37–8)

Frazer portrayed Artemis as "a goddess of fecundity, though not of wedlock" — amoral, promiscuous, powerfully sexual, and justifiably so because of her crucial role in ensuring survival of the species. He was unique among his male colleagues in seeing that in pre-Olympian matriarchal religions, women were not defined by their roles in relation to men; rather, men were defined by their roles in relation to women: "she who fertilises nature must herself be fertile, and to be that she must necessarily have a male consort" (39). Women were not passive, but the primary active force in survival, and their power was based upon their sexuality. As novel as this view may have been, however, Frazer's rendition still confined the female archetype to its traditional position in Western binaristic thinking: woman = body. He may have exalted images of female sexuality, but he also viewed female power as limited *to* sexuality.

Jane Harrison's rendition of female archetypes was more wholistic; she evaded patriarchal binarisms as much as one immersed in late Victorian culture could have by portraying the archetypes as they evolved in all their multifariousness. In *Prolegomena to the Study of Greek Religion* she analyzed their development from the most primitive animalistic bogeys called Keres, to their flowering as anthropomorphic expressions of the female life-cycle, finally to their mystical apotheosis in the union of Dionysian and Orphic mysteries with the Eleusinian ritual of Demeter and Kore. Certainly her interpretations were established on a foundation of Frazerian materialism. She understood thoroughly the importance of fertility in ancient ritual and the powerful role of goddessess and priestesses in those rituals: "As Dr. Frazer has well said, if man the individual is to live he must have food; if his race is to persist he must have children. ... These two things, therefore ... were

what man chiefly sought to procure by the performance of magical rites
for the regulation of the seasons" (*AAR* 50). For example, in *Prolegomena*, she describes in detail the "Women's Festivals," precursors of the
Eleusinian Mysteries, such as the Thesmophoria, involving "the magical
impulsion of fertility by burying *sacra* [sacred objects] in the ground,"
and the Haloa, a harvest festival of dancing and feasting on the threshing-floor (120–150). But when Harrison moves on to the "The Making
of a Goddess," Frazerian materialism is left behind.

The Keres began as ghosts — underworld bogeys, bringers of evil,
disease, death, old age, revenge. The purpose of many primitive rituals, such as the beating and sacrifice of the *pharmakos*, was to placate
these powerful spirits. They evolved into the familiar female archetype of woman as death-bringer, in such forms as Harpies, Sirens,
Gorgons, Sphinx, and Erinyes. But how did the archetype evolve from
Medusa, the terrifying Gorgon with pendant tongue, lethal eye, and
writhing snakes, to Athene, that picture of calm virginal rationality,
carrying the Gorgon's head on her shield as a last vestige of her
matriarchal past? Harrison is the only one among her colleagues who
regrets this passage from "barbarity" to rationality, which for her signifies the triumph of patriarchy:

> We are apt to regard the advance to anthropomorphism as nec-
> essarily a clear religious gain. A gain it is in so far as a certain
> element of barbarity is softened or extruded, but with this gain
> comes loss, the loss of the element of formless, monstrous mys-
> tery. The ram-headed Knum of the Egyptians is to the mystic
> more religious than any of the beautiful divine humanities of
> the Greek. ... Xenophanes put his finger on the weak spot of
> anthropomorphism. He saw that it comprised and confined the
> god within the limitations of the worshipper.   (258)

It is interesting to contrast Frazer's and Harrison's characterizations
of Demeter. Frazer asks "why did the Greeks personify the corn as a goddess rather than a god? why did they ascribe the origin of agriculture
to a female rather than to a male power?" (V, i, 113). Harrison asks how
the omnipotent Earth-mother, the "Lady of the Wild Things" became
more strictly limited to the agricultural "Grain-Mother" (271–2). Both
ascribe to a current theory that in very primitive societies women performed all the agricultural tasks while men hunted, which resulted
naturally in the agricultural deity being imagined as female. The fact

that women bear children also naturally associated them with fertility. Harrison concludes, "Such seems to have been the mind of the men of Athens who sent their wives and daughters to keep the Thesmophoria and work their charms and ensure fertility for crops and man" (272). Frazer, although willing to attribute the "greatest advance in economic history" (farming) to women, finds the agricultural theory too "far-fetched and improbable" to explain the Greek concept of Demeter: "I prefer to suppose that the idea of the corn as feminine was suggested to the Greek mind, not by the position of women in remote prehistoric ages, but by a direct observation of nature, the teeming head of corn appearing to the primitive fancy to resemble the teeming womb of woman" (130). To be sure, Frazer's version is more poetic!

Both Frazer and Harrison stress that Demeter and Kore are two aspects of one goddess and that in art they are often indistinguishable. But for Harrison this two-fold goddess is not confined to the "womb," i.e., to her function as symbol and guardian of the life-cycle of the grain. In her version, the two embody within themselves the cultural binarism usually expressed as female-body/male-spirit:

> The Mother takes the physical side, the Daughter the spiritual — the Mother is more and more of the upper air, the Daughter of the underworld. Demeter as Thesmophoros has for her sphere more and more the things of this life, laws and civilized marriage; she grows more and more human and kindly, goes more and more over to the humane Olympians, till in the Homeric Hymn she, the Earth-Mother, is an actual denizen of Olympus. The Daughter, at first but the young form of the mother, is in maiden fashion sequestered, even a little *farouche*; she withdraws herself more and more to the kingdom of the spirit, the things below and beyond. ... She passes to a place unknown of the Olympians, her kingdom is not of this world. (276)

Harrison's Persephone escapes the Olympian "family group of the ordinary patriarchal type" altogether through her return to the underworld and her absorption into a mystical faith that "concerned itself with the abnegation of this world and the life of the soul hereafter" (260, 276). Except for Persephone, however, Harrison describes all the "early matriarchal, husbandless goddesses," as once "noble and womanly, though perhaps not what the modern mind holds to be feminine," but limited and diminished "with the coming of patriarchal conditions"

(273). Demeter, Pandora, Athene, Hera, Aphrodite — all "are seques-
tered to a servile domesticity, they become abject and amorous" under
the gradual "superimposition" of Olympian theology (273). She objects
with particular vehemence to Hesiod's reworking of the Pandora myth:

> Through all the magic of a poet, caught and enchanted himself
> by the vision of a lovely woman, there gleams the ugly malice
> of theological animus. Zeus the Father will have no great Earth-
> goddess, Mother and Maid in one, in his man-fashioned Olym-
> pus, but her figure *is* from the beginning, so he re-makes it;
> woman, who was the inspirer, becomes the temptress; she who
> made all things, gods and mortals alike, is become their play-
> thing, their slave, dowered only with physical beauty, and with
> a slave's tricks and blandishments. To Zeus, the archpatriarchal
> *bourgeois*, the birth of the first woman is but a huge Olympian
> jest ...   (285)

One can almost hear Virginia Woolf thinking as she did about Char-
lotte Bronte, "She will write in a rage where she should write calmly"
(*AROO* 73). Of course this passage is no more or less clouded by emotion than Lang's "bestial buffooneries" or Frazer's "teeming wombs."
What it does admirably is express an/Other view. However, Harrison
herself seemed to feel she had gone too far, for quite uncharacteristi-
cally she tried in the following paragraph to efface the power of her
statement: "Such myths are a necessary outcome of the shift from
matriarchy to patriarchy, and the shift itself, spite of a seeming retro-
gression, is a necessary stage in a real advance" (285). She often felt
the force of her male colleagues' criticisms and sometimes tried to
accommodate them in the interest of appearing more "temperate"
and "reasonable" (i.e., less feminist), as she notes in the introduction
to *Themis*: "My critics have blamed me, and justly, for my intemperate
antipathy to the Olympians" (viii). After reading Murray's *Five Stages
of Greek Religion*, she admits to seeing "more clearly the debt we
owe to these Olympians for 'slaying the old blind dragon' still
unreasonably dear to me" (viii). But she never attenuated her views
without great "reluctance," and the overall impact of her oeuvre is a
strongly feminist recreation of a pre-patriarchal era she envisioned as
truly religious in a mystical sense.

For Harrison saw that the limitation of mythic female archetypes
to "domestic and amorous servitude" paralleled the limitation of

religious mysticism as expressed in ritual to a cold anthropomorphic theology that served patriarchal, political ends. This is why she so strenuously wished to restore the validity of mystical experience as she saw it in primitive worship, to dissociate it from rationalism and bring it to life again for her own spiritually bereft, and extremely patriarchal, age. As Harrison elaborated the ritual theory in *Ancient Art and Ritual*, describing the evolution of Greek tragedy from Dionysian ritual, she declared that primitive magic rituals could not have arisen out of rational or cognitive "conception," but expressed rather a collective emotional experience. In the following passage she pointedly disagrees with Frazerian theory:

> In discussions on such primitive rites as "Carrying out the Death," "Bringing in the Summer," we are often told that the puppet of the girl is carried round, buried, burnt; brought back because it "personifies the Spirit of Vegetation," or it "embodies the Spirit of Summer." The Spirit of Vegetation is "incarnate in the puppet." We are led, by way of speaking, to suppose that the savage or the villager first forms an idea or conception of a Spirit of Vegetation and then later "embodies" it. We naturally wonder that he should perform a mental act so high and difficult as abstraction.   (70–1)

Here she even mocks Frazer. How could beings so limited in rational capacity, as he so often imagines primitive people to be, "perform a mental act so high and difficult as abstraction"? Rather, for Harrison, the primitive doesn't need abstractions because he is "too busy living" fully. He "begins with a vague excited dance to relieve his emotion," but the dancer "does not 'embody' a previously conceived idea, rather he begets it." Magic ceremonies, therefore, are entirely experiential, based on "collectivity and emotional tension" (36; see also *T* 30–49). Unlike Frazer, Harrison's theory of magic was derived from contemporary psychological and sociological research, leaving behind all vestiges of 19th-century rationalism: "Sympathetic magic is, modern psychology teaches us ... not the outcome of intellectual illusion, not even the exercise of a 'mimetic instinct,' but simply, in its ultimate analysis, an utterance, a discharge of emotion and longing" (34).

Here Harrison parted from Frazer and never looked back; in her theory we see materialism evolve into a kind of psychologically based mysticism, with art gradually superseding religion as central to spiritual experience. One might argue further that in toppling hierarchic rationalism and substituting collective emotion as the human motivation for ritual, religion, and for art, lay Harrison's most daring feminist assertion. Again it comprises her attempt to reverse and heal the divisiveness of gender binarism, for she found it utterly false to partition human psychology,

> into a sort of order of merit or as it is called a hierarchy, with Reason as the head and crown, and under her sway the emotions and passions. The result of establishing this hierarchy is that the impulsive side of our nature comes off badly, the passions and even the emotions lying under a certain ban. ... A more fruitful way of looking at our human constitution is to see it, not as a bundle of separate faculties, but as a sort of continuous cycle. (38)

This fluid cycle described by Harrison consisted of perception, feeling, and action. Ratiocination, man's traditional "crown" of reason, she relegated to a practically nonexistent role, by first redefining *con*ception or knowledge as *per*ception, "receiving and recognizing a stimulus from without." Second, while perception "would seem to come first; we must be acted on before we can *re*-act ... priority confers no supremacy" (40). Emotion and action are equally, if not more, important than any cognitive process. As she examined primitive ritualistic dances, she concluded that "oddly enough, an impulse emotional in itself begets a process we think of as characteristically and exclusively intellectual, the process of abstraction" (42). For ritual is an abstraction from life, from the actual experience of hunt or battle, and art is a further abstraction: "The savage begins with the particular battle that actually *did* happen; but, it is easy to see that if he re enacts it again and again the *particular* battle or hunt will be forgotten, the representation cuts itself loose from the particular action from which it arose, and becomes generalized, as it were abstracted."

While both ritual and art rise out of the same emotional impulse, their difference lies in their respective distance from "immediate action." Ritual is "a re-doing or a pre-doing", but "always with a practical end." "Art is also a representation of life and the emotions of life, but cut loose from immediate action. ... The end of art is itself" (135). Thus Harrison saw ritual as one step removed from life and one step preceding art, "a bridge between real life and art." With the shift from ritual to art, she also saw — and deeply regretted — a shift from direct participation to passive speculation:

> In his actual life he hunts and fishes and ploughs and sows, being utterly intent on the practical end of gaining his food; in the *dromenon* [rites] of the Spring Festival, though his *acts* are unpractical, being merely singing and dancing and mimicry, his *intent* is practical, to induce the return of the food-supply. In the drama, the representation may remain for a time the same, but the intent is altered: man has come out from action, he is separate from the dancers, and has become a spectator. (135–6)

We shall see in Chapter 5 how Harrison traced the evolution of *dromenon* (literally "things done", or rituals) into Greek drama, using archaeological, as well as literary and historical evidence. She found "the history of the Greek stage" to be "one long story of the encroachment of the stage on the orchestra. ... The old circular orchestra shows the dominance of ritual; the new curtailed orchestra of Roman times and semicircular shape shows the dominance of spectacle" (143). Again, she regretted a cultural "advance" that excluded the people from active participation in communal ritual: "in the old ritual dance the individual was nothing, the choral band, the group, everything," while "in the heroic *saga* the individual is everything" (159). For Harrison, the experience of catharsis through art retains only a vestige of its original power as spiritual purgation and transcendence through collective ritual dance and song.

Among her other challenges to the status quo, Harrison refuted the Platonic dictum that art is imitation: "The whole 'imitation' theory ... errs, in fact, through supplying no adequate motive for a widespread human energy" (22). Art is an outpouring of "energy", not a conceptual copy or idealization of nature: "at the bottom of art, as its motive power and its mainspring, lies not the wish to copy Nature or even improve on her ... but rather an impulse shared by art and ritual, the desire, that is, to utter, to give out a strongly felt emotion or desire." (25–7). Human motive in commemorative rituals was not mimesis, but recreation of the original emotional experience: "it is not for the sake of copying the actual battle itself, but for the *emotion felt about the battle*. This they desire to re-live" (34):

> What they felt was not *mimesis* but "participation," unity, and community. It is the same with art. The origin of art is not

mimesis, but *mimesis* springs up out of art, out of emotional expression, and constantly and closely neighbours it. Art and ritual are at the outset alike in this, that they do not seek to copy a fact, but to reproduce, to re-enact an emotion. (46–7)

Aristotle, she claimed, "has been much misunderstood." When he says "Art imitates Nature," by nature "Aristotle never means the outside world of created things, he means rather creative force, what produces, not what has been produced. We might almost translate the Greek phrase, 'Art, like Nature, creates things'" (198). The function of art then, for Harrison, was certainly not instruction, nor even pleasure, but "something better called joy." And "true joy" she defined in her feminist way as "the consciousness of the triumph of creation" (213).

In Harrison's transposition of Aristotle's law we can see, prefigured, the artist as conceived by the Georgian writers. *Ulysses*, *The Family Reunion*, and *To the Lighthouse* all end in reaffirmation of "the triumph of creation" through art, just as Jane Harrison perceived it. And the fictional artists — Stephen, Harry, and Lily — through their sympathetic union with the "creative force," fittingly symbolized by the genetrices which dominate those works, learn that "Art, like Nature, creates things," and that art rises directly out of emotional experience.

Harrison's theoretical affinity with the Georgian writers is remarkable. Her regret that in the evolution of drama from ritual the audience had been divorced from participation, man "has come out from action, he is separate from the dancers," is strikingly similar to Yeats' plea, "How can we know the dancer from the dance?" For both Yeats and Harrison, dance was the art most united with life, the art in which life and the re-creation of life that is art cannot even be separated. "The dance in its inchoateness, its undifferentiatedness," Harrison wrote, "comes first." It was the art first to separate from pure ritual, the "meeting-point between art and ritual" (28, 171). Harrison's theory that art cannot be born out of a falsely hierarchical division of human faculties "into a sort of order of merit ... with Reason as head and crown," but must be experienced in those moments of "becoming" in which physical and imaginative selves are unified also parallels Yeats' characteristic repudiation of rationalism: "The body is not bruised to pleasure soul,/Nor beauty born out of its own despair,/Nor blear-eyed wisdom out of midnight oil" (Yeats, *CP* 214). Harrison described magical dances as primitive man's "work" (31); truly, like Yeats, she felt his "Labour is blossoming or dancing" (214).

Certainly, too, the young writer who boasted of replacing the "mystery of the Mass" with a new sacrament, "by converting the bread of everyday life into something that has permanent artistic life of its own" could have been her disciple (Ellmann 169). Like James Joyce, Harrison rejected the moribund dogma of 19th-century Christian theology, and insisted that the sacrament must be "a thing lived, experienced." Similarly, when D.H. Lawrence asserts the real novel's purpose is to remind readers of God's existence in "the very darkest continent of [the] body. ... And from Him issue the first dark rays of our feeling, wordless, and utterly previous to words: ... the first messengers, the primeval, honourable beasts of our being, whose voice echoes wordless ... down the darkest avenues of the soul, but full of potent speech" ("NF" 759), he echoes Harrison's oft-repeated insistence that religion and art both are "the projection of man's inner experience, vague and unanalyzed, into the outer world" (*AO* 168).

In 1915 Harrison read a paper entitled "Heresy and Humanity" to F.M. Cornford's Cambridge "Society of Heretics." She defined *hairesis* as "an eager, living word" and said: "If we are to be true and worthy heretics, we need not only new heads, but new hearts, and, most of all, that new emotional imagination ... which is begotten of enlarged sympathies and a more sensitive habit of feeling" (*AO* 27, 39). In 1924, Virginia Woolf read an equally heretical paper to the same society, her literary manifesto "Mr. Bennett and Mrs. Brown," also calling for a "new emotional imagination." For both Harrison and Woolf, art was not a mere copy of "the fabric of things", but the rendering of an imaginative "vision" that is ultimately truer to "the spirit we live by, life itself" (Woolf, "BB" 112, 119). For both, art comes out of an inchoate emotional "impulse." Woolf wrote that it is "very difficult to explain" precisely "what the impulse is that urges [novelists] so powerfully every now and then to embody their view in writing," but for her it is clearly emotional, even "an obsession" (97). So too for Harrison, the "impulse shared by art and ritual" is "to give out a strongly felt emotion or desire by representing, by making or doing or enriching" (*AAR* 26). Indeed, the title of Virginia Woolf's essay, "The Narrow Bridge of Art" is obviously taken from Harrison's metaphor of ritual as the "bridge" between religion and art. The call Woolf issues there for the novel to leave behind "fact-recording" and to become more "impersonal," to "give the relations of man to nature, to fate; his imagination; his dreams" seems inspired directly by Harrison's views (Woolf, "NBA" 18–19).

Ironically, Harrison praised the novels of Galsworthy, Masefield, and Bennett — the very generation of writers Woolf deprecated in her essay — because Harrison thought she perceived in them "signs that ... novel-writing is beginning again to realize its social function." She always stressed the collective emotional experience of primitive ritual and hoped to see art in her own generation assuming a similar socially cathartic function, "impatient of mere individual emotion, beginning to aim at something bigger" (*AAR* 245). By 1924, however, she was set straight: "Then, happily, I read *Mr Bennett and Mrs Brown*, and Mrs Woolf made me see that these Georgian characters, which I had thought were so unreal and even teasing, were real with an intimacy and a spirituality before unattempted" (*R* 25).

Both Lawrence and Woolf employed Harrison's trademark image of "leaping" as a signifier of ritual and artistic expression. Lawrence's description of "the life that bounds and leaps ... from out of the original dark forest within us ... the inbounding, inleaping life" (757), derives from Harrison's definition of the Dionysian dithyramb as "a leaping inspired dance" in both *Themis* and *Ancient Art and Ritual*, and her interpretation of the *Hymn of the Kouretes to Zeus*, in which god and worshippers leaped together to insure futurity and experience communal transcendence. While describing her fictitious Newnham in *A Room of One's Own*, Woolf paid this extraordinary tribute to Harrison:

> — and then on the terrace, as if popping out to breathe the air, to glance at the garden, came a bent figure, formidable yet humble, with her great forehead and her shabby dress — could it be the famous scholar, could it be J — H — herself? All was dim, yet intense too, as if the scarf which the dusk had flung over the garden were torn asunder by star or sword — the flash of some terrible reality leaping, as its way is, out of the heart of the spring.   (17)

This direct reference to Harrison, especially in a text where every other name is a fictional parody, reveals Woolf's great respect for the scholar, as well as her confidence that the identity of "J — H — " would be obvious to her audience, reinforcing the fact of Harrison's widespread reputation. Jane Marcus writes that Woolf's aunt introduced her to Harrison at Cambridge in 1904, and that Harrison became a "role model in scholarship and life, proving that women could master and understand Greek" (85). However, Woolf's "flash of some terrible reality leaping" does not refer to Harrison's achievements, despite the "chastity, outsidership, and poverty [that] were the conditions of life for the woman of genius," as Marcus imagines (86).

Like Lawrence, Woolf's reference evokes Harrison's beloved image of "leaping" in spring ritual invocations of the *daimon*, specifically to Harrison's *Themis*, inspired by the discovery of the *Hymn of the Kouretes to Zeus* or, as Harrison called it the "Zeus-Leap-Song" (*T* 4). The *Hymn* celebrates the protection of the infant Zeus from Kronos' destruction by the Kouretes, "armed and orgiastic dancers" (23). The youthful god is invoked as Kouros, the leader of the dancers, who "by leaping in conjunction with his worshippers is to bring fertility" and prosperity: "'To us also leap for full jars, and leap for fleecy flocks, and leap for fields of fruit, and for hives to bring increase'" (8–10). Leaping, or ecstatic tribal dancing, became for Harrison the quintessential expression of humanity's ritual, communal experience of the divine. "The dancers dancing together utter their conjoint desire, their delight, their terror, in steps and gestures," and in the "collective emotion" thus aroused "is the raw material of god-head" (45–6). Such a vital, experiential conception of divinity is the "terrible reality" Harrison found in the "heart of spring," that Woolf refers to. It is a vision she offered to the young modernist writers, who eagerly embraced it.

4: ELEUSIS AT ITHACA: MOTHER, MAID, AND WITCH IN JOYCE'S *ULYSSES*

The relation of these early matriarchal, husbandless goddesses, whether Mother or Maid, to the male figures that accompany them is one altogether noble and womanly, though perhaps not what the modern mind holds to be feminine. It seems to halt some-where half-way between Mother and Lover, with a touch of the patron saint. Aloof from achievement themselves, they choose a lo-cal hero for their own to inspire and protect. They ask of him, not that he should love or adore, but that he should do great deeds.

— Jane Ellen Harrison, *PSGR* 273

The comparative method of myth criticism is an appropriate ap-proach to modernists such as Joyce who consciously employed the "mythic method," finding in myth and ritual a rich substrate upon which to reconstruct the novel. One unfortunate result of Northrup Frye's long dominance in this critical methodology has been the loss to contemporary myth criticism of the anthropological specificity that so enlivened the work of the late 19th- and early 20th-century mythologists, due to his concern "not so much with the substance of myth as with their structures, that is, the narrative principles that are involved in their telling" (Warner 20). Another pervasive and extremely generalizing or reductive influence has been that of Jung. Myth criticism has been justly attacked for being too general, and nowhere is this more valid than when levied against archetypal interpretations of Molly Bloom, which typically devolve into Jungian stereotypes such as the "Eternal Feminine," "the generous, nurturing, all-embracing mother of the world," or "the mystery of animate Flesh, the Earth, Nature."[1] But by refering to Molly as "Gae-Tellus" Joyce could evoke a whole world of mythic meaning beyond Homer's Penelope that is no longer readily available to our imaginations (*U*17.2313).[2] For Joyce and others of his generation, the world of myth was not divorced from the world of temporal historicity or fictional naturalism, largely because of the pervasive influence of the ritual theory, by which myths were seen to have evolved out of seasonal rituals actually performed by people, in ages past all the way up to the present. A more precise understanding of Molly as "Gae-Tellus" and her archetypal relation to Bloom and Stephen, as well as their ritual roles, can be gained by looking beyond Homer to the myth of Demeter and Persephone and their ritual worship at Eleusis.

The "Da" of Da-mater has been etymologized as equivalent to the "Ge" of Gaia; Demeter *is* the Earth-mother, but as we have seen, she is a later, more specific incarnation — the agricultural deity whose function in bringing forth grain from the earth was vital to the ancient Greek. The *Homeric Hymn to Demeter*, discovered in a farmyard at Moscow in 1777, is the major source for the myth that tells, symbolically, of the religious rituals at Eleusis. "*Inter pullos et porcos labitat*," as Andrew Lang, ever mindful of Persephone's pigs, wrote: "the song of the rural deity had found its way into the haunts of the humble creatures whom she protected" (*HH* 53).

The hymn tells the story of Persephone's abduction by Hades to the underworld, Demeter's lamentation over the loss of her daughter, and her prolonged searching, fasting and blighting of the earth in her anger. She wandered to Eleusis where she was taken in and consoled by the king's wife and daughters, yet her "wrath" continued to render the earth sterile. "Now would the whole race of mortal men have perished utterly from the stress of famine" if Zeus had not finally sent Hermes to bring Persephone back from the underworld (200). Joyfully reunited, Demeter transformed the barren plains into rich fields of grain, but since Persephone had eaten Hades' pomegranate seeds she had to return to the world of the dead each year "for as long as the ears of corn were below the ground" (Witt 18). As Frazer stressed in his discussion of Demeter and Persephone, "the main theme which the poet set before himself in composing this hymn was to describe the traditional foundation of the Eleusinian mysteries by the goddess Demeter," and, at the conclusion of the hymn "the beneficent deity takes the princes of Eleusis ... [and] teaches them her mystic rites" (V, i, 35). Since the 1890s, archaeological information has supported the contention that the rituals experienced by initiates at Eleusis echoed Demeter's fasting, wandering, consolation, and reunion with her daughter closely. Further, the parallels between these ritual steps performed at Eleusis and Stephen and Bloom's "nocturnal perambulations" in "Eumaeus" and "Ithaca" are remarkable.

It would be strange if Joyce were unfamiliar with the Mysteries, since for 2,000 years they represented "the most widely influential of all Greek ceremonials" (Harrison, *PSGR* 120). References to them abound in classical sources, such as Euripides, Sophocles, Aristophanes, Plutarch, Pindar, Apollonius Rhodius, and Clement of Alexandria. It is clear from Joyce's notes that he studied the Demeter/Persephone myth in Wilhelm Roscher's encyclopedic 1886 *Ausführliches Lexikon der griechischen und römischen Mythologie* (Herring, *Buffalo* 27). He also knew the myth, in very general terms, from Professor Carl Witt's *Myths of Hellas: or Greek Tales*, the 1883 English translation of which he kept with him throughout his several moves (Connolly 41). The Mysteries have compeled excavation, study, and conjecture from their demise in early Christian times to the present day, and Joyce could have learned more about them by reading other German or French archeologists and classicists of the 1890s–1920s, or the English anthropologists. Frazer's second chapter of Part V, vol. i, "Spirits of the Corn and of the Wild", discusses the *Hymn to Demeter* and the Eleusinian mysteries in detail, but whether or not Joyce read Frazer's *Golden Bough* is problematic. "Unlike Yeats, Lawrence, and Eliot, James Joyce gives no explicit indication ... of having been acquainted with *The Golden Bough* or the other work of Sir James Frazer" (Vickery 326). At the same time, given the "pervasive influence" of Frazer's opus, it is hard to imagine that Joyce did not leaf through it at one time or another, and Vickery parallels the two works because both writers believed in "the way in which human and divine, literal and imaginative cohere with one another through the medium of myth" (370).

Yet for Frazer, as we have seen, the role mythic rituals could play in modern life was strictly limited to provincial peasant culture. For Joyce, however, ritual was an integral and daily part of all human life, from the simplest of acts such as defecation, to cathartic fantasy states in which the deepest psychological needs could be acted out and perhaps resolved. In this sense Joyce was theoretically much closer in spirit to Jane Harrison, who likewise believed that rituals form an essential "bridge" between actual life and its recreation in art. There is evidence that Joyce was familiar with Harrison's work since he owned her *Mythology* (Connolly 19). While this slim anthology of myths is a late production (1924), Joyce's possession of it does suggest a possible acquaintance with her earlier, more significant volumes, such as *Prolegomena to the Study of Greek Religion*, where she discusses the Eleusinian rituals in detail, from their origin as a simple harvest festival to their culmination as the dominant religious expression of ancient Greece.

Andrew Lang also provided Joyce with a source for the Demeter/ Persephone myth. Joyce relied on the Butcher/Lang translation of the *Odyssey*, and for the *Homeric Hymn to Demeter* it is quite likely he would have turned to Lang's lovely prose translation of 1884. In addition, the first volume Lang produced in his anthropological period, *Custom and Myth* (1884), contains an essay entitled "Moly and Mandragora" in which he discusses the primitive use of herbs and roots for magical purposes, including the potato: "the English magic potato, the German mandrake, the Greek moly, are all survivals from a condition of mind. ... that expects supernatural aid from plants and roots" (149– 150). This direct link of the folk "potato cure" with Homeric moly is convincing evidence that Joyce derived Bloom's keepsake from Lang's essay. His apparent familiarity with Lang's "anthropological" period argues a similar knowledge of Lang's *Homeric Hymn to Demeter*, published in 1899. But whatever source Joyce used, that he knew the hymn is proven by Stephen's drunken reference to "an old hymn to Demeter" in "Circe" (*U*15.2088). He mumbles, "The rite is the poet's rest," suggesting that Eleusinian ritual, symbolically enacted by Bloom and Stephen in "Ithaca," may affect his evolution as an artist. Through the psychological purgation offered by ritual acting out, the poet may finally come to rest.[3]

"In general by a mystery is meant a rite in which certain *sacra* [sacred objects] are exhibited, which cannot be safely seen by the worshipper till he has undergone certain purifications" (Harrison, *PSGR* 151). The first rites initiates experienced were purification in water and sacrifice of the pigs as "*pharmakoi*": "The bathing in the sea was a purification, a conducting out, a banishing of evil" (152). The following night "the torchlight procession, the all-night vigil" took place, which perhaps corresponds to the wanderings of Demeter as the initiates walked the 14 miles from Athens to the *telesterion*, or hall of initiation at Eleusis (Frazer 37). The hymn tells how Demeter fasted until she reached the palace of Eleusis where the queen offered her wine, which she refused, "saying that it was not permitted for her to drink red wine; but she bade them mix meal and water with the tender herb of mint, and give it to her to drink" (Lang 194). According to Harrison, this is because matriarchal rituals required offerings of more primitive agricultural products such as barley, wheat, oil, honey, milk, as opposed to the wine-based communions of later Olympian rituals (91–2; 156). At Eleusis the initiates purified themselves by fasting like Demeter, until the fast was broken by a communal drinking of the *kykeon*, "the solemn communion with the divinity by participation in a draught of barley-water from a holy chalice" (Frazer 37).

What happened next was a climactic visionary experience that confirmed the faith of initiates. Imagine the religious awe (not to mention the threats of legal prosecution) that kept thousands of initiates silent for hundreds and hundreds of years as to the "mysterious goings-on" in the *telesterion*! It is known that the hierophant, the ceremonial priest of the Eleusinian Mysteries, revealed something in a brilliant flash of light, but of the *sacra* thus revealed "we know nothing" (Harrison 157). Was it a revelation of the foods sacred to the Earth-mother, as the Christian Clement "contemptuously" suggested? (Ruck 80; Harrison 158), or was the myth of Demeter and Persephone "acted as a sacred drama," with initiates experiencing Demeter's loss and agony in the darkness, then rediscovering "Persephone herself," symbolically reborn, "flashed on the experient's soul, [in] the same flash of revelation [that] showed him his own continuity, the continued existence of all living things"? (Frazer 39; Kerenyi 142). Important in this context are the theories Joyce's likely sources espoused. According to Frazer, "the very heart of the mysteries consisted in shewing to the initiated a reaped ear of corn" (38). Harrison agrees, and cites evidence also for the enactment of a "Sacred Marriage and the Birth of the holy child," a son often associated with the infantile Dionysus, to Demeter/Persephone. She quotes an anonymous treatise describing the rites of the Phrygians:

"And following the Phrygians, the Athenians, when they initiate at the Eleusinian rites, exhibit to the epoptae [the highest level of initiate] the mighty and marvellous and most complete epoptic mystery, an ear of grain reaped in silence. And this ear of grain the Athenians themselves hold to be the great and perfect light that is from that which has no form, as the Hierophant himself, who is not like Attis, but who is made a eunuch by means of hemlock and has renounced all carnal generation, he, by night at Eleusis, accomplishing by the light of a great flame the great and unutterable mysteries, says and cries in a loud voice, 'Holy Brimo has borne a sacred Child, Brimos' " (549).

For Harrison, "the Marriage and the Birth were the culminating ritual acts, acts by which *union with the divine*, the goal of all mystic ceremonial, was at first held to be actually effected, later symbolized" (549). The "close conjunction" in which the grain was revealed and the child announced "makes it highly probable, though not absolutely certain, that the one, the human birth, was but the anthropomorphic form of the other," thus human eternity, through vegetative and sexual futurity, was assured (563). "Brimo," meaning Mighty One or Terrible One, is the epithet used for Demeter only in this context. Frazer's discussion of the sacred marriage focuses on attempting to clear it from the "reverend Christian scandal-mongers'" accusations of incest. It is crucial for him to prove that, if the bridegroom is Pluto, "his lawful wife [is] Persephone and not his sister and mother-in-law Demeter" (67). Frazer forgets, in this context, what he himself knows, that "the two persons of the godhead were one in substance" (68); as Harrison writes, "Brimo *is* a form of the Great Mother who is also the Maid" (551). On the final day of the events, two vessels filled with water were overturned, as "worshippers looked up to the sky and cried 'Rain!' and then looked down at the earth and cried 'Conceive!'" (Frazer 69). As Harrison concludes, "It was a fitting close to rites so primitive" (161).

Whatever the exact content of the Mysteries, they provided the spiritual consolation sought for in most religions. Initiates left Eleusis with a sense of joy, a diminished fear of the afterlife, and a reassurance of life's eternal renewal. " 'Thrice happy are those of mortals, who having seen those rites depart for Hades; for to them alone is it granted to have true life there; to the rest all there is evil,' Sophokles cries out exultantly. And to this Pindar with equal exultation answers: 'Happy is he who, having seen these rites goes below the hollow earth; for he knows the end of life and he knows its god-sent beginning' " (Mylonas 284–5).

It may be difficult today to conceive of a religion in which spirituality and physicality are not opposed but united. Yet vegetative fertility, human sexuality and life beyond death were inextricably bound in the ancient mind; this was the essence of the Eleusinian Mysteries and, most likely, the reason for its appeal to Joyce, for whom all that was metaphysical was first physical. The grain was worshipped in awed silence as civilization's primary food source and at the same time as the Kore. Both hold the potential of human fertility and futurity within. As the grain is buried beneath the earth, so Persephone descends into the underworld to experience death. There she eats the seeds of Hades; she is inseminated, and again like the grain, she brings forth life from death in an annually renewed miracle. In contrast to the Christian tradition, at Eleusis spiritual eternity is not achieved through the denial, but rather through the celebration of elemental material verities. In Leopold Bloom, Joyce created a character for whom physical realities such as food continually reaffirm spiritual confidence in the eternal coming of life from death.

At the end of "Scylla and Charybdis" Stephen passes the "dark back" of Bloom on the library stairs and then interprets in mythic ritual terms the "two plumes of smoke" he observes spiraling upwards from the rooftops: "Cease to strive. Peace of the druid priests of Cymbeline, hierophantic: from wide earth an altar" (*U*9.1221). This line appears to conflate two traditions of primitive worship: druidic and Hellenic, since only priests at Eleusis bore the name hierophant. Yet there are no druids in *Cymbeline*, no priests at all. Stephen's reference rather suggests a mythological time when Rome and Britain were one, as they are in *Cymbeline*, heralding Bloom, who is a pagan Briton and embodies the capacity for ancient ritual in a modern humanity.

Throughout "Scylla and Charybdis" Stephen had been arguing his theory of *Hamlet*, yet significantly he ends by recalling *Cymbeline*, a play that contains many of the same themes as *Hamlet* such as a ghostly father and the threat of adultery, but is a comic romance, not a tragedy. The chapter ends with a quotation from *Cymbeline*: "Laud we the gods/And let our crooked smokes climb to their nostrils/From our bless'd altars" (*U*9:1223). In Shakespeare's play these lines are uttered by Jupiter, called up in the hero, Posthumus', dream by the ghost of his father, Leonatus, who functions here as a kind of "druid priest".

Unlike the message of Hamlet's father, these words do not call for revenge, but assure the hero of his eventual happiness, should he trust to the gods and to ritual. Bloom is much closer in spirit to Leonatus, the father who appears in dream (as Bloom *has* appeared in Stephen's dreams) to reassure the son of a comic resolution through psychic ritual, than he is to the goading ghost of King Hamlet. To the discomfort of most of his compatriots in the library, Stephen has been arguing for the all-important power of the matriarchal lover such as Anne Hathaway, whose seduction stimulates the artist's creativity. He must now "cease to strive" and follow his own ghostly father and hierophantic guide through pagan ritual to union with just such a creative mother/lover, through which he will be reborn. Bloom's ritual role is the hierophant who has "'renounced all carnal generation,'" and who will guide Stephen, the initiate, through the "all-night vigil" of Eleusinian ritual to a final vision of Molly, the Earth-mother, behind the lighted window shade in "Ithaca."[4]

However, before Bloom can assume his archetypal role as hierophant he must himself undergo a violent purgative ritual in "Circe": he must face the vengeful "phallic mother" before he can lead Stephen to the generative Earth-mother, just as Stephen in "Circe" must face his own terrible fantasy of May Dedalus, the vampirish "devouring mother," before being rescued and guided by his hierophantic protector to Molly. It is a chapter of monumental mothers in various guises, that has been interpreted largely through psychoanalytic definitions of oedipal conflict, castration anxiety, and masochism.

The two classic psychoanalytic studies of Joyce, Mark Shechner's *Joyce in Nighttown* and Sheldon Brivic's *Joyce Between Freud and Jung*, both place the fantasies endured in Bella Cohen's brothel in the Freudian tradition of masochism, which holds that in the image of the phallic mother, woman has been fetishized to compensate for castration anxiety and that at the same time she stands in, as less threatening, for paternal punishment of oedipal desire (Shechner 67–9, 112–117; Brivic 126–137). Both use Freud's seminal essay, "On the Universal Tendency to Debasement in the Sphere of Love" to explain "the virgin/whore syndrome" so prominent in Joyce's work, the bifurcation of woman endemic to Western civilization that is rooted in forbidden oedipal wishes and fears: "one is idealized and loved, but cannot be defiled by sex, while the other is physically approachable, but can never be respected" (Shechner 94; Brivic 40). Shechner applies this "striking demonstration of castration anxiety" to his analysis of Joyce's letters to Nora, in which she plays both roles; while Brivic uses it to analyze Stephen's oedipal conflict and explain his paralyzed vacillations between "temptress and virgin." Neither apply it to the images of women in "Circe," but according to an early Jungian analyst William Walcott, they are similarly bifurcated: "as the generous, nurturing, all-embracing mother of the world, the well-spring of life and creativity, [Molly] is the opposite to the archetypal witch mother, the dark, evil, sinister, overpowering, devouring woman who is personified by Circe" (41).

Part of the problem is that the Freudian paradigm denies inherent maternal power, attributing all manifestations of power to the father. The phallic mother punishes only through borrowed whips and furs; she is dressed by the son in symbolic phalluses to compensate for her patriarchal castration, a fate the son fears, and desires, will be applied to himself. For Shechner, then, there is not much to say about "Circe" beyond that Bella Cohen is "the phallic mother *par excellence*" and "Bloom imaginatively assumes a submissive and feminine role and projects upon Bella the role of a cruel and castrating male figure, the monstrous Bello" (112–13). But this ignores entirely the "plump ... pouter pigeon," the Marian mother-image who "saunters" through Bloom's fantasies urging poor Poldy "to get his stick out of the mud," as well as the myriad other images of women, from sympathizing Mrs Breen to scolding Mrs Mervyn Talboys (*U*15.352–53). Joyce, at this point, was able to leave behind the simplistic bifurcated female archetypes of *Portrait of the Artist*: in "Circe" there are no virgins. All the women are sexual, most are mothers, although Joyce contrasts the fertile feminized mother, Mrs Marion, with the sterile masculinized mother (or, in mythic terms, the witch), Bella/Bello.

Brivic evades such problems by abandoning the Freudian model altogether and resorting to Jung in his analysis of Bloom. For Brivic, Shechner's view of Joyce is disturbingly solipsistic. Despite seeing Bloom's masochistic fantasies as "therapeutic," Shechner's conclusions condemn Bloom (and Joyce) to a sexual stasis of autoerotic fantasy, unable ever to overcome the relative safety of masturbation for actual sexual intercourse (149). Shechner sees Joyce's compensatory mastery of language as sublimation, a Freudian view that leaves out, for Brivic, "the enormous sense of the affirmation of human value and love that readers find in Joyce's later works" (5). So Brivic turns to Jung for a system in which to place the mythic transcendence of spirit manifested in Bloom, but this analysis, too, is reductive of the marvelously varied archetypes of woman expressed in "Circe," for Molly becomes again limited to one facet, "Phenomenon, the material world, which is for [Bloom] both benevolent god and mother" (142).

As Frances Restuccia has so admirably shown, the Deleuzean model of masochism, "based directly on the writings of Leopold von Sacher-Masoch," is far more applicable to Joyce and to Joyce's work than the Freudian (101). Deleuze could not understand "why so many psychoanalysts insist on ... detecting the presence of the father behind the woman torturer" (Deleuze 55). Instead, he realized that it is in sadism that "the paternal and patriarchal theme undoubtedly predominates" (59), whereas the masochist tries to "to ensure that the temporal order of reality and experience will be in conformity with the symbolic order, in which the father has been abolished for all time" (60, 66). The masochistic image of the punishing mother does not represent the father; in fact she is constructed to oppose everything he represents. For Deleuze the masochist "atones for ... his resemblance to the father and the father's likeness in him" (60–1). Therefore, what is being beaten in masochism is not the child, but "the image and likeness of the father" within: "the masochist thus liberates himself in preparation for a rebirth in which the father will have no part" (66). This is accomplished through a tripartite fantasy image of the mother, a "symbolic transfer or redistribution of all paternal functions to the threefold feminine figure"; thus the "father is excluded and completely nullified" (61).

Deleuze describes the tripartite maternal image as consisting of two "symbolic margins," the "uterine" or "hetaeric" mother at one end and the oedipal "sadistic" mother at the other. "Between them and moving from one to the other is the oral mother," the "good" mother, "the core of the fantasy" (62, 66). The oral mother is "invest[ed] with an amplitude which repeatedly brings her very close to the figures of her rivals" as she alternately subsumes them (67). "Respectable and pure, [she] must assume the function of prostitute normally reserved for the uterine mother." She also takes over the "administration of cruelty" from the sadistic oedipal mother and "is thus profoundly transformed and put to the service of the masochistic ideal of expiation and rebirth" (62).

Interestingly, the Deleuzean model of the tripartite maternal image is virtually identical to the archetypal female trinities so prevalent in Hellenic myth: the generative Earth-mother is the "uterine mother" and the Kore or maid is the "oral mother," while the "sadistic oedipal mother" is the witch. As in the Deleuzian model, these archetypes shift and meld into one another. The maiden Kore can give birth, as at Eleusis, through association with her fecund mother; the usually nurturing Earth-mother, when wronged, can punish violently through association with the witch. These tripartite images express intensely ambivalent feelings toward the mother that most likely derive from the preoedipal period, when object relations begin as "the child comes to recognize that its mother is a separate being," creating deep longing to remerge with the "good" oral mother (along with deep fear of her omnipotence), as well as hostility toward the assertive, separate "sadistic" mother, even though autonomy is desired by the child as well (Chodorow 69–91). Harrison explains that the matriarchal trinities originated in just such a "primitive doubleness," characterizing the *daimones* from which they evolved, death-bringers to be feared and life-givers to be courted (185). "It is immediately obvious," for instance, "that the triple Gorgons are not really three but one + two" (187). A goddess, "to the primitive Greek, took a twofold form ... shifting and easily interchangeable" and "the trinity-form grew out of the duality." Harrison concludes that "dualities and trinities alike seem to be characteristic of the old matriarchal goddesses" (286).

Joyce would have found a detailed analysis of these trinities in Jane Harrison's *Prolegomena to the Study of Greek Religion*. In the first chapters Harrison delineates the difference between chthonic and Olympian ritual, and explains the genesis of the powerful female archetypes that dominate primitive Hellenic religion. In short, the object of chthonic ritual was "placation" of underworld ghosts that had the power to curse and destroy, and "purification" of the worshipper to ward off such vengeful spirits. The ultimate goal of this "physical and moral purgation" was the "promotion and conservation of fertility," so essential to survival and so constantly threatened by death and disease in a primitive society (ix, 53). In several fascinating chapters Harrison traces the development of the malevolent underworld *daimones* called "Keres," portrayed in vase-paintings as tiny grotesque winged demons flying out of open graves, jars, and trenches, bringing disease, blindness, madness, old age, and death, into Harpies, "the Snatchers, winged women — demons, hurrying along like the storm wind and carrying all things to destruction" (165–176). Such trinities of winged bird-women are common in Greek art and mythology, whether portrayed as hideous Gorgons, seductive Sirens (originally birds, not mermaids), or bloodthirsty Erinyes.

Yet Keres bring good as well as evil: "The Harpies not only snatch away souls to death but they give life, bringing things to birth" (179). The soul of life is the breath, winged on the wind, and the lucky man is "Ker-nourished" (185). "Fructifying Keres" also evolved into gentler tripartite goddesses, patronesses "who bring the blessings of marriage and of fertile breezes" (252) such as the Eumenides, "Kindly Ones," the Semnae, "Venerable Ones," and the Korai, "Charites" or gift-givers. Just as in Aeschylus' *Oresteia*, when the demands for retribution according to the ancient blood-law are satisfied, the punishing Erinyes are converted into beneficent Eumenides, protectors of marriage and childbirth.

The Eleusinian Mysteries were no less the worship of three: Demeter, Persephone, and "threefold Hecate of the underworld" (288), always portrayed at a crossroad of "three ways" or with "three bodies" (Ruck 103). In the *Homeric Hymn to Demeter*, it is Hecate who hears Persephone's screams as she is seized by Hades, and first brings comfort to Demeter: "which of the heavenly gods or deathly men hath ravished away Persephone, and brought thee sorrow?" she asks the grieving mother. Her words hint at the witch's traditional role of vengeance for transgressions against blood ties, and Demeter "answered her not, but swiftly rushed on with her, bearing torches burning in her hands" (Lang 186), as they are united in revenge. As Harrison goes on to explain, Demeter's ritual epithet Brimo links her with Hecate, the "Thessalian Kore" of the underworld (hence her association also with the Kore Persephone). When associated with rage and revenge, Demeter *is* Brimo: "Brimo then, some said, meant the Mighty, some the Angry One. ... the Angry-Raging One is own sister to the Angry Demeter, Demeter Erinys" (552–3). As in the Deleuzian paradigm, in her rage over the violation of her daughter, the mother assumes the witch's traits, becoming the punisher. She is worshipped as "Demeter Erinys," until she bathes in a river, signifying renewal through purification by water, and returns to her identity as the generative Earthmother: "Demeter at Thelpusa had two surnames and even two statues. When she was wroth they called her *Erinys* on account of her wrath, when she relented and bathed they called her *Lousia*" (Harrison 214; Kerenyi 150). In her aspect as Queen of the Underworld, Persephone is united with Hecate who becomes her constant companion. Thus both Demeter and Persephone are Hecate, "for that goddess is the third that completes and joins the sacred duo of mother and daughter" (Ruck 103; Kerenyi 143).

At Eleusis the participant first suffers the Earth-mother's loss, her wrath, and her revenge as "Demeter Erinys" before the cycle of life is affirmed with the reunion of Demeter and Persephone. The witch must be appeased, sins must be purged, before the mother can bring her gifts of health and fertility. Such purgation is the purpose of Joyce's comic rendering of matriarchal ritual in "Circe." The ultimate end even of Bloom's fantasy emasculation is renewed fertility. Bloom's terrible sense of failure over his son's death, his fear of engendering another doomed child, his subsequent sexual deprivation of Molly, and his adulterous fantasies — all are transgressions against fertility that cry for punishment. Yet Bloom cannot bear to imagine Molly as punisher (and perhaps Joyce couldn't either); Molly must remain the nurturing, fecund, "oral"/"uterine" mother. So his purgation is accomplished in fantasy just as it is in myth and ritual, and just as it is in the Deleuzian model: the good mother is associated with others who punish and castrate, in a threefold amplification from Marion, to Circe, to Bella.

Mrs Marion (Molly) maintains the image of the "good" mother who has subsumed the fecundity of the "uterine" mother, while her identification with Circe shows her as associated with the other "margin" as well. Bella/Bello is the full-fledged Brimo, the sadistic oedipal mother, "put to the service of the masochistic ideal of expiation and rebirth." Although scolding, Marion never loses her femininity, while Bella becomes the whip-wielding, masculine Bello; Marion is softened by Bloom's plight, whereas Bello squats on him and castigates without mercy. So Bloom psychically merges creative and destructive images of woman, while keeping them separate at the same time, an associational process that serves the same ritually purgative function as it did in Greek myth: the mother can punish, scold, or destroy by assuming the witch's traits, without violating her own identity as life-giver and friend.

Joyce drew clear distinctions between Molly/Circe and Bella/Circe. Bloom dresses Molly in pants in his dream and fantasy, but she never becomes masculine as does Bella/Bello, because that would violate her essential fecundity. In his second dream fragment he recalls that Molly "had red slippers on. Turkish. Wore the breeches. Suppose she does" but he immediately confirms her as the erotic "hetaeric" mother by thinking of buying her a gift: "Petticoats for Molly. She has something to put in them" (*U*13.1240–45). "Mrs. Marion" does not lose her association with sexuality and fertility in his Circean fantasy either: "(He looks up. Beside her mirage of datepalms a handsome woman in

Turkish costume stands before him. Opulent curves fill out her scarlet trousers and jacket slashed with gold. A wide yellow cummerbund girdles her ...)" (*U*15.297). Here is the Eastern goddess dressed in red that Bloom's dream foreshadowed. But, although she wears "scarlet trousers," her "opulent curves" fill them out. She never truly becomes the sterile witch or the sadistic mother.

Although Mrs Marion enters Bloom's fantasy speaking "sharply" and aiming a blow at him, just as Circe threatened emasculation with her magic powers, she exits calling his name "softly" and hinting at love with a line from *Don Giovanni* (*U*15.347–51). She sympathizes with the whimpering figure cowering before her, crying: "O Poldy, Poldy, you are a poor old stick in the mud! Go and see life. See the wide world" (15.329). Just so Homer's Circe ended by encouraging Odysseus to overcome his fear and journey to Hades. The treatment essential for de-clawing a witch, as Hermes stresses in advising Odysseus, is not to "resist and refuse the bed of the goddess, /For so she will set free your companions, and care for you also" (Lattimore 160). In creating a parallel Circe in Bloom's fantasy of Mrs Marion, Joyce suggests that much the same kind of treatment is needed to mollify Molly and that subconsciously Bloom knows it. When Bloom's fantasy self, Poldy, says "At your service," after Marion's entrance, he means, as he tentatively mumbles a few lines later, as a "business menagerer" (*U*15.296, 325). But he must really "service" his wife and stop being merely her "menagerer," a word with multiple layers of meaning: 1) her business manager, 2) her housekeeper (*ménage*), and 3) her panderer, supplying her with a sexual menagerie, pornography and beasts such as Boylan, instead of doing the job himself. And Bloom's fantasy Marion says as much when she teases, "Has poor little hubby cold feet waiting so long?" (*U*15.307) — is fear keeping him from performing his sexual role as a husband?

Two other aspects of Bloom's Marion/Circe vision are particularly interesting and emphasize again his preservation of Molly as haeteric mother rather than sterile witch. In "Oxen of the Sun," Bloom recalls his dream a third time: " ... a strange fancy of his dame Mrs Moll with red slippers on in a pair of Turkey trunks which is thought by those in ken to be for a *change* (*U*14.508–12, my italics). The narrative then proceeds, without punctuation break, to "Mistress Purefoy" who "got in through pleading her belly." In "Circe" Mrs Marion also refers to this mysterious "change." Apropos of nothing she says, "So you notice some change? (Her hands passing slowly over her trinketed stomacher)"

(*U*15.328). In the first quotation, this "change" might indicate a sex-change, since the "Turkey trunks" are thought to be necessary for it. However, since the narrative immediately describes Mistress Purefoy's pregnancy in great detail, and since Marion's hands pass "slowly over her trinketed stomacher," that is, the yellow cummerbund encircling her waist, it most likely refers to a pregnancy. Subconsciously, Bloom either fears that Molly has been impregnated by Boylan, or knows that he must get his "stick out of the mud" and impregnate her himself, or, most probably, both. Soon after, Marion/Circe again enters Bloom's fantasy, accompanied by a curious camel:

(... Beside her a camel, hooded with a turreting turban, waits. A silk ladder of innumerable rungs climbs to his bobbing howdah. He ambles near with disgruntled hindquarters. Fiercely she slaps his haunch, her goldcurb wristbangles angriling, scolding him in Moorish.) ... (The camel, lifting a foreleg, plucks from a tree a large mango fruit, offers it to his mistress, blinking, in his cloven hoof, then droops his head and, grunting, with uplifted neck, fumbles to kneel. Bloom stoops his back for leap-frog.)   (*U*15.313–23)

The camel is obviously one of Circe's transformed beasts, a desert animal that Haroun al Rashid might ride, and this imagery suggests that the camel is Bloom, or rather, another substitute fantasy self. Mrs Marion "slaps his haunch" and scolds him, just as Bella will later berate Bloom. And, as the camel plucks the "large mango fruit" and "offers it to his mistress," he echoes, in dumb, brutish parody, Haroun al Raschid's offering of the melon to Stephen. This offering of fruit by Haroun in Stephen's dream has been interpreted by McCarroll and others as an invitation to sexual experience, since "Bloom holds his own face against the 'melons' of Molly's rump," and "Molly's rump, in Bloom's mind, is virtually a symbol for Molly and his conception of the female" (McCarroll 174). In this case, the Camel/Bloom's offering of a mango — a more uterine-shaped fruit, containing one large seed — *to* Molly suggests a sexual invitation that will in the end be fruitful, i.e., reproductive. Thus, Joyce provides another symbolic indication that Bloom's subconscious mind is reassuring him of his wife's essential fecundity, and telling him to impregnate her. As Marion "saunters" offstage, "plump as a pampered pouter pigeon," Bloom tries to follow, but an "elderly bawd seizes his sleeve," like a witch with "the bristles of her chinmole glittering" and her "wolfeyes shining" (*U*15.356–69). Bloom's greatest transgression, as accused by his own fantasy of the fertile husband, Theodore Purefoy, has been "to frustrate the sacred ends of nature" (*U*15.1742). He will not see the fecund, feminine Earth-mother again until he has been punished in the witch's underworld of Nighttown.

Bloom's entrance into the dreamscape of Nighttown begins his matriarchal purgatory. The world of witches is fittingly guarded by a "wolfdog" that follows him as "he walks on toward hellsgates" (*U*15.577). The dog is Hecate's beast, associated also with Cerberus, guardian of the gates of hell, just as Hecate is associated with Persephone, Queen of the Underworld. The dog's association with women is underscored as it approaches Bloom, "his tongue outlolling," just as the "gaudy dollwomen loll in the lighted doorways" of Nighttown, and Bloom thinks, "Strange how they take to me. ... Like women they like *rencontres*" (*U*15.633–71). A prudent ritualist, Bloom seeks to placate this hound of Hecate with the "crubeen and trotter" he has been carrying. He then sees a "covey of gulls" rising "hungrily from Liffey slime," recalling his similar kindness to animals earlier in the day when he fed the gulls (15.683). Yet at the same time, shrieking taloned birds are another traditional manifestation of the witch as Harpy. Bloom's kindness, like his pampering of Molly with breakfast in bed, is revealed as a sop to his conscience, guilty over his various peccadillos and sexual failures, since he immediately finds himself "Caught in the act," collared by the "watch," and put on trial, like a comic Orestes, for his sexual transgressions, sins against the mother (15.680). First Bloom's epistolary flirt, Martha, screams, "Henry! Leopold! Lionel, thou lost one! Clear my name" and threatens to charge him with "Breach of promise" (15.753–765), then Mary Driscoll, the Blooms' servant whom Molly fired, appears on the witness-stand to "tax" him with masturbation: "I was discoloured in four places as a result." (15.871–88) Bloom denies all charges, really the convictions of his own conscience: "Gentleman of the jury, let me explain. A pure mare's nest. I am a man misunderstood. I am being made a scapegoat of" (15.875–76). He has indeed found himself in a psychic "mare's nest," persecuted by women, but he continues "pleading not guilty" before the very phantasms of his own guilt, in order to avoid the impending punishment, which he of course at the same time desires.

Joyce's use of the word "scapegoat" in this context links Bloom with the ritualistic scapegoats often described by the anthropologists. In *The Literary Impact of the Golden Bough*, Vickery finds many parallels with Frazer's descriptions of the ritual scapegoat, or dying and reviving god, in primitive fertility festivals. While Vickery's discussion is illuminating, again I find more convincing similarities with Harrison's discussion of the Hellenic scapegoat, or as she rendered it in Anglicized Greek, the "*pharmakos*," particularly in the emphasis both she and Joyce give to ritual beating and whipping. She cites Ovid, who "goes straight to the question of what the Romans meant by the word *februum*" in "the opening words of the second book of the *Fasti*" (51). *Februum* were "'any thing by which the soul was purged,'" and "to strike with a sacred thing, whether with a strip of skin from a victim or a twig from a holy tree," was to purify by expelling evil. Spring was the time of purification in the ancient world — the Greek Anthesterion and the Roman Lupercalia, both celebrated in February, included cathartic rituals. Indeed, Harrison notes that our name of the month "February" derives from the "strips of skin ... known as *februa, purifiers*," with which celebrants scourged one another, and "by their purifying power they became fertility charms" (52). The human scapegoat, sacrificed at the Thargelia, was annually chosen from among criminals, slaves, or captured foreigners, fed or draped with the traditional matriarchal foods — barley cakes, figs, cheese — led outside the city and beaten with rods, usually of leeks, "fig sprigs," or other medicinal branches. "The beating of the pharmakoi," Harrison writes, "was a point of cardinal importance," and she stresses that while "we associate beating with moral stimulus," for the ancients its purpose was "clearly expulsive," to drive out moral and physical "pollution" (100–103). The *pharmakos* bore all the evil, sin, and disease of the community; by leading him out, beating and eventually killing him, the city was purified. As in all matriarchal ritual, such purification ultimately led to fertility: "The primary gist of the sacrifice is to appease and hence keep off evil spirits; it is these evil spirits that impair fertility: in a word purification is the placation of ghosts ... that fertility might be promoted, fertility of the earth and of man himself" (53–4).

That Joyce portrays Bloom particularly as *pharmakos* is suggested by Bloom's fantasy lawyer's description of him as "a poor foreign immigrant ... of Mongolian extraction and irresponsible for his actions" (*U*15.942–56), just the sort of "'scum' of humanity," as Aristophanes put it, that the Greeks chose to die for their cities' ills (Harrison 102).

"By Hades," J. J. O'Molly, declares, "I will not have any client of mine gagged and badgered in this fashion by a pack of curs and laughing hyenas" (*U*15.967–69), but Hades *is* the realm of Hecate's "curs," and the *pharmakos* must be "gagged and badgered" in fulfillment of his ritual role, purification leading to renewed fertility. So, a trio of avenging Erinyes enters Bloom's fantasy scenario — Mrs Yelverton Barry, Mrs Bellingham, and Mrs Mervyn Talboys — hurling more of the defendant's sexual transgressions at the court. Being three in number, predatory and vengeful, sporting all the accoutrements of the "sadistic oedipal mother," they are clearly associated with the three taloned, whip-bearing Erinyes, particularly as portrayed in Aeschylus' *Oresteia*. A comic Orestes, Bloom too has sinned against the mother and violated blood-law. Backed by her sister Erinyes, Mrs Mervyn Talboys threatens to "scourge the pigeonlivered cur ... flay him alive" and "flog him black and blue in the public streets" just like the *pharmakos* (*U*15.1081–1117), but Bloom's fantasy purgation through matriarchal ritual is interrupted. His emasculation will not be carried out by the three Erinyes, but by the apotheosis of his avenging witches, Bella Cohen. Like all witch figures, her retribution is extremely violent as she dominates and emasculates Bloom. "Henceforth you are unmanned and mine in earnest, a thing under the yoke," she says as Bloom dons his fantasy "punishment frock" and becomes a servant-girl trampled by bawds and witch goddesses (15.2963–67).

Critics have, naturally, focused on Bloom's emasculation and offered various explanations for it, usually deriving from Joyce's use of Leopold von Sacher-Masoch's *Venus im Pelz* and from the theories of masochism discussed above. Certainly Bloom's, and perhaps Joyce's, titillation by masochism and transvestism are evident, but the text also functions on a mythic level where rituals of beating and castration do not enact emasculation as punishment for oedipal desire. Quite the opposite: they signify a devotion to the mother and her generative purpose. Frazer's view was that the ritual "custom of castration" among priests of the great matriarchal goddesses was "designed to meet a constantly recurring need. ... the maintenance of the fruitfulness of the earth" (IV, i, 283). As Stuart Gilbert suggested long ago, prompted by Joyce, Bloom and Stephen may be seen as "Korybantes", priests of the Asian Earth-mother Cybele, "whose rites were frenzied excitement and self-castration, in which the votary made himself the serving-woman, handmaid of the goddess" (334). Frazer describes these castration rites in a vivid passage that clearly shows the goddess' duality as witch and mother:

Wrought up to the highest pitch of religious excitement they dashed the severed portions of themselves against the image of the cruel goddess. These broken instruments of fertility were afterwards reverently wrapped up and buried in the earth or in subterranean chambers sacred to Cybele, where, like the offering of blood, they may have been deemed instrumental in recalling Attis to life and hastening the general resurrection of nature, which was then bursting into leaf and blossom in the vernal sunshine. (268–9)

All the great matriarchal goddesses had male consorts — Cybele and Attis, Isis and Osirus, Aphrodite and Adonis — who were cruelly killed, castrated, or dismembered, but (and this is Frazer's entire thesis) ultimately resurrected as a sign and an agent of the annual resurrection of nature. Such rites as described by Frazer seem to be a symbolic enactment, not of castration, but of sexual intercourse, as the goddesses' "male ministers ... impersonated her divine lovers" by burying their phalluses within her (269).

Along with castration, transvestism also played a significant role, very different from today's conception, in ancient ritual. It was not an expression of homosexuality, but a way to identify with the mother, and through her with the creative life-force. Some discussions have focused on Joyce's use of the "couvade" ritual whereby "the father of the child simulates the confinement of the wife, often behaving as if he were actually giving birth" (Walkley 55). Joyce certainly parodies couvade, as Bloom, pronounced the "new womanly man," cries, "O, I so want to be a mother," and fantasizes giving cosmic birth to eight children, much as Gaia spouted giants and nymphs (*U*15.1817). R. Barrie Walkley shows that Joyce could have "run across a description of couvade anywhere," since, like many primitive rituals, it was first named and documented by E.B. Tylor, then much debated and popularized, but he determines that Joyce used Ernest Crawley's (a disciple of Tylor and Frazer) anthropological study of marriage customs, *The Mystic Rose* as his source. However, Walkley's interpretation of couvade as "a piece of symbolism whereby the father asserts his paternity against the maternal" is a questionable and inaccurate paraphrase of Crawley's argument (57).

Crawley summarizes earlier theories, J.J. Bachofen's and Tylor's, that through couvade "the father asserts his paternity, and accordingly his rights as a father, as against the maternal system of descent and inheritance," therefore marking a transitional stage in the shift of the matriarchal social system, where lineage is traced through the mother, to patriarchy (421). Yet Crawley goes on to *disagree* with this explanation, which,

> like many another explanation of marriage customs and systems on legal lines, really errs in not taking into account the woman's side of the question. They show a sympathy with the father and with the child, but forget the mother, and are thus a modern document illustrating the history of woman's treatment by man.   (422)

Instead Crawley bases his interpretation of couvade on the Tylorian notion of magic through the association of ideas: "Things and persons that have been or are in contact of any sort" retain their "*material* bond" even in *conceptual* or simulated performances, "and either party can thereby sympathetically influence the other" (422). Thus, by imitating the mother, the father magically participates in and takes on the terrors and dangers of childbirth, assisting and protecting both child and mother (425). Such primitive "sympathy expressed by contact is always tending to pass into substitution and exchange of identity" (425), so we see couvade explained as a matriarchal ritual, in which transvestism is a form of identification with woman in order to share her pain and participate in her creative power, hardly, as Walkley asserts, "paternity stressed at the expense of maternity" (61).

This more accurate understanding of Crawley's work accords better with Joyce's characterization of Bloom, whose empathy with women, as critics have frequently discerned, is well-marked throughout *Ulysses*, to the point where he even experiences the sluggish depression of "monthlies." It also accords with the many recent critics, such as Joseph Allen Boone, Suzette A. Henke, Cheryl Herr, and Carol Siegel, who see the androgynous Bloom, the "new womanly man" who emerges at the end of "Circe," not as castrated, but as sexually vital in a new way.[5] And his counterpart, the "phallic mother," is not a masculinized substitute for the father, but functions in her own right, as a purifying female eminence. Bloom's fantasy sex-change into a servant-girl and a prostitute is, in part, comic parody, but Bloom is also performing a sympathetic ritual identification with the lowest and most abused women in patriarchal society in order to experience female pain, and ultimately participate in her creative power. Boone's point that "'recovery' for Bloom cannot be measured in conventional terms of virility" is well-taken: it would be a violation of his most "positive" feminine characteristics to view him returning to Molly after his fantasy purgation as "the type of virile 'man' who conquers adversity, and women, through force" (79, 80). Yet many Joyceans want to believe that there will be some material change in his sexual relations with Molly after all the exhaustive psychic rituals of his day, particularly those in "Circe." Mythic and ritual parallels suggest that Bloom's return home as the "womanly man," the feminized priest of matriarchal ritual, will lead to renewed sexual fertility for both goddess and consort.

As Joyce told his sister Eva a few years after Giorgio was born, "The most important thing that can happen to a man is the birth of a child" (Ellmann 212). Bloom's autoeroticism, his adulterous fantasies and masturbation, are sterile, a violation of the mother-goddess Molly and of the "sacred ends of nature." As in matriarchal myths and rituals, Bloom's castration and transvestism in "Circe" are an enactment of justice, a purgation, and an identification with woman — and thus a psychic liberation from sterility. Bloom cries out, "Moll! I forgot! Forgive! Moll! ... We ... Still" (*U*15.3151). With this plea to the benevolent goddess for forgiveness, he leaves the realm of the witch to return to the mother: "Let me go. I will return. I will prove ... " (15.3191). As a sign that his Hecatean purgation is complete and his return to the mother imminent, he gets back the talismanic potato, "a relic of poor mamma" (15.3513). Purged by the witch, he can be reunited with Molly in her archetypal role as mother-goddess. He has been punished by Bella/Circe, allowing Marion/Circe to remain "plump as a pampered pouter pidgeon" — the generative Earth-mother to whom he will guide Stephen throughout "Eumeus" and "Ithaca." In "Circe" he ascends from lowly archetypal *pharmakos* to dignified archetypal hierophant, the modern/ancient Briton/pagan priest who will lead Stephen through Eleusinian ritual to Molly and to creation.

Eleusinian ritual begins with purification in water and from the beginning of "Eumaeus," Bloom, with his initiate in tow, seeks water for their "ablutions" (*U*16.7). Throughout "Eumaeus," Bloom as hierophant urges Stephen toward the three elements essential to the experience at Eleusis: grain (*sacra*), drink (*kykeon*), and "the female form" (Demeter/Persephone) (16.895). Stephen has expressed the desire for something to drink, probably alcohol, but Bloom's idea is "some drinkables in the shape of a milk and soda or a mineral," the unfermented liquids of matriarchal ritual (16.5–10). As Stephen's pagan hierophant, Bloom inhales with joy the "very palatable odor indeed of our daily bread ... the staff of life" and as "the more experienced of the two" he rejects the "supernatural God" as revealed in "Holy Writ" (16. 56–9, 771–77). His attention is focused instead on "eatables," the more material divinity behind primitive Hellenic ritual, as he urges Stephen repeatedly to eat and drink: "Can't you drink that coffee, by the way? Let me stir it and take a piece of that bun ... Try a bit" (16.784–804). Urged by his "good genius," Stephen attempts "a sip of the offending beverage" in the cab shelter, but coffee is not the ritual drink to answer Stephen's physical or spiritual needs. As if sensing the inadequacy of these offerings, Bloom adds, "Still, it's solid food. ... You ought to eat more solid food. You would feel a different man" (16.810–14). The point here, as many critics have noted, is that Stephen needs to be transformed into a "different man" through discovering the spirituality that inheres in physicality, the ultimate reassurance achieved by the initiate at Eleusis.

Bloom's disparagement of whores in "Eumaeus" reverberates with mythic connotations beyond his characteristic medical prudence, for, as one of Joyce's notes for "Circe" asks: "LB what kind of child can much fucked whore have" (Herring, *Buffalo* 17). Bloom as hierophant knows that the ultimate end of all primitive ritual is fertility, sexual as well as vegetative. It is as "paterfamilias" that Bloom feels whores should be "medically inspected," to guard against blighted procreation (16.743–44). It is "a thousand pities" that "the young fellow ... should waste his valuable time with profligate women" (16.1553–55). Bloom feels that Stephen needs to experience a sexuality of fecundity rather than sterility, of creative renewal rather than ennervating onanism. So, Bloom presents him with the photograph of Molly/Demeter, fecund Earth-mother.

As with the *sacra* at Eleusis, the symbolic "likeness" of the photograph to the goddess should "speak for itself" so that the initiate can "drink in the beauty for himself," or ritually experience the universal "female form" (16.1457–59, 1449). Molly's incarnation as Hellenic goddess here is emphasized by the parallel drawn in Bloom's mind between the photograph and the "Grecian statues" in the National Museum. Unlike the photograph, he thinks, the statues really "do justice to her figure," to its "opulent curves," but the photo seems sufficient to stimulate the admiring hierophant, who feels he may have to go outside to "satisfy a possible need by moving a motion" if he looks at it much longer (16.1445–64). Like the coffee, however, it is insufficient to move Stephen. Bloom worries over Stephen's mother-lessness, picturing him "rooked by some landlady worse than any stepmother," and over his need for food and drink, "were it only an eggflip made on unadulterated maternal nutriment" (16.1566–70). Clearly, Stephen's need for "maternal nutriment" — physical, sexual, and mythical — cannot be adequately fulfilled by the rank coffee and stale bun of the cabman's shelter, nor even by the photograph of Molly. Finally, when Bloom learns that Stephen has been fasting (as do the initiates at Eleusis) for two days, the hierophant realizes he must bring his initiate to the *telesterion* at 7 Eccles Street.

Every action performed in "Ithaca" corroborates Bloom's role as hierophant. The words of his dream: "Come in. All is prepared" achieve actuality as he stands "in the open space of the doorway" holding the "portable candle," his hierophantic torch (17.107, 116–17). As "waterlover, drawer of water, watercarrier," he performs the "ablutions" first hinted at in "Eumaeus" (17.183). It is as if, in Joyce's accretive, "scientific paeon" to water even the reader is made to experience the sea bath of the initiates (Madtes 456). At Eleusis, the initiates are cast into darkness until the hierophant orchestrates the visionary experi-ence in a brilliant flash of light. To facilitate this, he prepares the *kykeon* that reenacts Demeter's drinking at the palace of Eleusis and brings communion with her. As at any holy communion, the "'symbols of this initiation,'" including the "cymbal" from which initiates drink, were of sacred importance (Harrison 158). So Bloom "relinquish[ed] his symposiarchal right to the moustache cup of imitation Crown Derby presented to him by his only daughter, Millicent" and "substituted a cup identical with that of his guest" (*U*17.361–63). Bringing "light to the gentiles," hierophant Bloom joins Stephen in the rite of drinking, although as the leader he has "the advantage of ten seconds at the *initiation* ... " (17.353, 378, my italics).

Joyce loads the chapter with words connotative of Greek ritual — "sign" "pyre" "vessel" "chant" "rite" — to indicate that a more an-cient ritual than the one established at the Last Supper is here taking place. Joyce's use of the word "symposiarch," like his earlier use of "hierophantic," is redolent with Eleusinian significance. As Richard Madtes has noted, "the word comes from *syn-posis* 'a drinking together'" (456); in addition, however, Ruck defines "symposiarchos" as the lea-der at "a symposium or social drinking party" who "ceremoniously determines" the "intensity of inebriation" by deciding "what ratio of dilution would be used" (90). Thus, "symposiarch" emphasizes Bloom's hierophantic role of determining the visionary experience of the participant, just as Bloom "prepare[s] a collation for a gentile," carefully measuring out "two level spoonfuls, four in all, of Epps's soluble cocoa" (*U*17.354–56). Madtes cites Joyce's note, "SD cocoa 'creatura'", as proof that in the line "Epp's massproduct, the creature cocoa," Joyce intends their drinking to echo the Eucharist (456). However, Joyce deliberately departs from Christian symbolism here, and Eucharistic associations give way to a richer pagan substrate. For these initiates drink milk, the more primitive unfermented fluid requisite to matriarchal ritual, not wine. As if to stress that Stephen finally receives the "unadulterated maternal nutriment" symbolic of Molly, Joyce writes that Bloom does not only add boiling water to the soluble cocoa, but also "served extraordinarily to his guest and, in reduced measure, to himself the viscous cream ordinarily reserved for the breakfast of his wife Marion (Molly)" (*U*17.363–65). Bloom has already rejected Holy Writ and the hierophant and his initiate drink milk not wine; thus, their goal in the ritual is not to experience communion with the asexual man-god, Christ, but rather in Frazer's words, a "solemn communion with the divinity" of Demeter, the generative Earth-mother of all "creatura."

Yet the Eleusinian Mysteries were a celebration of both mother and daughter. Where is Persephone? Throughout *Ulysses* Milly is conspicuous by her absence. She has gone to Mullingar to work for a photographer, and like Persephone's abduction, this absence coincides with her sexual initiation, as Bloom intuitively fears from his daughter's letter mentioning "a young student" related to Boylan (*U*4.426–31). For Bloom has not only lost a son, Rudy, but he has lost a daughter as well, and, while the loss of a child to sexual maturity is much less traumatic than the loss of a child to death, yet it is still baffling and painful, as Joyce suggests by these crucial lines given at the end of the chapter. After Rudy's death,

> there remained a period of 10 years, 5 months and 18 days during which carnal intercourse had been incomplete, without ejaculation of semen within the natural female organ. By narrator a limitation of activity, mental and corporal, inasmuch as complete mental intercourse between himself and the listener had not taken place since the consummation of puberty, indicated by catamenic hemorrhage, of the female issue of narrator and listener, 15 September 1903, there remained a period of 9

months and 1 day during which in consequence of a preestablished natural comprehension in incomprehension between the
consummated females (listener and issue), complete corporal
liberty of action had been circumscribed. (17.2282–92)

There has been no physical intercourse between Bloom and Molly
since Rudy's death, but the onset of Milly's menstruation has disturbed
the "mental intercourse" between them. This is because of the "preestablished natural comprehension in incomprehension between the consummated females": menstruation is "preestablished" "natural" and
to the male "incomprehensible," yet through this incomprehensible
mystery mother and daughter share a "comprehension" which excludes
Bloom; they are "consummated." While Bloom blames himself for
Rudy's death, he may blame Molly for the loss of his daughter; hence
the estrangement from their usual mental intimacy. That Joyce intended Bloom to feel his women had united against him is revealed by
the notesheets for "Ithaca": "Molly & Milly both turn on LB" (Herring, *BM* 429).

Milly's symbolic presence, however, permeates the ritual of "Ithaca,"
just as Persephone's does the Eleusinian ritual. Stephen has just heard
in the hierophant's "chant" the "accumulation of the past" (*U*17.765,
777). Being "secluded, reassured, the decocted beverages ... having
been consumed," just as initiates in the *telesterion*, Bloom encourages
Stephen to "chant in a modulated voice a strange legend" (17.795–
800). He does not appear to be disturbed by the anti-Semitism of
the song about "Little Harry Hughes" who "broke the jew's windows
all" (17.802–07). But in the "second part" of the song, "the jew's
daughter" leads the "pretty little boy ... by the lilywhite hand" where
"none could hear him call," took a "penknife out of her pocket/And
cut off his little head" (17.813–28). Now Bloom, "the father of Millicent" is filled with "mixed feelings" and "unsmiling" as he envisions
his daughter, "all dressed in green," performing such a horrific role
(17.830–31).

The words of the song, "Where none could hear him call," echo the
narrator's description of Bloom and Stephen sitting "where none could
hear them talk" (17.797). Like Harry Hughes they are alone, facing
through this rite a goddess who, as they both know from "Circe,"
can be fiercely destructive, as the song appears to express both men's
fear of a violent Cybelean castration. Milly, the "jew's daughter," has
danced through Bloom's fantasy before, "greenvested," to taunt him

during his emasculation by Bello: "My! It's Papli! But. O Papli, how old you've grown!" Bloom at first confused her with Molly, until corrected by Bello: "That's your daughter, you owl, with a Mullingar student," or, in other words, your daughter in a sexual role, similar to her mother (15.3165–71). In Stephen's song, Milly is envisioned in the castrating, destructive role of the archetypal witch. Here, as at Eleusis, the witch is the third manifestation of mother and daughter: Milly/Persephone is associated with both Molly/Demeter and Bello/Hecate. Her green clothing, however, signifies the positive side of her sexuality, i.e., Persephone's rebirth in spring and the renewal that comes after the witch's destruction, just as Demeter Erinys returns to Demeter Lousia.

Stephen's "commentary" on the song is a difficult passage that reveals his increasing awareness of pagan ritual. He refers to the little boy of the song, associated here with himself, as the "victim predestined," i.e., the *pharmakos* (17.833). He "challenges his destiny," as it might be said both Bloom and Stephen are doing, but destiny in turn "challenges him reluctant ... holds him unresisting" and "leads him to a strange habitation, to a secret infidel apartment, and there, implacable, immolates him consenting" (17.834–7). Clearly Stephen refers to himself here, in the "apartment" of the "infidel," and implies his "consent" to the "immolation" or violent purgation demanded by matriarchal ritual before it imparts spiritual affirmation. The narrator's denomination of the "host" also as "victim predestined" and "secret infidel" indicates Bloom as accessory initiate and hierophant in the ritual. Although "unresisting," Bloom is also "sad," "reluctant" and "silent" (17.838–843). His conscious reason for resisting the ritual castration told by Stephen's "legend" is his characteristic dislike of "ritual murder" (17. 844), yet unconsciously the song disturbs him because it shows his daughter with a woman's full sexual power: Persephone has become one with Hecate and with Demeter.

The symbol most evocative of Milly's change and Bloom's loss of his daughter to womanhood is the photograph, an image already highly charged with female sexuality from its relation to Molly in "Eumaeus". Bloom's thoughts progress in "Ithaca" from "infantile memories" of Milly to memories of her "adolescence," which are recorded chronologically. First "she relegated her hoop and skippingrope to a recess," then, "entreated by an English visitor, she declined to permit him to make and take away her photographic image (objection not stated)" (17.864–78). The "objection," however, is made clear from one of

Joyce's notesheets for "Ithaca": "Milly feared her photo part of self" (Herring, *BM* 420). Like the photograph of Molly, it would have the power to "speak for itself" of her budding sexuality. And Milly's newly acquired sexual instinct warns her that photographs of women can be used for sexual titillation by men. For Bloom, who hides erotic postcards in his desk drawer, not to recognize Milly's motivation in refusing to be photographed, reveals the father attempting to repress full acknowledgment of his daughter's sexuality.

But the photograph of Molly conveys her spiritually as well as sexually. Molly appears in her photo as the universal "female form," the Earth-mother Demeter. So too Milly's refusal to permit a man to take her photograph is a manifestation of her divinity as "Kore," the Maiden who is traditionally hidden and protected from view. It is a mythological commonplace (i.e. Actaeon) that men who have the misfortune to spy a virgin goddess while she is bathing suffer an awful fate, usually death. The significance of Milly's job in a photographic studio now becomes obvious. Like Persephone she has crossed the river into death and sexuality: "I am getting on swimming in the photo business now. Mr Coghlan took one of me and Mrs will send when developed" (4:400–03).

As noted, Frazer and Harrison both stress the remarkable pictorial similarity between Demeter and Persephone. "Greek artists ... frequently represent the Mother and Daughter side by side in forms which resemble each other so closely [as to be] ... almost indistinguishable" (Frazer 67). To Frazer the reason for this similarity was obvious: how can we "divide exactly the two persons of the divinity," for "at what precise moment does the seed cease to be the Corn Mother and begin to burgeon out into the Corn Daughter?" (58) Harrison describes how "matriarchal goddesses reflect the life of women . ... woman as maiden, bride, mother and grandmother" (262). She differs from Frazer in pointing out that Demeter and Kore "are not Mother and *Daughter*, but Mother and Maiden ... in fact, merely the older and younger form of the same person." But she agrees that "primitive art never clearly distinguished" between them, "never lost the truth that they were one goddess" (274). To enter into communion with Demeter at Eleusis was, therefore, to experience Persephone at one and the same moment, since "the two persons of the godhead were one in substance" (Frazer 67).

Thus Bloom's fond memories of Milly lead him to ask Stephen "To pass in repose the hours intervening between Thursday (proper) and

Friday (normal) on an extemporised cubicle in the apartment immediately above the kitchen and immediately adjacent to the sleeping apartment of his host and hostess" (*U*17.931–34). The "father of Milly" offers both his daughter and wife to Stephen, just as the hierophant at Eleusis offered a visionary experience of both Demeter and Persephone to the initiate. After asking Stephen to stay overnight, Bloom lists the "various advantages" which might result from the "prolongation" of the arrangement. For himself one advantage would be "vicarious satisfaction" and for Molly a result might be "disintegration of obsession," presumably her obsession with Boylan (17.935–39). Just as hierophant and initiate shared a symbolic communion with the goddess by drinking together, so Bloom imagines that sharing Molly sexually with Stephen may also grant him "vicarious satisfaction." And,

> Why might these several provisional contingencies between a guest and a hostess not necessarily preclude or be precluded by a permanent eventuality of reconciliatory union between a schoolfellow and a jew's daughter?

> Because the way to the daughter led through the mother, the way to mother through daughter.   (17.940–44)

The schoolfellow here is, of course, Stephen, and the question reveals Bloom's hope that the young man might form a "permanent ... union" with his daughter, a marriage. Joyce's understanding of the essential unity of mother and daughter at Eleusis is acute. In Bloom's imagination Stephen's affair with Molly should in no way preclude his union with Milly, since, in a line that might have come from any text describing the Eleusinian mystery, "the way to daughter led through mother, the way to mother through daughter."

Furthermore, not only are mother and daughter one, but father and son are also. Most of the sexual paths Bloom opens for Stephen, are routes he needs to follow himself. Bloom will gain a son through physical rapprochement with Molly; he will regain his daughter through spiritual rapprochement with Molly, since mother and daughter have united in an intimacy which excludes him. And, just as imagining Stephen, the son, as a substitute for himself in the arms of the mother grants Bloom "vicarious satisfaction," so resuming sexual relations with Molly will grant him the vicarious satisfaction of sexual relations with his daughter, a fantasy that may lurk behind his fear of his daughter's sexual maturation.

Why does Joyce make the onset of Milly's menstruation occur exactly 9 months and 1 day prior to the events of June 16, 1904? The answer can only be that after this obvious period of gestation there will be a birth, not an actual child born to Milly, but, since mother and daughter are "a single divine substance," the mythic child that concluded the mysteries at Eleusis, the "divine boy" Brimos, or in Joyce's version, Stephen. For, not only are mother and daughter one, but the lover or the "husband" and the child are also. Brimos is the undifferentiated son of Brimo, but he is identified with different male figures associated with Eleusis, in the *Homeric Hymn* with Ploutos, another manifestation of Hades, his father. "The old matriarchal couple, the Mother and the Maid, who though they were two persons were yet but one goddess, had for their foster-child now one local hero, now another, now Demophon, now and chiefly Triptolemos," writes Harrison, and later, in the union of two cults, the infant Dionysus. As she concludes, his identity "is a question that can never certainly be answered. He is the young male divinity of Eleusis, the nursling of the goddesses; beyond that we cannot go" (562–3). On June 16, 1904 both father and son, Bloom and Stephen, conjoin with and are ritually reborn through Earth-mother and Maiden-daughter. Their experience in the garden at 7 Eccles Street is, like Eleusis, a celebration of the undifferentiated act of creation and perhaps signals the rebirth of two creators, father and poet.

As Bloom and Stephen pass through the "door of egress" to the final rites in the garden, the hierophant leads carrying his ritual torch, the "Lighted Candle in Stick borne by Bloom" (*U*17.1021–33). He leaves the "candlestick on the floor," for, as at Eleusis, with "'torches extinguished ... the vast and countless assemblage believe[s] that in what is done ... in darkness is their salvation'" (Harrison 563). So Bloom and Stephen "emerged silently, doubly dark from obscurity by a passage from the rere of the house into the penumbra of the garden," in an image of rebirth, to where they are illuminated generally by the fecund, celestial light of Molly, the "humid nightblue fruit" (*U*17.1036–39). Yet her archetypal apotheosis as Demeter is symbolized by a more specific light, as it was at Eleusis where all sources agree, the mystery was revealed "by the light of a great flame" (Harrison 550). So, in Joyce's paeon to Molly/Demeter, the "visible luminous sign" appears first to Bloom the hierophant, "who attracted Stephen's gaze" to where "In the second storey (rere) of his (Bloom's) house the light of a paraffin oil lamp with oblique shade projected on a screen of roller blind"

(*U*17.1171–74). Here Joyce ingeniously captures the essence of religious visionary experience, for Molly herself is "invisible" yet the initiate actually perceives her in the light which, to the uninitiate, would only be symbolic of her. Bloom, the conscientious hierophant, tries to "elucidate the mystery of an invisible person, his wife Marion (Molly) Bloom, denoted by a visible splendid sign, a lamp," but ultimately words fail (17.1177–78). Both men fall into "silent" worship of her and of their own unity in her — "theirhisnothis fellowfaces" — just as the Eleusinian initiates gazed in silence at the grain, united in the symbol of the universal continuity of life (17.1184).

The role of the male in creation is not forgotten at Eleusis, for the Earth-mother cannot give birth without the "Sacred Marriage," just as the grain cannot grow unless "fertilising showers quicken the seed in the furrows" (Frazer 69). So on the final day of the Mysteries, "two vessels called *plemochoae* are emptied, one towards the east, the other towards the west, and at the moment of outpouring, a mystic formulary was pronounced. ... looking up to the sky they cried aloud 'Rain,' and looking down to earth they cried 'Be fruitful'" (Harrison 160–1). Kerenyi adds that the water flowing east and west symbolized the directions of birth and death, "the two aspects of the primal element," water (149). These two aspects exist as well in Bloom and Stephen's dual aqueous tribute to the goddess, for urine is waste matter or decay, but at the same time it symbolizes rain and semen, both male-linked sources of life, and Joyce's association of urination with creativity is well-known. Significantly, this is the first ritual act initiated by Stephen, although, as with the drinking, both men participate in it equally: "At Stephen's suggestion, at Bloom's instigation both, first Stephen, then Bloom, in penumbra urinated" (*U*17.1186–87). Stephen, "hydrophobe" (17.237), declined involvement in Bloom's initial ablutions, but he has become fully participatory in this ritual celebration.

"What celestial sign was by both simultaneously observed?" A comet shoots "beyond the stargroup of the Tress of Berenice towards the zodiacal sign of Leo," symbolizing, perhaps, a "Sacred Marriage" between the goddess and her lover — between Molly, suggested (albeit faintly) by the "Tress of Berenice" and Leo/pold (17.1210–13). More important than the marriage, however, was "the holy rite enacted between the hierophant and the chief priestess of Demeter," their "holy congress" shrouded in mystery, but resulting in the symbolic birth of a divine son (Harrison 550). Such a ritual intercourse is enacted by Bloom "inserting the barrel of an arruginated male key in the hole of an unstable female lock" to open the "aperture" through which Stephen passes, symbolically reborn, to face his future as creator (17.1215–19). As many critics have discerned, and Jean Kimball has noted, "the spirit of the artist must participate in the flesh that passes; the word must become flesh ... [an] incarnation [that] can happen only in a woman's womb" (155). Through the guidance of his hierophant Stephen has found this maternal archetype in Molly Bloom, goddess of a religion in which physicality and spirituality are one, and he has been reborn through visionary union with her as lover and son. What, in actuality, will be Stephen's future, Joyce leaves open, but these Eleusinian parallels suggest an optimistic reading. As Jane Harrison writes, the matriarchal goddess asks of her male child/lover, "not that he should love or adore, but that he should do great deeds" (273).

5 : SWEENEY AND THE MATRICIDAL DANCE: THE EVOLUTION OF T. S. ELIOT'S DRAMA

"Man makes his demons in the image of his own savage and irrational passions."

— Jane Ellen Harrison, *PSGR* x

T. S. Eliot evolved his dramatic theory out of a wide knowledge of the entire field of anthropology, from its origin in E. B. Tylor through the Cambridge School of Anthropology. The influence of this group's ideas on Eliot, particularly Francis M. Cornford's connection of primitive ritual with the origin of Greek comedy, was first discussed by Carol H. Smith in her 1963 study, *T. S. Eliot's Dramatic Theory and Practice*, and in her updated, although essentially unchanged, 1984 article, "Sweeney and the Jazz Age." Smith decried the tendency of much Eliot criticism to consider his drama a lesser achievement than his poetry, as well as the critical inability to explain why Eliot turned to drama in the first place. But if, as the Cambridge classicists believed, the highly formalized conventions of Greek drama were survivals of religious rituals, communal expressions of the spiritual impulse, then drama would be a natural form for "a poet of spiritual experience" with a growing sense of the poet's "social mission" to choose, particularly one with "a compelling need to make some personal order out of the chaos which he found around him" (Smith 34, 24, 5).

Smith cites ample evidence of Cornford's and Murray's influence on Eliot from his 1923 essays, "The Beating of a Drum," "Four Elizabethan Dramatists," and "Marie Lloyd," in addition to a 1924 letter to Arnold Bennett, the 1926 introduction to his mother's poetic drama *Savonarola*, his 1933 letter to Hallie Flanagan, who was attempting to produce *Sweeney Agonistes* at Vassar, and "The Use of Poetry and the Use of Criticism" published the same year. However, the impact of the ritual theory — Harrison's explication of the evolution of drama out of Dionysian ritual — on Eliot's dramatic theory must also be considered not only as filtered through her disciples, but directly, since Eliot was just as well acquainted with her work as theirs.

The "Sweeney" poems and their culmination in the dramatic fragment "Sweeney Agonistes" show Eliot's application of the ritual theory to his art, as well as his incipient exploration of Aeschylean themes. Sweeney is a precursor to Harry, the young agonist of *The Family Reunion*, since Eliot associated both with Orestes, and the parallels with Aeschylus' *Oresteia* in that play need to be explicated. Eliot's female archetypes transform from the hideous Gorgonesque witch of "Sweeney Erect" to the maiden Kores, Agatha and Mary, of *The Family Reunion*, just as Aeschylus shows the transformation of vengeful Erinyes into beneficient Eumenides. Unlike Joyce, Eliot denies the Earth-mother and the validity of physical renewal promised through fertility, idealizing instead a purely spiritual patroness aligned with the father-god, much like the motherless Olympian, Athene. Most analyses of the Sweeney poems and their culmination in *The Family Reunion* have focused on Eliot's ultimately Christian vision, while the powerful female archetypes in those works and their Hellenic parallels have been largely misunderstood or dismissed.

In *Ancient Art and Ritual*, Jane Harrison traced the evolution of "*dromenon*" (literally "things done" or rituals) into Greek drama, beginning with Aristotle's statement that tragedy "'originated with the leaders of the Dithyramb'" (76). The dithyramb was "the song of the birth of Dionysos in the spring, the time of the maypole, the time of the holy Bull" (101–2), and it was celebrated at the Great Dionysia in Athens, established by the tyrant Peisistratos as the state-sanctioned spring festival, much like the Eleusinian Mysteries had been absorbed by Athens as the chief harvest celebration. Both, of course, were based on primitive and ancient agricultural *dromena* long indigenous to the countryside. But by the time of Aeschylus "the belief in the efficacy of certain magical rites, and especially of the Spring Rite" had decayed (137). He found an ancient spring *dromenon* that was "well-nigh effete" and infused it with new life by adding the Homeric epic sagas to the old ritual forms, thus initiating the great era of Greek tragedy (146). This "decay of religious faith," leaving the "ritual moulds" empty and "ready for a new content," Harrison expressed beautifully (especially since Dionysus, the god of the drama is also the god of wine) in the metaphor of "old bottles" being filled with "new wine" (140, 146): "The amazing development of the fifth-century drama is just this, the old vessel of the ritual Dithyramb filled to the full with the new wine of the heroic *saga*; and it would seem that it was by the hand of Peisistratos, the great democratic tyrant, that the new wine was outpoured" (164).

She points to the visible "encroachment of the stage on the orchestra" in the archaeological remains of the Dionysiac theater in Athens as evidence of this evolution: "The old circular orchestra shows the dominance of ritual; the new curtailed orchestra of Roman times and semicircular shape shows the dominance of the spectacle" (143). Originally the Dionysian ritual was performed by "a band or chorus who dance together *with a common leader*," around whom "the emotion centres" (72). The "kernal and centre of the whole was the *orchestra*, the circular *dancing-place* of the chorus," just as the chorus, "the band of dancing and singing men ... was the centre and kernal of and starting point of the drama" (123). There was no division "between actors and spectators; all are actors, all are doing the thing done, dancing the dance danced," but with the infusion of Homeric epic, the focus of the drama increasingly came to be on the individual, not on the group (126). Thus, the "prologues and messengers' speeches and ever-present choruses" in Greek drama are survivals: "ritual forms still surviving at a time when the drama has fully developed out of the *dromenon*" (122).

Twenty-eight years later Gilbert Murray's work still reflected the impact of Jane Harrison, as he described a possible performance of Aeschylus' *The Suppliant Women*, "far the earliest Greek play that has come down to us," giving a vivid picture of this proto-drama derived from communal rituals:

Now in the *Supplices* the Chorus consists of the fifty daughters of Danaus. ... But that is by no means all. The fifty Danaids are pursued by the fifty sons of Aegyptus. ... Furthermore, the fifty Egyptians are put to flight by the Argive army, which must, therefore, at a modest estimate, be reckoned at least at another fifty. ... There are no other characters ... only three Choruses, each fifty strong, each with its Director, or Exarchon. ... Thus we have no actors, no stage, but at least a hundred and fifty-three persons engaged in a complex of dances on the old danc-ing-floor of Dionysus. (*ACT* 48)

To Harrison's theoretical backbone Murray and Cornford added flesh, respectively tracing the survivals of ritual in tragedy and com-edy. "It seems clear," Murray wrote in his "Excursis on the Ritual Forms preserved in Greek tragedy" included in Chapter VIII of Harrison's *Themis*, and employing her concept of the "Eniautos-Daimon," "that Comedy and Tragedy represent different stages in the life of this Year Spirit; Comedy leads to his Marriage Feast, his *Komos*, Tragedy to his death and *Threnos* [lamentation]" (*T* 341). Murray then identified the ritual components of tragedy, combining Frazerian and Aristotelian nomenclature in refering to the "*Agon* or Contest" as the "Year against its enemy," the "*Pathos* of the Year-Daimon, generally a ritual or sacri-ficial death," the "Messenger," the "*Threnos* or Lamentation," the "*Anagnorisis* — discovery or recognition — of the slain and mutilated Daimon, followed by his Resurrection," resulting of course "with a *Peripeteia* or extreme change of feeling from grief to joy" (343). Murray examined the plays of Euripides, Aeschylus, and Sophocles, culling evidence of these forms, and echoed Harrison's metaphor in his con-clusion: "the vessels of a very ancient religion overfilled and broken by the new wine of reasoning and rebellious humanity, and still, in their rejection, shedding abroad the old aroma, as of eternal and mysterious things: these are the fundamental paradoxes presented to us by Greek tragedy" (362–3).

Cornford built on Murray's and Harrison's edifice, finding that "the ritual drama lying behind Comedy proves to be essentially of the same type as that in which Professor Gilbert Murray has sought the origin of Tragedy" (*OAC* vii). Comedies begin with an expository "Prologue" followed by the "*Agon*," often a "dramatised debate" (73) or "fierce 'con-test' between the representatives of two parties or principles" (2). Nearly all of the Aristophanic comedies "end with an incident no less canoni-cal than the *Agon* — a festal procession (*Komos*) and a union which I shall call a 'Marriage'. ... We shall also find in almost every play two other standing incidents which fall between the *Agon* and the final *Komos* — a scene of Sacrifice and Feast" (3). In the sacrifice and feast, Cornford saw "traces of an older form of ritual in which the God himself ... is dismembered, and the pieces of his body are either devoured raw ... or cooked and eaten in a sacramental feast," again for the purpose of "regeneration" (99). Then the hero "is accompanied in the *Komos* by a person who ... is always mute," and appears nowhere else in the play; "sometimes a nameless courtesan, sometimes an allegorical figure, she is the temporary partner of the hero" so that a union may be celebrated (8), representing a survival of the "sexual union consummated or feigned" in ancient rituals, for instance at Eleusis, to stimulate "the two great agents of vegetable fertility, the Earth-mother and the Heaven-father" (16–19).

Thus, Cornford observes, comedy focuses on sexuality; tragedy on spirituality:

> In Tragedy ... the element of sex magic and consequent obscenity has, if it ever was there, been totally suppressed. The emphasis has come to fall on the death, the resurrection surviving only in rudiments. ... In Comedy the emphasis still falls on the phallic element and the fertility marriage. (68)

This dichotomy may be further illustrated by comparing Harrison's and Cornford's differing emphases on Aristotle's "famous sentence": "'Tragedy — as also Comedy was at first mere improvisation. The one originated with the leaders of the dithyramb, the other with those phallic songs which are still in use in many of our cities'" (*T* 32). As we have seen, Harrison focused on the dithyramb in tragedy, a song celebrating the eternal renewal symbolized by Dionysian resurrection. Cornford, naturally, in explicating the origins of comedy, focused on "The Phallic Song," invoking "Phales, the companion of Bacchus in his nightly revels," or more precisely, an expression of Dionysus himself in his purely sexual form — "little more than the emblem of human procreation, the *phallus*, barely personified" (*OAC* 19, 36–8). This difference in emphasis becomes important when considering the influence of the Cambridge classicists on Eliot's drama. As Carol Smith established, Eliot's first attempt at drama, "Sweeney Agonistes/Fragments of an Aristophanic Melodrama," with its "Prologue" and "Agon," was clearly influenced by Cornford's *The Origin of Attic Comedy*. Indeed, Eliot advised Hallie Flanagan that the book was "'important to read before you do the play'" (Smith 62). However, while "Sweeney Erect" is a comic poem, "Sweeney Among the Nightingales" is more ambivalent, and after *Sweeney Agonistes*, Eliot turned to tragedy as his dramatic model, so that thereafter Harrison became a much profounder influence than Cornford.

Unlike Joyce, Eliot's use of mythic archetype and ritual does not recall the pre-Olympian matriarchal rites like Eleusis, with their emphasis on sexuality and eternity through material regeneration. Rather, his source was Greek tragedy, a later development that came long after the ancient ritual "bottles" had been filled with the "new wine" of Olympianism, with its worship, not of the fecund, familial Earthmother, but of the hierarchic, spiritual father, Zeus. This accords with Eliot's marked preference for the "arch-mystic" Aeschylus (as Harrison called him), also "a monotheist and ... 'all for the father' " (*T* 386), over Euripides whose tragedies hearkened back to the more primitive matriarchal rites, as in the *Bacchae*.

Harrison always preferred ancient matriarchal rituals and the "vague *daemones*" of pre-Olympian worship, but not for their message of sexual renewal. Rather she yearned for the "living spirit" expressed through the communal emotional release of primitive ritual as she imagined it (thus it was entirely characteristic that she moved away from Frazerian materialism, with its consistent emphasis on fertility). Harrison envied the primitive dancers whose "limitations of personality fall away," who could create a "mystery-god" out of "*collective* feeling," a theory she derived from the French sociologist Émile Durkheim and anthropologist Lucien Lévy-Bruhl. She loved the cult of Dionysus, which she regarded as matriarchal. For instance, around the turn of the century, the British archaeologist Arthur Evans had shown her clay tablets unearthed at the Cretan palace of Cnossos portraying the "Great Mother" with the "human king — God wearing the mask of a bull," that is Dionysus, which deeply moved her (*R* 71). Her emphasis was not on the phallic energy of Dionysus, nor on the material renewal of fertility ritual, but always on the mysticism and communal worship of the matriarchal *daimones*, among which he is preeminent. This predilection is unique to her among the Cambridge Anthropologists, and because Eliot was also influenced by French sociology, his dramatic theory is closer in spirit to Harrison than to Cornford or Murray. He shared her desire to evoke a collective spiritual experience through resurrecting the ancient ritual "mould" inherent in Greek drama, not only in theory but on the modern stage.

There is ample evidence for Eliot's familiarity with the ritual theory of the Cambridge group, particularly his 1923 article entitled "The Beating of a Drum," in which he reviewed a "Miss Busby's" study of "the Fool in Elizabethan comedy." Criticizing Miss Busby, Eliot expresses his belief that one should not merely be a "chronicler," but rather an "anthropologist of Folly." He directs his readers to Cornford's *The Origin of Attic Comedy*, finding in the Fool a stock character similar to Cornford's Cook or Learned Doctor, with "more than a suggestion of the shaman or medicine-man." Carol Smith draws attention to two key terms, essential to an understanding of Eliot's dramatic theory, that emerge in this article: rhythm and abstraction (47–9). "Critics are agreed that Eliot ... stood firmly against realism and favored instead an art which used devices of abstraction," but "there is very little agreement on what the poet meant by such terms as rhythm" (32). Both terms "took on important theoretical significance for Eliot" (12) as "The Beating of a Drum" reveals:

> If Mr. Cornford's theory is correct — and I believe it has the support of Mr. Gilbert Murray — the original dramatic impulse ... is neither comic nor tragic. The comic element, or the antecedent of the comic, is perhaps present, together with the tragic, in all savage or primitive art; but comedy and tragedy are late, and perhaps impermanent intellectual abstractions. Now my own conclusion (for which I would not hold anyone else responsible) is this: that such abstractions, after developing through several generations of civilization, require to be replaced or renewed. The essentials of drama were, as we might expect, given by Aristotle: poetry, music, and dancing constitute in Aristotle a group by themselves, their common element being imitation by means of rhythm. ("BD" 139)

Commenting on this passage, Smith rightly observes that "Eliot was seeking beneath the usual classifications of drama for something basic and elemental upon which the contemporary poet could rebuild dramatic art. Beneath tragedy and comedy lay primitive religious rites and beneath these rites lay rhythm and man's innate fascination with it" (49). However, neither Cornford nor Murray ever emphasized rhythm. They agreed, certainly, that the substrate of both tragedy and comedy was religious ritual, but they did not equate ritual with rhythm. To understand the significance of rhythm in drama for Eliot, we must turn to the connection Jane Harrison habitually made between them: "All these ritual forms haunt and shadow the play, whatever its plot, like ancient traditional ghosts; they underlie and sway the movement and the speeches like some compelling rhythm. Now this ritual mould, this underlying rhythm was once shaped and cast by a living spirit" (*AAR* 138). It is possible, therefore, that Eliot's "own conclusion" for which he "would not hold anyone else responsible," owes quite a bit to his reading of Harrison.

In addition, the term "abstraction" is not to be found in Murray's or Cornford's work, yet we have already seen what a key term it was in Harrison's theory of the ritual bridge between art and life. Ritual, as an abstraction from life, she felt, stood mid-way between life and art. Both ritual and art, therefore, represent stages in a process of distancing, or formal abstraction, from life: "oddly enough, an impulse emotional in itself [ritual] begets a process we think of as characteristically and exclusively intellectual, the process of abstraction" (*AAR* 42). The movement from ritual to art she regretted as a movement away from direct emotional experience to arid intellectualization, and she sought to reverse it in her own way by re-establishing the original connection between ritual and art. For ritual always began for Harrison in "the desire to utter, to give out a strongly felt emotion," and it is this "common *emotional* factor that makes art and ritual in their beginnings well-nigh indistinguishable" (26).

How uncharacteristic for the author of "Tradition and the Individual Talent," written four years earlier, to refer to intellectual abstractions as "impermanent," and to want to "replace or renew" the formal abstractions in drama that took "several generations of civilization" to develop! That Eliot should want to strip drama down to its most elemental, emotional basis — rhythm — argues for Harrison's influence. Like Harrison, he saw the restoration of rhythm to drama as a return of the "living spirit," and in the communal catharsis of rhythm they both saw a human expression of divinity. The conclusion of "The Beating of a Drum" is even more reminiscent of Harrison. Eliot finds it a "pity" that one scholar who has written "a study of primitive religious dances ... falls into the common trap of interpretation, by formulating intelligible reasons for the primitive dancer's dancing." Instead, Eliot asserts, "primitive man acted in a certain way and then found a reason for it." This sounds extraordinarily similar to Harrison's insistence, in opposition to Frazer, that the primitive dancer does not dance to embody a "Spirit of Vegetation," since he does not "perform a mental act so high and difficult as abstraction." Rather he "begins with a vague excited dance to relieve his emotion," and only then "the abstract idea arises," gradually, out of the act (71).

However, it may be wrong to insist that Eliot derived this understanding of primitive humanity's "pre-logical" mentality solely from Harrison, since he, like she, knew Durkheim's studies in the sociology of primitive religion and Lévy-Bruhl's research in primitive cognition quite well. In fact, modern criticism has paid little attention to how deeply knowledgeable Eliot was of the *entire* field of anthropology, from Darwin and Tylor through the French sociologists and Cambridge classicists. The repeatedly cited influences of Frazer, Cornford, and Weston merely scratch the surface of his knowledge. In "The Beating of a Drum" Eliot tells literary critics that "instead of perpetually perusing the writings of other critics," they would gain a better understanding of literature by studying its sources in "such books as 'The Origin of the Species' itself, and ... 'Primitive Culture'" (11). In a 1924 article for *Vanity Fair*, in which he praises Frazer, Eliot reveals his wide reading in Mannhardt, Sir E.B. Tylor, Robertson Smith, Miss Harrison, Miss Weston, A.B. Cook, F.M. Cornford, Dr. Rendel Harris, Hartland, and others (29). Even earlier, in a 1919 review for *The Athenaeum*, "War-Paint and Feathers," Eliot asserts that, while it is "not necessary, perhaps ... to peruse all the works of Miss Harrison, Cooke [*sic*] Rendel Harris, Lévy-Bruhl or Durkheim ... one ought, surely, to have read at least one book such as those of Spencer and Gillen on the Australians, or Codrington on the Melansians" (1036). Here, four years before commending Joyce for his use of the "mythic method," Eliot's extensive knowledge of anthropology had already convinced him that "primitive art and poetry can even, through the studies and experiments of the artist or poet, revivify contemporary activities."

In a 1920 review of Gilbert Murray's translation of *Medea*, Eliot charts the growth of anthropology into all the various branches of modern science, which

> began, in a sense, with Tylor and a few German anthropologists: since then we have ... watched the clinics of Ribot and Janet, we have read books from Vienna and heard a discourse of Bergson; a philosophy at Cambridge and we have a curious Freudian-social-mystical-rationalistic-higher-critical interpretation of the Classics and what used to be called the Scriptures. ... Few books are more fascinating than those of Miss Harrison, Mr. Cornford,

or Mr. Cooke [*sic*], when they burrow in the origins of Greek
myths and rites; M. Durkheim, with his social consciousness,
and M. Lévy-Bruhl, with his Bororo Indians who convince
themselves that they are parroquets, are delightful writers. A
number of sciences have sprung up in an almost tropical exu-
berance ... and such men as Tylor, and Robertson Smith, and
Wilhelm Wundt, who early fertilised the soil, would hardly
recognize the resulting vegetation.   (38–43)

Clearly, there was no major theorist in anthropology and in the
related fields of sociology, psychology, and classicism with whom Eliot
was not familiar, but the influence of Lévy-Bruhl was particularly important. As early as 1913 Eliot wrote an essay at Harvard entitled
"The Interpretation of Primitive Ritual," based on Lévy-Bruhl's theories, in which he "argued against the tendency, in studies of primitive
tribes, to explain belief or practices only as rationalizations of ritual."[1]
Eliot's graduate work in philosophy introduced him to Lévy-Bruhl,
who was originally a philosopher before turning to anthropology in
1910 with *Les Fonctions Mentales dans les Sociétés Inférieures* (*How Natives
Think*), from which Eliot derived his essay. Lévy-Bruhl reconsidered
primitive cognition and opposed the "English School of Anthropology,"
in particular Tylor and Frazer, so steeped in Darwinian and Spencer-
ian evolution that they could only explain primitive mental functions
as a "rudimentary" form of their own rationality (16–17, 26–27).
Rather, he introduced several concepts that impressed Eliot so much
they formed an integral part of his dramatic theory twenty years later,
and they also reveal the basis of his theoretical affinity with Harrison.
First, in conjunction with Émile Durkheim, Lévy-Bruhl proposed that
all primitive mental "representations" are collective rather than individual:

Myths, funeral rites, agrarian practices and the exercise of magic
do not appear to originate in the desire for a rational explanation: they are the primitives' response to collective needs and
sentiments which are profound and mighty and of compulsive
force. Being collective, they force themselves upon the individual; that is, they are to him an article of faith, not the product
of his reason. ... The ensemble of collective representations which
master him and excite in him an intensity of feeling which we
cannot even imagine, is hardly compatible with that disinterested

contemplation of matter which a purely intellectual desire to probe into its cause would demand.   (23–5)

Thus, in Lévy-Bruhl's terms, primitive humanity is "pre-logical" and deeply mystical, experiencing a kind of unity with creation through what he called the "law of participation." Primitives do not perceive contradictions or oppositions between entities, so when the Bororo tribe claim as their totem the red parakeet, "it is not a name they give themselves, nor a relationship that they claim. What they desire to express by it is actual identity. That they can be both the human beings they are and the birds of scarlet plumage at the same time, [we may] regard as inconceivable, but to the mentality that is governed by the law of participation there is no difficulty in the matter" (77–8). Harrison is clear about her debt to French sociology and anthropology in the introduction to *Themis*. The "two ideas" that inform the work are Bergsonian *durée* and Durkheim's theory that "religion reflects *collective* feeling and *collective* thinking" (*T* xiii). In addition, she paraphrased and quoted (but did not credit) Lévy-Bruhl's theory of participation when describing the ecstatic dancing of a tribe identified by the kangaroo totem in *Ancient Art and Ritual*:

> The men-kangaroos when they danced and leapt did it, not to *imitate* kangaroos — you cannot imitate yourself — but just for natural joy of heart because they *were* kangaroos; they belonged to the kangaroo tribe, they bore the tribal marks and delighted to assert their tribal unity. What they felt was not *mimesis* but "participation," unity and community.   (*AAR* 46)

The kangaroo dancers are just another example of Lévy-Bruhl's "Bororo Indians who convince themselves that they are parroquets," which Eliot found so "delightful." Indeed, his choice of the word "delightful" is revealing. Both Eliot and Harrison stressed the joy of spiritual expression through unity and community, which they felt was more available to the simple, unconscious participation of primitives or "lower class" people than to the "listless apathy with which the middle and upper classes regard any entertainment of the nature of art" (Eliot, "ML" 174). Like Harrison, Eliot viewed the joyful spiritual catharsis of the "uneducated," for instance at the music-hall, with an almost nostalgic longing. Thus, we can trace the origin of Eliot's rather surprising remark, "I myself should like an audience which could neither read nor write," as well as his frequently quoted theory of the several levels in drama that can appeal to and unite "as large and miscellaneous an audience as possible," and his growing sense of the "social 'usefulness' for poetry [in] the theatre" to Lévy-Bruhl — an influence he shared with Harrison — rather than to the ritual parallels traced by Murray and Cornford in Greek drama ("UP" 94).

From Eliot's enthusiastic praise of the music-halls in his tribute to the comedienne and singer Marie Lloyd, Smith concludes that "Eliot found in the song-and-dance teams, the jazz patters ... and even in the art of the jugglers the rhythm" he felt was so essential to drama, and "in addition he found ... there still remained a social unity in the relationship between the performer and the audience that had disappeared in other forms of dramatic art" (53–4). But to this it must be added that Eliot described vaudeville at its best as a form of joyful spiritual participation through unconscious communal ritual: "It was, I think, this capacity for expressing the *soul* of the people that made Marie Lloyd unique, and that made her audiences, even when they joined in the chorus, not so much hilarious as *happy*" (172, my ital). Marie Lloyd was "the expressive figure of the lower classes" and Eliot described the "working man who went to the music-hall" much as Harrison envisioned the kangaroo dancers or worshippers singing the dithyramb at the Great Dionysia: "joined in the chorus, [he] was himself performing part of the act; he was engaged in that collaboration of the audience with the artist which is necessary in all art and most obviously in dramatic art" (174). Eliot turned to drama seeking "some direct social utility" as a poet, "to convey the pleasures of poetry, not only to a larger audience, but to larger groups of people collectively," hoping that there might be "some fulfilment in exciting this communal pleasure" (95), a spiritual fulfilment not to be found in the highly personal and isolated voice of lyric poetry (see also "The Three Voices of Poetry," 1953).

Smith's argument rests on Eliot's "pursuit of order." She emphasizes that Eliot found in drama a "capacity to present a completely ordered world," beginning with his 1924 essay, "Four Elizabethan Dramatists" (10). In the passage Smith analyzes, Eliot praises Aeschylus as the only dramatist whose poetry is thoroughly dramatic, contrary to the division between poetry and drama often perceived in Elizabethan drama by Lamb, Swinburne and "Mr. William Archer": "for all modern opinion rests upon the admission that poetry and drama are two separate things" ("FED" 116). However, in Aeschylus, "every style of utterance in the play bears a relation to the whole and because of this relation is dramatic in itself" (117). From this Smith concludes that Eliot objected to realistic drama because "he desired in a work of art an ideal relationship of the parts to the whole which he believed could be achieved only by abstraction from reality" (11). While this is true, Smith neglects a stronger chord running throughout this article and throughout Eliot's dramatic theory. For Eliot, an escape from realism was an escape from personality into universality: "No artist produces great art by a deliberate attempt to express his personality" ("FED" 120). It was not so much the ordered world of dramatic convention that Eliot sought, but rather the collective participation possible only through the ritualistic conventions of drama. Dramatic convention frees writer and actor alike from personality, and Eliot makes it clear that by "convention" he means "any form of rhythm imposed upon the world of action," i.e., poetry and dance.

How closely his ideas here echo Harrison can be seen from the following, which might have been lifted verbatim from *Ancient Art and Ritual*: "on the one hand actual life is always the material, and on the other hand abstraction from actual life is a necessary condition to the creation of the work of art" ("FED" 118). Indeed, he shares Harrison's inordinate admiration for dance because of a similar conviction of its spiritual potential, and devotes the bulk of "Four Elizabethan Dramatists" to praising dancers over actors. Because the dancer is limited to "strict form," there is less possibility for his or her personality to intrude. When we watch "one of the great dancers of the Russian school," we do not witness a human personality, but "a being who exists only during the performances ... [filled with] a vital flame which appears from nowhere, disappears into nothing and is complete and sufficient in its appearance" (119). It is clear that "abstraction from reality," enforced by the strict formal movements and rhythms of dance — conventions Eliot hopes to bring to drama — allow the performer (and ultimately the audience) to empty him or herself of humanity, in order to be filled with the "vital flame" of divinity:

> The differences between a great dancer and a merely competent dancer is in the vital flame, that impersonal, and, if you like, inhuman force which transpires through each of the great dancer's movements. So it would be in a strict form of drama; but in realistic drama, which is drama striving steadily to escape the conditions of art, the human being intrudes.   (120)

Ideally, dramatic art for Eliot is an abstraction from life, formalized by rhythm just as ritual is, and allowing spirituality to enter into human expression. For Jane Harrison, too, humanity can only experience divinity by transcending the limitations of individuality through communal rhythmic expression:

> The dancers dancing together utter their conjoint desire, their delight, their terror, in steps and gestures, in cries of fear or joy or lamentation ... being a collective emotion it is necessarily felt as something more than the experience of the individual, as something dominant and external. The dancers themselves by every means in their power seek to heighten this effect. They sink their own personality and by the wearing of masks and disguises, by dancing to a common rhythm, above all by the common excitement, they become emotionally one, a true congregation, not a collection of individuals. The emotion they feel collectively, the thing that is more than any individual emotion, they externalize, project; it is the raw material of godhead.   (*T* 45–6)

That Eliot, like Harrison, regarded dance as the art form most expressive of spirituality is also revealed in a 1925 review "The Ballet," in which he asserts that the ballet and the mass both evolved from "dancing amongst primitive peoples": "For is not the High Mass — as performed, for instance, at the Madeleine in Paris — one of the highest developments of dancing?" (441)

While "Four Elizabethan Dramatists" may appear to be the earliest expression of his desire to contribute "something of revolutionary influence on the future of drama," it is not (115). Smith does not discuss the 1920 review of Murray's *Medea*, playing then at the Holborn Empire, in which Eliot not only acknowledges the impact of anthropological classicism, but also announces its limitations and its demise — and in doing so, sketches his own future role in making Greek drama "as present to us as the present." Eliot praises "Miss Sybil Thorndyke" as Medea, while deriding Murray's translation with caustic wit:

> Miss Thorndyke, in order to succeed as well as she did, was really engaged in a struggle against the translator's verse. She triumphed over it by attracting our attention to her expression and tone and making us neglect her words; and this, of course,

was not the method of Greek acting at its best ... and the re-
fined Dalcroze chorus had mellifluous voices which rendered
their lyrics happily inaudible. All this contributed toward the
highbrow effect which is so depressing; and we imagine that
the actors of Athens ... would have been pelted with figs and
olives had they mumbled so unintelligibly as most of this troupe.
But the Greek actor spoke his own language, and our actors
were forced to speak in the language of Professor Gilbert
Murray.   ("EGM" 36–7)

His criticism of Murray is as generational as Woolf's criticism of
the Edwardian novelists: "it is inconceivable that anyone with a genu-
ine feeling for the sound of Greek verse should deliberately elect the
William Morris couplet, the Swinburne lyric, as a just equivalent"
(38). Every age adapts the classics to suit its own ear and its own
values, and Eliot's alarm at the "pernicious influence" of Murray's outdated translations is revealing. He insists it "is really a point of capital
importance," because "the Greek language and the Latin language,
and, *therefore*, the English language, are within our own lifetime passing through a critical period" (37). The classics "have lost their place
as a pillar of the social and political system ... [and] if they are to
survive, to justify themselves as literature, as ... the foundation for the
literature we hope to create, they are very badly in need of persons
capable of expounding them." Again, three years prior to his
recommendation of Joyce's mythic method, Eliot is calling for "educated poets" (himself?) who can render classical poetry in a truly modern idiom, so that it can have a "vitalising effect" upon "the literature
we hope to create." In deriding Murray's translations, Eliot opens the
way for his own future role as a poet who builds a drama of "furnished
flat sort of people" upon a substrate of Greek myth.

Particularly interesting is that, nearly two decades prior to *The Family
Reunion*, Aeschylus' *Oresteia* was already beckoning to Eliot. We have
seen his preference for Aeschylus in "Four Elizabethan Dramatists."
In this review, he expresses regret that no translator has "yet shown
himself competent to attack the 'Agamemnon,' " the first play in
Aeschylus' Oresteian trilogy ("EGM" 243). And, from the hauteur of
the editorial "we," he forgives Murray for choosing Euripides over
Aeschylus, implying thereby that only an idiot would do so: "We do
not reproach him for preferring, apparently, Euripides to Aeschylus.
But if he does, he should at least appreciate Euripides" (38). In fact,

Murray had done more than anyone to revolutionize the 19th-century tendency, typified by Harrison's Cambridge professor A.W. Verrall, to regard Euripides as a "rationalist," even an atheist.

But it is not as a classicist that Eliot objects to Murray, only as a poet. Murray is "the most popular Hellenist of his time," and as such he is "very much of the present day, and a very important figure in the day," but "as a poet, Mr. Murray is merely a very insigificant follower of the Pre-Raphaelite movement" (37–8). For Eliot, it is time for the scientists — classicists, anthropologists, sociologists, *et al* — as "useful and important in their own phase" as they are, to give way to a new generation of poets and their rendering of the classics, both in translation and in their own creative work. For Professor Murray has no "creative instinct," and only the "creative eye" can render the past "so lively that it shall be as present to us as the present." Thus, Eliot forecasts his own role over a decade later in bringing the "vitalising effect" of classical drama, and its capacity to convey the "vital flame" of divinity through ritualistic conventions, to the modern stage. But while these early critical essays reveal Eliot's desire "to attack the 'Agamemnon,'" he had much maturing to do, both as a poet and as a man, before he could recast Aeschylus' great trilogy. That process of maturation, particularly as it relates to Aeschylean themes, may be traced in the "Sweeney" poems and in Eliot's first dramatic effort, *Sweeney Agonistes*.

Sweeney's dual nature has been much discussed: he is both primal ape and upright man. Although evidence in "Sweeney Erect" of his spiritual redemption is tenuous at best, and the climactic stanzas portray disturbing images of sexual violence, critics have generally downplayed Sweeney's sexual brutality and overstressed his spiritual potential. Typically they find the overt sexual reference of the title negligible and identify a spiritual heroism in Sweeney's misogyny. For Kinley E. Roby, Sweeney is a spiritual "pilgrim" who "escapes" "the baited trap that would imprison him," the "seduction" represented by women (11–13), while Charles Peake sees him as the "Emersonian hero," finding the " 'self-command' Sweeney exhibits in a difficult situation," his "philosophic calm" in evading " 'the female temperament' ... worthy of the hero or great man described in 'Self-Reliance' " (53). Indeed, it is notable that Sweeney's defeat of female entrapment is frequently identified by male critics as heroic, while his "murderous ... cruelty" is frequently excoriated by female critics as a "degradation of the human capacity for love" (Baldridge 48; Hargrove 149–156).

The most definitive analysis of the poem to date is William Arrow-smith's "The Poem as Palimpsest: A Dialogue on Eliot's 'Sweeney Erect.'" Arrowsmith records an exhaustive discussion of the poem's allusions among five academics, whether fictional or actual is hard to tell and probably irrelevant; it is a refreshing format for literary analysis. For these discussants, all of Sweeney's avatars — Poe's shaving orang-outang in "Murders in the Rue Morgue," Rousseau's orang-outang from the appendix to the *Discourse on Inequality*, Ovid's "pastoral-comic Polyphemus in the tale of Acis and Galatea in *Metamorphosis*" (36) — suggest "the nameless savage memories, the animal lurking in all of us, buried at the base of the vertebrate spine" (26). But like Roby and Peake, while acknowledging the sexual violence of the poem, Arrowsmith emphasizes Sweeney's "emerging capacity for spiritual life" (23) and sees in the "shaving animal" the "instinct to evolve ... by shearing away the animal, the brute, the lout" (29).

None of these interpretations answers the question of why man's brutality, as expressed in this poem, is directed specifically at woman. Why does woman have to be sexually mastered, betrayed, abandoned, or even symbolically killed, for man to become "civilized"? Arrow-smith's discussants decide that, prefigured in the poem's references to Nausicaa and to Beaumont and Fletcher's *Maid's Tragedy*, the wom-an's "virginity is the point" (38). They see her sexual violation as Eliot's modern replay of the ancient ritual sacrifice of virgins: "Defloration as sacrifice will in fact be a kind of sacred violence practiced by a murder-ous priest (who does not regard himself as a murderer), in search of salvation of some kind, on a willing victim" (43). Thus, the "agency" of female annihilation allows male connection with divinity. However, Arrowsmith has confused two quite different kinds of ritual here. Some cultures do practice ritual defloration, but it is an initiation rite to mark passage into adulthood and to prepare for marriage, a ritual with an altogether different purpose from the sacrificial murder of a victim or *pharmakos* to achieve communal purification or divine appeasement. Sacri-ficial rituals are not sexual, although they may be done to engender fertility in the community by purging sterility, disease, famine. There is no evidence in any of Eliot's anthropological sources, from E. B. Tylor to Frazer or Jane Harrison, of sacrificial rituals involving sexual violation.

Arrowsmith attempts to bypass the intense misogyny of the poem by justifying or glorifying the masochism of women. Her "pain is min-gled with pleasure" and is acceptable since she too "crosses the fron-tier" into transcendence through being violated: "In the case of the

willing sacrifice, death is desired; the spirit desires the death, by morti-
fication, of the flesh that desires" (45). But there is no evidence in
"Sweeney Erect" that the woman is a "willing sacrifice," no evidence
that her "flesh" desires, nor that her "spirit desires death." She does
not desire; she is the object of desire, and as Eliot portrays it here,
male desire is indeed "mortifying" — but not of man's flesh, only of
woman's. Arrowsmith's interpretation sees the woman's supposedly
"epileptic" seizure as "the great 'sacred disease'... of the ancients" and
a sign of her "spiritual possession" (43). Like "Ariadne, abandoned by
her human lover," she is ravished by the god Dionysus, "ironically
manifest in the straight brandy and the sal volatile" (54). But it is
pushing the imagery of the poem beyond what it will bear to see Doris
and Mrs. Turner as "agents of conversion" and this interpretation still
evades the central question: why does Eliot equate sexuality with
murder? This theme, a key one in Eliot's early work, is most dramatically expressed in "Sweeney Erect," but it appears in *Sweeney Agonistes*
with Sweeney's desire to "cannibalize" Doris: "Any man has to, needs
to, wants to/Once in a lifetime, do a girl in" (80–3), and it appears in
The Family Reunion with Harry's fear that he has murdered his wife.
For Sandra Gilbert and Susan Gubar, Eliot's "fantasies of femicide,"
participate in a cultural backlash expressed generally in the work of
male modernists against the threatening achievements of feminists,
their "invasion of culture," the sexual demands implicit in women's
increased sexual freedom, and the aggression of the suffrage movement (31–2).

While this view has validity, the key to meaning in the poem is to
be found in the poem's mythic method, the technique Eliot so praised
in Joyce's *Ulysses*, "manipulating a continuous parallel between
contemporaneity and antiquity" ("UOM" 177). The mythic texts this
poem alludes to are just as misogynistic as Eliot's reworking of them,
and express the same universal theme: the violent antagonism between
the sexes that is, ultimately, an expression of male oedipal conflict. The
epigraph to "Sweeney Erect" from Beaumont and Fletcher's *The Maid's
Tragedy*, in which the jilted Aspatia compares her situation to the aban-
donment of Ariadne by the Greek hero Theseus, introduces this princi-
pal classical allusion of the poem. In "Sweeney Erect" violence against
women, matricidal in origin, and its heroic potential, liberation of the
son, are expressed through classical allusions to Theseus and Perseus,
just as they are in *The Family Reunion* through allusions to Orestes. While
the allusions to Ariadne and Nausicaa do admittedly identify the woman

with virginity, there are too many fearful images of vaginal engulfment in the poem for it to be strictly about the ravishment of an
innocent. And aside from the mythical allusions, there is no imagery
in the body of the poem to support the virginal innocence of this anonymous woman. The event takes place in a whorehouse, however
euphemistically dubbed by critics as "shabby-genteel boarding house
or house of assignation" (Arrowsmith 38), and she could as easily be a
prostitute, as other critics such as Nancy Hargrove and D.W. Rude
view her. But perhaps that is the point. Like the female archetypes of
The Waste Land, where "all the women are one woman", once a virgin
is bedded, she is found to be like all women — whore, mother, threat
(Eliot, *CPP* 52).

This is the only explanation that deals cogently with the baffling
issue of why Eliot equates sexual intercourse with murder. Sexual intercourse with any woman evokes the primitive/infantile past which is
bound irrevocably with the need to eradicate the mother who first
aroused forbidden desire. Sweeney/Orestes/Theseus — all must kill
the object of their desire lest they face castration by the father. While
it may seem that matricide and idealization of the father are the
opposite of the oedipal configuration, for the Freudian they merely
symbolize a more deeply repressed oedipal conflict: matricide expresses a desire to eradicate the unendurable arousal, shame, disgust, and
rage caused by the sexual, intrusive mother, and oversolicitous concern for the father masks a desire to see him as weak and take his place
(E. Jones 79, 92–94). So the mother is villified; the father is deified;
and castration anxiety is averted. Sweeney stands "upright" after devastating the virgin/prostitute because man cannot be "civilized" until
he has symbolically killed the lover/mother, and thereby extirpated
his own "original sin," his repressed incestuous desire. Thus both
Sweeney and his avatar Theseus are valiant misogynists who defeat
the engulfing mother and escape the ambivalent oedipal desire and
terror she arouses.

However, as Roby pointed out, "excessive solemnity in dealing with
Sweeney runs the risk of masking the comic elements" (10). For this is
a "Phallic Song" in which the "*Agon*" and the "*Komos*" have been com-
pressed into one, to use Cornford's terminology. The "nameless
courtesan" of the "*Komos*" is here the antagonist. As in the *The Waste
Land*, fertility ritual in the modern world has been rendered sterile.
Sweeney is no Dionysus, but a mock-epic hero of Attic legend like
Theseus, a great monster-slayer. And like yet another Greek hero,

Perseus, he slays a horrific Gorgon's head, a manifestation of the witch described in stanza four.

Theseus' misogynistic adventures began, fittingly enough, with his defeat of his father's second wife, the archetypical destructive mother and sorceress, Medea. When Theseus' mortal father, Aegeus, left his mother and returned to Athens, he buried his sword and sandals beneath a huge rock. For his son to inherit the sword/phallus, he must be strong enough to roll away the rock and take it to Athens, where Aegeus will formally recognize him. Meanwhile his father had married Medea, but when she attempted to trick him into poisoning Theseus, Aegeus recognized the sword and banished her, sharing the throne instead with his son. Here, the maternal threat is displaced onto a stepmother and, like the *Oresteia*, this myth presents a young man who conquers the mother to avenge or strengthen the father, and also charts the movement of Greek civilization away from vestigial matriarchal values to patriarchy. Eliot tells the same psychological and mythic tale, from Sweeney through Harry in *The Family Reunion* — the tale of the son who rejects the mother in order to embrace the values and authority of a patriarchal godhead, just as Orestes embraces Olympian Apollo. Of all the title's several meanings, therefore, its most important signifies Sweeney's erection, a mutual identification of son with father like Theseus' sword.

Theseus seems, like Sweeney, to be an incorrigible womanizer, but the pattern of his adventures with women expresses Greek idealization of asexual virgin daughters, of whom Athene is the prime example, and repulsion at mature, sexual, threatening mothers, of whom Hera is the prime example (Slater 66; Harrison 303). He pursues virginal women, but one by one they mature and express a sexual passion that is too threatening, and he must abandon or kill them to avoid being overwhelmed. Ariadne helps him penetrate the labyrinth to kill her brother, the Minotaur, but her great passion for Theseus is a dangerous reminder of Medea, who also murdered her own brother for love. He abducts the Amazon queen, Antiope, but when her sexual jealousy threatens his marriage to Phaedra, he kills her. Phaedra too becomes a sexual, destructive woman after their marriage, falling in love with her stepson Hippolyte and persuading Theseus to destroy the son who resists her seduction — a reflection of his father's relation to Medea. Ironically, both Sweeney's and Theseus's misogyny, which appears to victimize women, reveals a repulsion at female sexuality that has desire and fear at its root. It implies, not female helplessness, but rather female omnipotence in the male psyche.

The first two stanzas of Eliot's poem introduce a symbolic Greek landscape of threatening matriarchal monsters, indeed, of horrific vaginal imagery, that the poem will go on to develop. "The bold anfractuous rocks/Faced by the snarled and yelping seas" signify Scylla, herself a mythic image of the *vagina dentata*, with her six long necks surmounted by terrifying heads, each with a triple row of teeth that gnash and devour passing sailors. "Anfractuous" sends readers scurrying to the dictionary, but that cannot have been Eliot's main objective. Arrowsmith concludes that "the effect is to superimpose the labyrinth of Knossos on the stony maze of desert Naxos," to show Ariadne "in the anfractuosities of Naxos" entering a labyrinth like Theseus did on Crete, which is a "return to sources: the dark womb of earth, the earth's body, from which he was born" (57, 55). But in the myth it is Theseus who enters the maternal genital labyrinth to face the monster of his own oedipal desire, not Ariadne. Representative of the safely virginal daughter, she provides the hero's way out, as the myth attests. The rocks of Eliot's "cavernous" shore are symbols of male oedipal anxiety: sinuous, circuitous, winding, involuted, like Theseus' labyrinth they suggest an entrapping vaginal channel, which can only lead to a confrontation with the Minotaur, an image of overwhelming sexuality, a human bestiality that devours the innocent.

In stanza two, Eliot describes the "insurgent gales/Which tangle Ariadne's hair/And swell with haste the perjured sails." The image of Ariadne's tangled hair associates her now, not with the abandoned virgin, but rather with the engulfing mother, for tangled hair implies the power to entangle, like the sinous rocks and the long-necked heads of Scylla. The "perjured sails" suggest Theseus' lie to Ariadne that he would marry her if she guided him out of the labyrinth, thus signifying his escape from entanglement by abandoning her on the island, and foreshadowing Sweeney's similar victory over the prostitute. As another sailor who can shrewdly trick powerful women into helping him and then manage to escape, this line also associates Sweeney with Odysseus, implied further in the allusions of the third stanza.

Nausicaa and Polypheme are indeed an "unlikely pairing" since they have nothing to do with each other in any myth (Peake 52). Donald Rude provides the most convincing explanation, showing that in Chapman's Homer, a likely source for Eliot, Nausicaa compares the

naked, seaweed-encrusted Odysseus to the Cyclops in trying to calm
her handmaidens' fears (57). Odysseus is adept at getting what he
wants from women like Nausicaa and the goddesses Calypso and Circe,
and then escaping their inordinate sexual desire for him (or in the case
of Nausicaa, her desire for marriage), just as Sweeney turns his back
on the prostitute. In the case of Polyphemus, Odysseus again escapes
a trap through his craftiness, and the tremendous pointed log with
which he gouges the Cyclops' eye may be applicable to Sweeney's
exaggerated phallicism. The Cyclops is a multi-determined image,
however. He appears to be masculine, another "ancient avatar of the
simian or savage Sweeney," while his eye can be interpreted as "the
carnal or phallic eye" (Arrowsmith 36, 51). Indeed, the eye, with its
gaze that penetrates, is traditionally associated with masculinity; however the Cyclops' eye *is* penetrated. As Thalia Feldman has pointed
out, "there is a curiously suspect female side to his character," which
reveals his possible derivation from the predominantly female bogeys
of the Greek imagination: his cannibalism, his shaggy hair, and his
one eye all associate him with the vaginal imagery of the devouring
mother (493–4).

Vaginal imagery culminates strikingly in stanza four:

> This withered root of knots of hair
> Slitted below and gashed with eyes,
> This oval O cropped out with teeth: (*CPP* 25)

Like Scylla's heads, the imagery of stanza four portrays, with a kind of
"gigantism" similar to Joyce's Cyclops chapter in *Ulysses*, phallic
vulnerability and dread of engulfment by an all-powerful vagina. The
head is not generally referred to as the "root" of a human being, but is
more commonly described as the crown. The genitals are the "root,"
of life, and "this withered root of knots of hair," suggests the vulva
with its kinky hair and perhaps "withered" looking labia. Significantly,
"knots of hair," like Ariadne's "tangles," suggest the power to knot, to
entangle. The teeth serve the same gnashing, castrating purpose as
Scylla's heads, while "slit" and "gash" are both slang terms for female
genitalia, with added connotations of blood suggesting a horror of
menses that Eliot may indeed have felt, according to Peter Ackroyd
(67).

Critics have missed the *vagina dentata* envisioned here; usually these
lines are interpreted as a description of the prostitute's face, or even of

Sweeney's face. Many accept the denotative meaning of "epileptic" unquestioningly; however, Eliot has planted an alternative interpretation, "hysteria," in stanza ten, and epilepsy may be merely a metaphor for the physical violence of her retaliation to the violence that has been committed upon her. We find additional evidence that "hysteria" represented "the female temperament" at its most threatening for Eliot in a prose-poem entitled "Hysteria," written in 1915:

> As she laughed I was aware of becoming involved in her laughter and being part of it, until her teeth were only accidental stars with a talent for squad-drill. I was drawn in by short gasps, inhaled at each momentary recovery, lost finally in the dark caverns of her throat, bruised by the ripple of unseen muscles... I decided that if the shaking of her breasts could be stopped, some of the fragments of the afternoon might be collected, and I concentrated my attention with careful subtlety to this end. (*CPP* 19)

As Ackroyd notes in his biography of Eliot, the narrator here "feels that he is being engorged by a woman," another image of the "threatening and salacious females" common to Eliot's early poetry, and perhaps derived from the failed sexuality of his marriage to Vivienne Haigh-Wood (66; Roby 11). Teeth "with a talent for squad-drill" can kill, especially if one is "drawn in" to the mouth, which clearly symbolizes an engulfing, castrating vagina with its "dark caverns" (i.e. the "cavernous waste shore") and "unseen muscles." Only if "the shaking of her breasts," emblems of her threatening femaleness, can be stopped — only if the sexual mother can be slain or eluded — will the narrator survive, and he concentrates with Odyssean "subtlety to this end."

Female hysteria in this poem, however, is far less potent. Impervious to the danger of an "oval O" fitted out with teeth, Sweeney has wielded his "jackknife" phallus victoriously, leaving his foe impotently "clawing at the pillow slip." Clearly she has lost this visceral battle between the sexes, for Sweeney is an alter-ego of the prose-poem narrator of "Hysteria", as well as of Prufrock: the terrified male's projection of the conquering male. He is a Theseus who can penetrate to the center of the labyrinth and come back alive. However, the imagery of stanza four links him with yet another Greek matriarchal bogey slayer, Perseus, for it describes all the monstrous attributes of the Gorgon's head: "knots of hair" like Medusa's writhing snakes, eyes, teeth, and particularly the "oval O" — at once the gaping mouth and the "Evil Eye" that turns men to stone with a single glance.

We have seen that, according to Harrison, Harpies, Gorgons, Sirens, and Erinyes are all triplicate winged women-demons evolved out of generic Keres, chthonic spirits who bring evil and good to mankind. But these sister divinities came to represent only the witch, the destructive Keres, separate from the life-giving mother: "the bird-woman became a death-demon, a soul sent to fetch a soul, a Siren that lures a soul" to its death (*PSGR* 201). In the case of the Gorgons,

> the two unslain sisters are mere superfluous appendages due to convention; the real Gorgon is Medusa, the most evil of the three, slain by Perseus. ... In her essence Medusa is a head and nothing more; her potency resides in the head, a grinning mask with glaring eyes and protruding beast-like tusks and pendent tongue. (187)

At one time, the Gorgon's head represented "the ugly bogey-, Erinys-side of the Great Mother," but as "the highest divinities" of chthonic religion became mere monsters in the Olympian canon, the "Gorgoneion" became a matriarchal relic, a leering mask that could turn men to stone, to be conquered by a young Greek hero (194). In "tooth and eye resided its potency," especially the "malign effluence" from its eyes: "it is clear that the Gorgon was regarded as a sort of incarnate Evil Eye. The monster was tricked out with cruel tusks and snakes, but it slew by the eye, it *fascinated*" (194–6). "More monstrous, more savage than any other of the Ker-forms," the Gorgon "lacks wholly the gentle side of the Keres, and ... lent some of its traits to the Erinys, and notably the deathly distillation by which they slay: 'From out their eyes they ooze a loathly rheum' " (197 — Harrison quotes from Aeschylus' *Eumenides*). Indeed, in the final scene of the *Choephoroi* (the second play in the Oresteian trilogy, quoted by Eliot in *Sweeney Agonistes* and *The Family Reunion*), when Orestes first sees the Erinyes, he cries: "they come like gorgons, they/wear robes of black, and they are wreathed in a tangle/of snakes" (Lattimore, *AIO* 130). In "Sweeney Erect," the imagery of stanza four suggests all the monstrous attributes of the Gorgoneion: "knots of hair" like Medusa's writhing snakes, eyes, teeth, and particularly the "oval O," a mouth, but also the Evil Eye, like Polyphemus', that kills by its "malign effluence." In order to destroy Medusa, Perseus must avert his eyes from the gaze that turns men to stone and observe her in the polished surface of his shield, just as Sweeney ignores the prostitute's raging and faces a mirror. In slaying this Gorgon, Sweeney/Perseus/Orestes overcomes the mother in one of her most monstrous witch manifestations.

Clearly this is an image that haunted Eliot. In his poem, as in the myth too, the Gorgon's disembodied head represents maternal genitalia, as Freud detected. But for Freud it was "a representation of woman as a being who frightens and repels because she is castrated," and the boy's sight of maternal genitalia reinforces his own fear of castration by the father. The writhing snakes are compensatory phallic symbols, as is the turning to stone, a "stiffening" which "reassures him ... he is still in possession of a penis" (105–6). Freud's inability to recognize the inherently castrating potential of the vaginal image is characteristic: if woman appears as castrating, as in masochistic fantasies, it is only as a substitute for man's displaced anxiety about the more fearful father. But Karen Horney countered Freud in her 1932 paper, "The Dread of Women":

> Freud's account fails to explain this anxiety. A boy's castration-anxiety in relation to his father is not an adequate reason for his dread of a being whom this punishment has already over-taken. Besides the dread of the father there must be a further dread, the object of which is the woman or the female genital. (349–351; see also Slater, 17–18)

Subsequently, feminist psychoanalysts such as Nancy Chodorow and Dorothy Dinnerstein, have stressed that oedipal anxiety is deeply informed by earlier preoedipal fears of maternal omnipotence deriving from the narcissistic period of intense mother-child bonding and dependence.[2] Medusa's snakes thus represent the entwining power of the "phallic mother" (as the mother of the narcissistic period is frequently called), and her power to turn her infant to stone indicates a paralysis, a refusal to nurture, that can hardly be "reassuring." The Gorgoneion suggested by the imagery of Eliot's poem, representing maternal genitalia as well as the looming, huge maternal head, unites both infantile origins, oedipal and preoedipal, of male fear of female sexuality.

Like Theseus at the labyrinth, Perseus must have virginal female aid in order to defeat the maternal bogey. Three Naiads, or nymphs, give him the prophylactic devices necessary to survive his encounter with the sexual mother unscathed: the cap of invisibility, the winged

shoes, and the wallet for hiding the Gorgon's head. Perseus tricks the
three Graia, or grey-haired sisters, who guard the cave of the Gorgons
by donning the cap of invisibility and snatching the one eye they share
(again reminiscent of Cyclops). Entering Medusa's cave, Perseus cuts
off her head with his sword, stows it in the wallet, and flies to freedom
on the winged shoes, escaping the pursuit of the other Gorgons. That
this is a myth of infantile liberation from the maternal threat is obvious. Once Perseus has the maternal genital safely in his possession it
becomes an apotropaic device, protecting him rather than threatening
him with its power. The boy's complete oedipal triumph is achieved
when he uses it to turn both his stepfather and his grandfather to
stone. Perseus' tale is one of infantile phallic triumph and sole possession of mother, as Philip Slater has written: "By 'castrating' the mother,
the hero gains potency; destroying her sexuality engenders his own"
(380).

Like the myth of Perseus, "Sweeney Erect" celebrates a grandiose
phallic triumph. The poem is a paean to Sweeney's phallicism: his
"jackknife" or "razor," like Perseus' sword, vanquishes the Gorgon
that threatens to engulf him. Like Perseus, too, Sweeney is surrounded
by compensatory, protective women. The "ladies of the corridor," while
undoubtedly not virginal, fill Athene's role: they are hostile to the
shrieking prostitute, "deprecate the lack of taste," and support Sweeney's cause with prophylactic sal volatile and "brandy neat." Critics
have interpreted Sweeney "addressed full length to shave" as a paradigm expressing man's bestial/spiritual duality, but the image of
Sweeney "Broad-bottomed, pink from nape to base" suggests a baby
as well as the shaving ape. Thus it expresses the paradigm of man's
dual infantilism and yearning for adulthood, his fear of impotence and
longing for phallic power. Although this poem is indeed intensely
misogynistic, offense at Sweeney's "chauvinistic, superior, and entirely
unsympathetic attitude toward the epileptic" is misplaced (Hargrove
154). Like the myths it engages, "Sweeney Erect" does not portray
actual relations between the sexes, but a catharsis of infantile terrors,
a comic mock-heroic world where omnipotent feats can be achieved
and overwhelming fears purged.

"Sweeney Among the Nightingales," first published in 1918, also
charts acute tension between male and female. In Roby's view, Sweeney
represents a successful "escape mechanism," just as he does in "Sweeney
Erect," from the "two women, who seem still linked to the violent and
fallen world of the bloody wood" (13). Roby emphasizes the Christian

connotations of the word "host" in stanza nine, and his view rests on interpreting the "indistinct" person conversing with the host as "the presence of Christ in the poem" (17). Thus Sweeney "escape[s] through grace from the endless repetition of lust, violence, and death [that is] human history ... [and] the fate of Agamemnon in the bloody wood." While there may be Christian implications in the imagery of stanza nine, Sweeney in this poem is not victorious as in "Sweeney Erect." Sexual violence is more subtly evoked here, but it is not resolved in male triumph, nor in a clear "escape." Sweeney is not yet identified with Orestes, the son who kills his witch/mother and finds spiritual sanctuary in the mercy of a patriarchal god. Instead he is identified in this poem with Agamemnon when he is stabbed by Clytemnestra, an association that plainly implies Sweeney has not escaped the fate of men caught in the imagined trap of female sexuality and anger. Eliot's epigraph, "a deep, a mortal blow," taken from Agamemnon's dying words, makes this unequivocal.

The poem is filled with potent witch emblems, particularly in its bird imagery. As we have already seen, the bird-woman is a manifestation of the witch, as exemplified by the Harpies and the Erinyes. Eliot explained the "bloody wood" in a letter to the *Sunday Times* of April 6, 1958 as "the grove of the Furies at Colonus ... bloody because of the blood of Agamemnon at Argos" (Hargrove 162). While it may seem that Eliot is confusing Sophocles and Aeschylus, he is not, for both dramatists were portraying the same tradition. Clytemnestra is identified with the Furies throughout the *Oresteia*; she is herself a manifestation of them as she enacts the vengeance of their strict blood-law by stabbing her husband. Old, blind, and exiled, Sophocles' Oedipus "finds a home among the sacred Furies" in their grove at Colonus, where "the nightingales make sweet music," because he also seeks revenge, "a curse on those who have driven me away." In Sophocles' version, nightingales guard the grove of the Furies, and their singing portends these "dreadful ... divinities, most feared/Daughters of darkness and mysterious earth". ... "Ladies whose eyes/Are terrible" (Fitzgerald 80–83). So too, Eliot's nightingale imagery — in addition to its often-noted allusions to prostitutes and Ovid's Philomela — signifies the Furies.

Another harpy appears in the Raven of Death of stanza two, which is in turn echoed by "Rachel *née* Rabinovitch," yet another witch with her "murderous paws." As George Whiteside intriguingly proposes, "Her name suggests a rabid animal. In particular, with letters transposed it sounds like 'Raven-a — bitch': a bitch dog with ravenous hunger" (64). As we have seen, the dog is another animal manifestation of the witch, just as Orestes calls the Erinyes "the bloodhounds of my mother's hate" (Lattimore 131). Indeed, I have little to add to Whiteside's "Freudian Dream Analysis of 'Sweeney Among the Nightingales.'" According to him, the plate of fruit represents genitalia, "a woman's belly and vulva (oranges and figs) next to male's phallus and testicles (bananas and grapes)," so that, as Rachel "Tears at the grapes," she presents "an image of a female castrator" (65). I also agree with Whiteside's interpretation of the silent figures in this drama, the man in brown and the caped woman, as images of the inexpressible desires of the named characters, Sweeney and Rachel. His very namelessness argues that the man is an alter-ego of Sweeney, or, as Whiteside suggests, "a strange dream image" of Sweeney's phallus: "'mocha brown' in color ... a 'silent vertebrate' that suddenly 'Contracts and concentrates'" (65), while her cape provides a subliminal vaginal image.

However, Whiteside fails to notice that this phallus "Contracts and concentrates and *withdraws*" (my italics). If the man in brown is phallic, then he is an image of detumescence, even impotence. For Whiteside, the poem is filled with images of "sadistic oral aggression." The man in brown "is an image for the dreamer's [Sweeney's] sexual impulse, yet ultimately that is an impulse to bite" (65). We have seen oral aggression in Eliot's imagery before, in the prose-poem "Hysteria" and in the *vagina dentata* of "Sweeney Erect," but in both cases it is attributed only to women. Whiteside's reading of the man in brown as a phallus capable of "penetration" does not accord with Eliot's description of him as "contract[ed]" and "withdraw[n]," nor with the lines in stanza seven, where he "Declines the gambit, shows fatigue" (*CPP* 36). Rather than betokening an aggressive "impulse to bite," his "grin" celebrates a passive sexual evasion: he has escaped the "gambit" of the two women "thought to be in league."

Unlike "Sweeney Erect," the phallicism here is passive, suggesting impotence and evasion rather than sexual triumph. And, in the last two stanzas the bird-women have the final victory, as the "nightingales are singing" and "let their liquid siftings fall/To stain the stiff dishonoured shroud." As has often been noted, "liquid siftings," refers to the birds' excrement, but it also recalls the "loathly rheum," the "malign effluence" that drips from the Erinyes' eyes and kills. Eliot's use of the word "stiff" brings phallic connotations to Agamemnon's shroud, indicating that in this poem, contrary to "Sweeney Erect," the vicious sexual war has been won by women or, to put it in psychoanalytic terms, oedipal issues have been reinforced by preoedipal fear of maternal omnipotence. If Eliot's hero is to psychically kill the witch and find peace from the erotic tensions that threaten to engulf him, he will not do it through physical or sexual power, traditionally the realm of women in the binaristic world Eliot portrays. Sweeney must become Harry, and enter the spiritual realm of the father.

Sweeney Agonistes, Eliot's first attempt at verse drama, was written some ten years after the Sweeney poems and published in 1926 and 1927 in the *Criterion*. These were crucial years, during which Eliot began to find the strength to separate from Vivien and the constant burden of her mental instability, and found a new life in his conversion to Anglicanism. So too, Sweeney evolved in this fragmentary drama to represent "the forces of spiritual purgation and reawakening" (Smith 68), or, in Roby's words, "renunciation and suffering for a spiritual purpose" (13). His growth is made clear in the two epigraphs. The first quotation is Orestes' exit line in the *Choephoroi* when he first becomes aware of the Furies, who haunt and pursue him after his murder of his mother: "You don't see them, you don't — but *I* see them: they are hunting me down, I must move on." Since "Sweeney Among the Nightingales," Eliot's focus has shifted from the *Agamemnon*, the first play in Aeschylus' trilogy, in which the king returns from Troy to be murdered by his wife, to the *Choephoroi* and the *Eumenides*, the second and third plays in the trilogy, in which Orestes avenges his father's death. In other words, Eliot's interest has progressed from the horrific violence of sexual relations between man and woman, to the painful, solitary, spiritual purgation or quest that follows matricide. Unlike the Sweeney poems, the dramatic event of *Sweeney Agonistes* is not evasion or murder of a threatening female archetype, but rather Sweeney's effort to communicate the spiritual meaning of that murder after it has been committed.

According to the turn-of-the-century Cambridge classicist A.W. Verrall, the *Choephoroi* "is essentially a legend of religion ... [and] everything in the Aeschylean version has been shaped with the purpose of converting Orestes into a minister of Pytho" [the oracle of Apollo at Delphi] (x–xiii). So, too, Eliot shapes his version to show Sweeney/Harry's painful conversion into the "minister" of a patriarchal faith. For Aeschylian Olympianism and Christianity have this in common — both promise spiritual eternity through repudiation of the "dark Earth." Therefore, Eliot aptly equates Orestes' spiritual quest with Christian mysticism in his second epigraph, from St. John of the Cross, as Smith attests: "Hence the soul cannot be possessed of the divine union, until it has divested itself of the love of created beings," which is, "part of the instruction to the novice who wishes to pass through the first stage of the mystic path — the dark night of the senses in which purification of all human desires must occur before the next stage can be reached" (60). *The Oresteia* presents a story similar to Christian sacrifice and redemption, for Orestes is chosen to do Zeus' will, to suffer because of that deed, and eventually to find mercy and sanctuary, in the third play of the trilogy, through his faith in Apollo, an "exponent of his father's will" (Harrison, *T* 387) like Christ.

The Pythian priestess' opening lines in the *Eumenides* describe the "sequence of cults at Delphi from Gaia to Apollo" — that is, the superseding of matriarchal religion by patriarchal religion — from Gaia, the original Earth-mother with her violent, retributive blood-law, to Apollo, spokesman of his father's new, rational justice tempered with persuasion and mercy:

> the real *agon* of the play [is] the conflict between the new order and the old, the daimones of Earth, the Erinyes, and the *theoi* of Olympos, Apollo and his father Zeus, and further necessarily and inherently the conflict of the two social orders of which these daimones and *theoi* are in part the projections — matriarchy ... and patriarchy. (*T* 386)

According to Murray's interpretation of the *Eumenides*, the accession of patriarchal religion dramatized by Aeschylus marks "a conception of a God who is above the Law and can therefore forgive," and "the substitution of humane beings, who can love man and understand his best thoughts, for the blind and monstrous forces" of the more primitive religion (*ACT* 201, 81). It is no wonder that Eliot was so drawn to Aeschylus, for "the supremacy of Zeus was to Aeschylus the keystone of his beautiful faith in a right that was beyond might, a thing to be preserved even in the face of seeming facts," a faith in an eternal truth beyond "all the facts" of physical reality (Harrison, *T* 386).

Therefore, although Eliot and Joyce both used the mythic method, their approach to Hellenism was very different. Bloom and Stephen experience rebirth through union with an embodiment of the female principle in which spiritual eternity is not separate from physical life. But Eliot's mythic model was the drama of Homeric heroes and

Olympian gods that filled the old, empty ritual "bottles" in fifth-century Athens, as it is epitomized by its greatest poet of "philosophic or religious truth" (Murray, *ACT* 18). For Eliot, after his conversion, spiritual eternity must come through denial of the female, as it did for Aeschylus, who attempted to justify through his art the dominance of Apollo and of Olympian patriarchy. As Sweeney tries to tell Doris, existence is meaningless when reduced to "the facts when you come to brass tacks" — "birth, and copulation, and death" (*CPP* 80). Physical life is merely death — "Death is life and life is death" — and spiritual rebirth cannot be experienced until it is renounced or "killed" (84). Unlike Bloom, who is reborn through submission to the generative maternal archetype, Sweeney must exterminate the mother and the physical life she represents to achieve spiritual rebirth through the father. This inescapably takes on a misogynistic tone because physicality is always symbolically embodied by woman:

> I knew a man once did a girl in
> Any man might do a girl in
> Any man has to, needs to, wants to
> Once in a lifetime, do a girl in.
> Well he kept her there in a bath
> With a gallon of lysol in the bath   (83)

In Smith's view, Sweeney's tale tells of his purgation according to the epigraph from St. John of the Cross, the "divestment of the love of created beings ... in order to achieve rebirth and union" (71). In tracing the parallels between the ritual survivals Cornford identifies in *The Origin of Attic Comedy* and the structure of *Sweeney Agonistes*, Smith, like Arrowsmith, deemphasizes the misogyny in Eliot's murder imagery, interpreting it "in the ritualistic sense, [as] the agony of the old and impotent god who suffers death and mutilation before the regeneration of resurrection" (62). The "Fragment of an Agon," obviously, corresponds to Cornford's agon "the conflict between good and evil principles, Summer and Winter, Life and Death" (Smith 67). Doris supplies Sweeney's antagonist, representing "the old life of the senses in the battle with spiritual forces." She "drew the COFFIN very last card" (*CPP* 83), and knows, in Smith's words, that she "is due for the same murder as the girl in Sweeney's tale" (71). With images from cooking that also echo Cornford, Sweeney asserts, " 'I'll convert *you*!/ Into a stew./A nice little, white little, missionary stew,'" offering Doris "a painful regeneration by a sacramental means," and painting a picture of the pointlessness of life "without a spiritual rebirth" (Smith 68–9).

But Sweeney is alone in his perception that life on the "crocodile isle" — purely physical life — "is death" (*CPP* 82–3). When Doris twice replies, "A woman runs a terrible risk," she trivializes her own fear and makes fun of Sweeney's grandiose misogyny. Sweeney tries to communicate the real meaning behind this grotesque murder, to suggest that it is metaphoric for an experience that did not occur in physical, temporal reality, where all the other characters live. When Swarts wants to know how the story ended according to its narrative surface, "What did he do?", Sweeney tells him, "That dont apply." He is not telling a chronological story of events, but describing a psychic state. "But I've gotta use words when I talk to you" — how else can he communicate the experience? He chooses a lurid newspaper tale of a woman's murder in a London flat to convey his attempt to kill the female principle of sexuality and physicality within himself, or in Smith's words, "the mystic's process of killing desire in order to bring to birth the spirit" (71).

Sweeney is a mystic in transition, however. He has attempted to extirpate the female, but has not yet found Apollo, as male and female still battle within him:

> He didn't know if he was alive and the girl was dead
> He didn't know if the girl was alive and he was dead
> He didn't know if they were both alive or both were dead   (84)

At the conclusion, the "full chorus" affirms that Sweeney is still "in the middle of the night," in "a hell of a fright," in a "cream of a nightmare dream and you've got the hoo-ha's coming to you" (84). As Smith points out, the "hoo-ha's serve the same function as the relentless Furies in their pursuit of Orestes," the "pursuit of the penitent by purgatorial forces" (72). *Sweeney Agonistes* ends precisely where *The Family Reunion* begins, for Harry also believes he has murdered a woman — i.e., exterminated the female principle — only to find the witch howling within him.

6: ORESTES IN THE DRAWING-ROOM: MOTHER, MAID, AND WITCH IN T.S. ELIOT'S *THE FAMILY REUNION*

The solution he gives us in the prologue is utterly Aeschylean and in a sense strangely modern. There has been not a fight but a development, not even, as in the agon of the play, a reconciliation and sudden conversion, but a gradual emergence and epiphany of godhead from strength to strength, from Gaia to Zeus.

— Jane Ellen Harrison, *T* 386

Eliot's attempt to bring the conventions of Greek drama into a naturalistic English drawing-room setting in *The Family Reunion*, written throughout 1937–8 and produced in the spring of 1939, has generally been considered a failure. Reviewers following opening night felt emphatically that "Christian and pagan do not mix" (Brown 376). Expecting "naturalistic stagecraft" they found that the chorus of aunts and uncles destroyed "the last refuge of willing make-believe in us" (Brown 376; MacCarthy 373). An exasperated Desmond MacCarthy asked, if Eliot's theme is Christian sin and expiation, "why introduce Greek mythology at all? It is maddening" (374). Maud Bodkin, a more knowledgeable classicist than other early reviewers, attempted to answer this criticism in her review by finding the Erinyes' traditional role as "pursuers that avenge not private but communal crime" a fitting symbol for the modern age, then enduring the "horror" of World War II (Grant 386). However, Bodkin's defense of Eliot's Eumenides broke down in her longer study two years later because the play is not about "communal crime," but rather an individual conscience haunted by a personal, though perhaps universal, sense of sin.

Later criticism did not surmount these difficulties. Like the earliest reviewers, F.O. Matthiesen was disturbed by "the break between the surface of the play and the depth it is meant to symbolize" (169). Again, for Matthiesen, naturalism collides with the symbolism of Harry's spiritual quest when he takes off to "follow the bright angels" in "the highpowered car in which his faithful valet, after returning to pick up his Lordship's cigarette case, drives him away" (169). Like Bodkin, Matthiesen felt that "Eliot could not contrive to endow his Eumenides with any of the collective significance that they possessed for the Greeks"; therefore they fail as an "'objective correlative'" for Harry's experience (173). Critics like Matthiesen and C.L. Barber began to voice a third objection: Harry's lack of "remorse" for his wife's death, whether accidental or not, and his "ruthlessness towards his mother" seem to Matthiesen "unnatural" (170–1), to Barber "appalling" (430). Barber also found that the "Eumenides fail as an objective correlative because Harry's relation to them exists exclusively on a symbolic level which cannot be adequately dramatized in social terms" (427). Indeed, criticism through the years has focused so completely on Eliot's failure to transform the avenging Erinyes into benevolent Eumenides as Aeschylus did, that other Aeschylean parallels have been virtually ignored.

Those who emphasize Eliot's Christian theme have provided the most sympathetic interpretations of *The Family Reunion*. Since they submerge Hellenic parallels under Harry's Christian quest to escape the "dominion of the senses," they avoid many of the difficulties encountered by earlier critics (Smith 134). For instance, David E. Jones dismisses analogies between the *Oresteia* and *The Family Reunion*, since "even where the parallel is closest, the action is transformed in the light of Christian dispensation" (90–1). Carol Smith also believes that "all of the Greek sources which Eliot has used" appealed to him primarily because they seemed "rich in ... Christian meaning." Like Jones, she found in *The Family Reunion*, "the curse on the house of Atreus becomes original sin, and the father being revenged becomes the heavenly Father," while the Eumenides are necessary guides in "the self-inflicted ordeal of the mystic path." However, although the *Oresteia* and *The Family Reunion* share the theme of purgation, for Smith "attempts to push the analogies further" encounter too many "difficulties. ... Nor have the scenes involving Mary, Agatha, and Dr. Warburton counterparts in the *Oresteia*" (129–34).

As we have seen, Smith convincingly established the influence of F.M. Cornford's *Origin of Attic Comedy* on Eliot's first dramatic fragment *Sweeney Agonistes*. She also attempts to explain *The Family Reunion* through Cornford's Frazerian "ritual plot with its agon between the sin-laden and impotent representative of the old year and the reborn and sin-free god of the new year." For Smith, "Amy represents the old principle which must be destroyed before the new principle can be born," and again she attenuates Eliot's "long fascination with the symbolic meaning of murder" by associating Harry's imagined murder of his wife with "the ceremonial meanings of murder in the fertility rituals where the god-figure was actually mutilated or dismembered in order to purify him of the iniquities acquired in his sojourn among men," which she parallels with "Christ's Passion, Crucifixion, and Resurrection" (123).

While Eliot's subliminal message of Christian redemption cannot be ignored, I agree with Maud Bodkin that "in writing a play so permeated by awareness of a spiritual world, yet with no direct reference to Christian forms of faith, Eliot had meant to avoid any unnecessary limiting of the communication of his thought" to Christian meaning (39). After *Murder in the Cathedral*, he refused "invitations to write further religious or historical plays" (Browne 90), determined to "take a theme of contemporary life, with characters of our own time living in our own world," primarily a secular world (Eliot, "PD" 141). Thus Eliot's message of Christian redemption should not be overemphasized at the expense of the Hellenic parallels that he obviously thought, however mistakenly, would universalize the themes of spiritual purgation and quest for his largely secular audience. Furthermore, by the time Eliot wrote *The Family Reunion*, his interest had long since progressed from Cornford's ritual origins underlying Aristophanic comedy to the epic themes, the "new wine" that filled the "old ritual bottles," of Greek tragedy.

It is most important to realize that Amy is not only "the old principle which must be destroyed before the new principle can be born," she is Harry's mother, which is why Aeschylus' *Oresteia* provides such an important mythic substrate for this play. In the ritual agon between the forces of the old year and the new, both agonist and antagonist are male, sometimes father and son, just as Frazer's Dying God, priest, or king, reborn anew with the spring, is always male. In ancient fertility rituals the mother is never killed — that would be a contradiction of the very purpose of the ritual, which is to ensure her fertility. Yet Eliot's fascination with murder centered on the murder of women, envisioned in the Sweeney poems as rapacious and engulfing — qualities that similarly describe Harry's mother:

Harry

Everything has always been referred back to mother.
When we were children, before we went to school,
The rule of conduct was simply pleasing mother;
Misconduct was simply being unkind to mother;
What was wrong was whatever made her suffer,
And whatever made her happy was what was virtuous —
Though never very happy, I remember. That was why
We all felt like failures, before we had begun.
When we came back, for the school holidays,
They were not holidays, but simply a time
In which we were supposed to make up to mother
For all the weeks during which she had not seen us
Except at half-term, and seeing us then
Only seemed to make her more unhappy, and made us
Feel more guilty. ...   (*CPP* 259)

Harry's imagined murder of his wife is his first step toward psychically murdering this engulfing mother, and *The Family Reunion* is in fact a denial of the cyclical physical renewal promised through fertility. Both mother and family estate are intolerable to Harry, who must "kill" familial bonds if he is to heed his purely spiritual vocation. But he will never be "liberated from the human wheel" until he frees himself from his mother, so the Furies' "divine" role is to drive him back from the imagined murder of his wife to Wishwood, to confront his real mother. To be liberated Harry must first confront the ties binding him to earth, to the controlling mother who "has only lived for your return to Wishwood." Like Orestes he must be purged of the pattern of family tragedy if he is to be free to pursue his spiritual calling. Thus the play cannot be understood without a detailed comparison to the *Oresteia*, the Greek trilogy in which the laws and customs of the old matriarchal, earth-bound religion are emphatically declared to be dead, superseded by a patriarchal religion of the spirit in which father displaces mother and godhead is above nature:

Apollo

I will tell you, and I will answer correctly.
The mother is no parent of that which is called
her child, but only nurse of the new-planted seed
that grows. The parent is he who mounts. A stranger
she preserves a stranger's seed, if no god interfere.
I will show you proof of what I have explained.
              There can
be a father without any mother. There she stands,
the living witness, daughter of Olympian Zeus,
she who was never fostered in the dark of the womb
yet such a child as no goddess could bring to birth.
              (Lattimore, *AIO* 157–8)

In particular, the powerful role women play in *The Family Reunion* must be examined in comparison to the *Oresteia*, for in both a man's destiny is first dominated and blighted, then resolved, by women. Both plays tell of defending and identifying with the father, but both are dominated dramatically by female archetypes. Clytemnestra and the Erinyes, witch-figures representing the matriarchal blood-ties of the ancient Earth-mother, are portrayed in Eliot's play by Amy. They are supplanted by a purely spiritual mother without ties to the "dark earth," a patroness who resolves the violence of blood-bondage, represented in Eliot's play by Agatha, just as Aeschylus' Erinyes, "Angry Ones," are transformed into the "Kindly Ones," Eumenides, by the intervention of the motherless goddess Athene. Like Aeschylus, Eliot resolves the matricidal impulse, the "long fascination with murder" that has haunted his poetry.

Not only are the two works analogous in such broad thematic ways, but, contrary to Smith's assumption, the scenes involving Mary, Agatha, and Dr. Warburton all have "counterparts" in the *Oresteia*. But while there are many analogies between Eliot's play and his ancient source, it is necessary to keep in mind the difference Bodkin first pointed up in these two works between the communal, historical, grand scale of Aeschylus' world and the personal, psychological, intimate scale of Eliot's. For instance, Clytemnestra stabs her husband three times and glories in the "driven rain of bitter savored blood," words that perversely parody springtime fertility ritual, whereas Amy and her husband were "never very happy together:/They separated by mutual consent" (Lattimore, *AIO* 80; Eliot, *CPP* 260).[1] However different the scale, the effect is the same: a mother has deprived a son of his father, dominated and blighted the life of her children and her entire community, whether it be the city-state of Argos or the family estate of Wishwood.

Amy is clearly parallel to Clytemnestra in more specific ways than those already noted. A great villainous character must have motives that, at least in their origin, compel sympathy, and this is true of both these towering matriarchs. So true is it of Amy, that many years later Eliot admitted "my sympathies now have come to be all with the mother, who seems to me, except perhaps for the chauffeur, the only complete human being in the play" ("PD" 144). Clytemnestra had much just cause to hate Agamemnon: he sacrificed their eldest daughter, Iphigeneia, to placate the winds to carry his troops to Troy on a mission of war that utterly drained his community. In avenging her daughter's death, Clytemnestra defends the matriarchal system, in which bonds of blood take precedence over any other ties, including matrimony. When Apollo challenges the Chorus of Erinyes persecuting Orestes, they reply that it is their "duty" to "drive matricides out of their house" and defend this value system:

Apollo

Then what if it be the woman and she kills her man?

Chorus

Such murder would not be the shedding of kindred blood.

(142)

Again, when Orestes asks during his trial why the Erinyes did not "descend" on his mother for the murder she committed, they reply:

Chorus

The man she killed was not of blood congenital.

Orestes

But am I then involved with my mother by blood-bond?

Chorus

Murderer, yes. How else could she have nursed you beneath
her heart? Do you forswear your mother's intimate blood? (156)

Amy too is a great matriarch, upholding the primal importance of
physical regeneration:

Amy

I do not want the clock to stop in the dark.
If you want to know why I never leave Wishwood
That is the reason. I keep Wishwood alive
To keep the family alive, to keep them together,
To keep me alive, and I live to keep them.
You none of you understand how old you are
And death will come to you as a mild surprise,
A momentary shudder in a vacant room.
Only Agatha seems to discover some meaning in death
Which I cannot find.   (227)

The last two lines signify that Agatha, like Athene, "was never fostered
in the dark womb" of nature. She finds life after death in the spiritual
eternity promised by the patriarchal god, unlike Amy, who sacrifices
everything to propagation in order to ensure physical eternity in the
face of death, even "Forcing sons upon an unwilling father."

In the magnificent concluding scene, these two female archetypes
finally collide, as Amy accuses Agatha of taking her husband and her
son:

Amy

You knew that you took everything
Except the walls, the furniture, the acres;

Leaving nothing — but what I could breed for myself,
What I could plant here. Seven years I kept him,
For the sake of the future, a discontented ghost,
In his own house. What of the humiliation,
Of the chilly pretences in the silent bedroom,
Forcing sons on an unwilling father?...
I *would* have sons, if I could not have a husband: ...
I forced myself to the purposes of Wishwood ...   (282)

Amy's language shows her matriarchal principles: Agatha took everything of a spiritual nature, including her husband's love, but left the
material objects that ensure familial prosperity and symbolize physical regeneration, "the walls, the furniture, the acres." For these, for
the futurity of Wishwood, Amy as Earth-mother, "forced herself" to
"breed" and to "plant." And, like Clytemnestra when Agamemnon
returned with Cassandra, Amy had to endure her husband's love for
another.

Yet, while their original cause is just, both Clytemnestra and Amy
become mothers out of control, so that their righteous defense of fecundity becomes perverted into a dominating will that corrupts and
destroys. Clytemnestra's cause begins in defense of familial ties that
Agamemnon violated, but ultimately her will crushes the husband
whom ten years of war could not defeat, and destroys the family it is
her duty as matriarch to protect. She has already exiled her son before
Agamemnon's return, so that she can enact her revenge and rule Argos
without interference, with her lover Aegisthus. Her confrontation with
Agamemnon is one of the greatest scenes of reversal in all literature,
as she urges him to step from his chariot and walk upon purple tapes-
tries into the palace. In effect, she tempts him to give into his *hubris*,
for purple was reserved for the gods as Agamemnon well knows. In
bending to her will, Agamemnon seals his fate: the purple robe becomes "the folded web's/entanglement" with which she "pinions him ...
in the watered bath," and which so galls Orestes, who displays it in
disgust after he has avenged his father (70):

Spread it out. Stand around me in a circle and
display this net that caught a man. So shall, not my
father, but that great father who sees all, the Sun,
look on my mother's sacrilegious handiwork. ...

But she, who plotted this foul death against the man
by whom she carried the weight of children underneath
her zone, burden once loved, shown hard and hateful now,
what does she seem to be? Some water snake, some viper
whose touch is rot even to him who felt no fang
strike, by that brutal and wrong daring in her heart. (128–9)

Orestes' speech shows the perversion of Clytemnestra from the mother who gives life, carrying "the weight of children beneath her zone" to the "viper whose touch is rot," bringing death and corruption. "Even to him who felt no fang" refers to himself, since he was not stabbed, but his life was nonetheless blighted by "that brutal and wrong daring in her heart." Similarly, Harry tries to explain "the filthiness" with which he has been infected, expressing a disgust at parental sexuality that reveals the oedipal origin of his matricidal impulse: "I can clean my skin,/Purify my life, void my mind,/But always the filthiness, that lies a little deeper ..." (269). Clytemnestra forced Agamemnon to bend to her will, just as Amy extracted her emotional revenge for a loveless marriage: "Seven years I kept him ... a discontented ghost,/In his own house. ... Forcing sons on an unwilling father." These "putrescent embraces," this "unspoken voice of sorrow in the ancient bedroom" (277, 234), reach out to contaminate the next generation, just as Orestes cannot escape the curse of his familial past. As Eliot's chorus sings: "whatever happens began in the past, and presses hard on the future. /The agony in the curtained bedroom, whether of birth or of dying,/Gathers in to itself all the voices of the past, and projects them into the future" (270–1).

Just as Argos is subject to Clytemnestra's tyranny, so too the Mon-chensey family convenes obediently at Wishwood "at Amy's command, to play an unread part/in some monstrous farce, ridiculous in some nightmare pantomime" (231). The "nightmare pantomime" is Harry's forced accession to family head, which Amy has planned as part of her birthday celebration. After "Thirty-five years designing his life" and "Eight years watching, without him, at Wishwood" (283), she makes one final effort to coerce Harry to her will, as she did his father: "For the sake of the future: Harry is to take command at Wishwood" (230). The pathos of Amy's character lies in its terrific irony: the very futurity she fought so relentlessly to ensure has been blighted through her own "indomitable will," as the chorus sings:

I am afraid of all that has happened, and of all that is to
                                                    come;
Of the things to come that sit at the door, as if they had been
                                            there always.
And the past is about to happen, and the future was long
                                        since settled.
And the wings of the future darken the past, the beak and
                                    claws have desecrated
History. Shamed
The first cry in the bedroom, the noise in the nursery,
                                                mutilated
The family album, rendered ludicrous
The tenants' dinner, the family pic-nic on the moors.
                                                Have torn
The roof from the house, or perhaps it was never there.
And the bird sits on the broken chimney. I am afraid. (256–7)

We have seen the significance of bird imagery in Eliot's Sweeney poems, and here again it symbolizes the rapacious harpy, mother as witch. Amy has "long since settled" Harry's future, but under the dark wings of her domination, the past, blighted and "shamed," can only be repeated. The "beak and claw" of her greed have "desecrated" familial "history," "mutilated" and "torn" those very traditions she sought to preserve. She has destroyed Wishwood itself, or "perhaps it was never there" — perhaps it was never the bastion she imagined and tried so singlemindedly to recreate. Like the nightingales excreting on Agamemnon's shroud, this destructive female archetype sits upon a "broken" phallic symbol, just as Clytemnestra, "Standing above the corpse, obscene/as some carrion crow she sings/the crippled song and is proud" (83).

There is another child in this family whose future has been blighted by the mother's "indomitable will": Mary, Harry's second cousin, a poor relation who lived at Wishwood as a child and therefore functions in part as a sister figure to Harry, counterpart to Electra. While Orestes, a son who might command power in Argos, had been exiled, Electra, a harmless daughter, was "kennelled like a dog," imprisoned in the palace like a "slave" after her father's death (97, 108). Like Electra, Mary is too weak to fight and remains a prisoner of Amy's schemes and a slave to her whims as "a housekeeper-companion": "What Cousin Amy wants, she usually gets ... /I suppose I could have gone, if I'd had the moral courage,/Even against a will like hers" (245).

The second scene of Part I, in which Harry and Mary meet and share what Eliot called the first of two "lyrical duets" in the play, is a scene of recognition, identification, and affirmation, analogous to the first scene of the *Choephoroi*, in which Orestes returns after his years of exile and meets Electra by the grave of their father. He has come to mourn and lays a token strand of his hair across the grave, then hides at the approach of the women, the "libation bearers." Electra recognizes the hair, identical to her own. Mystified, not daring to hope that Orestes has returned, Electra sees "another sign," the footprints that are "like the prints I make" (Lattimore, *AIO* 100). Orestes reveals himself but he is disguised, and Electra expresses her fear in the recurrent metaphor of deception so central to the trilogy: "Is this some net of treachery, friend, you catch me in?" Orestes replies, sealing their mutual identification: "Then I must be contriving plots against myself" (101). After identification and recognition comes affirmation, as brother and sister each gain strength through sharing their mutual suffering:

Orestes

Zeus, Zeus, direct all that we try to do. Behold
the orphaned children of the eagle-father, now
that he has died entangled in the binding coils
of the deadly viper, and the young he left behind ...
I, with my sister, whom I name, Electra here,
stand in your sight, children whose father is lost. We both
are driven from the house that should be ours.   (102)

In this scene Orestes and Electra share a lyrical duet, "a song sung to the gods beneath us," telling of the "cruel, cruel/all daring mother" and invoking their father's ghost to aid their revenge. This "great invocation of the dead, is in short a species of sacrament, the appointed means of entering into communion with the unseen world" (Verrall xxi). While Orestes calls on his father to join him in "battle on the side of those/you love," Electra begs for his pity, in a splendid reversal of the net imagery:

Electra

Here one more cry, father, from me. It is my last.
Your nestlings huddle suppliant at your tomb: look forth
and pity them, female with male strain alike.

Do not wipe out this seed of the Pelopidae.
So, though you died, you shall not yet be dead, for when
a man dies, children are the voice of his salvation
afterward. Like corks upon the net, these hold
the drenched and flaxen meshes, and they will not
drown.   (111)

Mary and Harry also share a mutual identification in discovering
that both have suffered alike under Amy's rule, and each finds affirmation and strength through acknowledging this shared experience.
At first, like Orestes and Electra, they seem alien and unsure, unknown to one another. Mary, afraid of Harry's desire to speak with
her, awkwardly attempts to leave the room but he detains her:

Harry

No, don't go just yet. ... There was something
I wanted to ask you. I don't know yet. ...
It seems I shall get rid of nothing,
Of none of the shadows that I wanted to escape;
And at the same time, other memories,
Earlier, forgotten, begin to return
Out of my childhood. I can't explain.
But I thought I might escape from one life to another,
And it may be all one life, with no escape. Tell me,
Were you ever happy here, as a child at Wishwood?

Mary

Happy? not really, though I never knew why:
It always seemed that it must be my own fault,
And never to be happy was always to be naughty.
But there were reasons: I was only a cousin
Kept here because there was nothing else to do with me.
I didn't belong here. It was different for you.
And you seemed so much older. We were rather in awe of

you —

At least, I was.   (247)

Here both express a shared sense of imprisonment. One child departed and one remained, but both were similarly caught in the net of

familial tragedy. Like Orestes, Harry finds there is "no escape" from the "shadows" of the past that haunt his life and he must return to battle them; and Mary, like Electra, finds herself "kept here because there was nothing else to do with me." Like Electra, Mary is slow to trust, remaining in "awe" of the hero she has idolized over the years, but Harry, like Orestes, seals their identification in mutual suffering by using the first person plural pronoun, which Mary then echoes:

Harry

Why were we not happy?

Mary

Well, it all seemed to be imposed upon us;
Even the nice things were laid out ready,
And the treats were always so carefully prepared;
There was never any time to invent our own enjoyments. ...

Harry

I was part of the design
As well as you . ... But do you remember

Mary

The hollow tree in what we called the wilderness

Harry

Down near the river. That was the block house
From which we fought the Indians. ...

Mary

It was the cave where we met by moonlight
To raise the evil spirits.

Harry

... Of course we were punished for being out at night
After being put to bed. But at least they never knew
Where we had been.   (248)

While beautifully evocative of childhood, the imagery here is also richly pagan. The children had discovered the real "wishwood," the "sacred wood." Here they share "a species of sacrament ... entering into communion with the unseen world," to use Verrall's words, calling up underground Keres from the cave or *megara*, "evil spirits" of the dead, but also bringers of life. Had they been left to "invent their own enjoyments," they might have eventually found love, marriage, sexual union, and the regeneration of Wishwood as a natural result of their shared, "secret" world in the wilderness symbolic of fertility. However, Amy decimates this wood in her effort to control the children, to bend them to her will, an example of Eliot's poignant irony. The mother who wishes for Wishwood's continuity above all else in fact destroys the seeds of its renewal. Like Clytemnestra, her dominating will has perverted her from the purposes of fertility into a harbinger of sterility:

Mary

They never found the secret.

Harry

Not then. But later, coming back from school
For the holidays, after the formal reception
And the family festivities, I made my escape
As soon as I could, and slipped down to the river
To find the old hiding place. The wilderness was gone,
The tree had been felled, and a neat summer-house
Had been erected, 'to please the children.'
It's absurd that one's only memory of freedom
Should be a hollow tree in a wood by the river.   (248)

Mary, like Electra, gains strength from this reunion. Her despair, an "ordinary hopelessness" that has enveloped her life under Amy's dominion, gives way to a hope she tries to share with Harry:

Mary

That sudden comprehension of the death of hope
Of which you speak, I know you have experienced it,
And I can well imagine how awful it must be.
But in this world another hope keeps springing
In an unexpected place, while we are unconscious of it.   (249)

It is significant that for Mary "hope keeps springing" like the regeneration of spring itself "in *this* world," the physical world, earth with its promise of annual renewal.

While Orestes' prayers are focused on the bloody battle he must face, Electra sees beyond revenge to future life, to the "seed of the Pelopidae," made suddenly possible should Orestes finally end the familial curse. Orestes calls on "Earth" to release his father's spirit to aid him in battle, while Electra responds in turn, "Persephone, grant still the wonder of success" (110). By calling on Persephone, Electra evokes all the manifold symbolic richness of that goddess: like her brother, she wants the Queen of the Dead to grant them the power of ghosts below, but unlike Orestes she invokes "the wonder of success," the wonder of renewed life that Persephone also signifies in her annual return from the underworld. For Electra "children are the voice of salvation" after death, and with Orestes' return she discovers her own identity, hitherto blighted by her mother's domination, as the archetypal Kore, the maiden who holds the possibility of futurity in her womb.

Mary too is a Kore, who finds her identity with Harry's return. She is also equated with Persephone through her association with springtime, from the moment she enters the stage at the beginning of Scene II carrying flowers in her arms:

Mary

The spring is very late in this northern country,
Late and uncertain, clings to the south wall.
The gardener had no garden-flowers to give me for

this evening. ...
I had rather wait for our windblown blossoms,
Such as they are, than have these greenhouse flowers
Which do not belong here, which do not know
The wind and rain, as I know them.   (244)

Mary embodies the spirit of the wilderness, of the free "wind-blown blossoms," as opposed to Amy's forced, sterile "greenhouse flowers." Persephone's abduction by Hades, at once into the underworld and into sexual initiation, occurred when she was picking flowers during "Anthesterion, the Flower Month, roughly our February, but in Greece the cold winter season when bulbs bloom" (Ruck 85) and also the time of these events, as Amy's words indicate: "Will the spring never come? I am cold" (225).

In her newfound identity as Kore, Mary urges Harry to abandon his "infatuation" with "loathing" and turn from hate to love, from death to life. He describes her voice in metaphors appropriate to her as nature goddess: "the distant waterfall in the forest" and the "usual noises/ In the grass and leaves, of life persisting." He is both attracted and frightened by the spring she offers: "Perhaps you are right, though I do not know/How you should know it. Is the cold spring/Is the spring not an evil time, that excites us with lying voices?" (251). Here we are reminded that "April is the cruelest month"— cruel because physical birth leads inexorably to death. Spring "excites us" with the promise of new birth, but "with lying voices," for death lies hidden in its germ. Mary's first verse is filled with language "throbbing" with the "pain" of birth:

Mary

The cold spring now is the time
For the ache in the moving root
The agony in the dark
The slow flow throbbing the trunk
The pain of the breaking bud.
These are the ones that suffer least:
The aconite under the snow
And the snowdrop crying for a moment in the wood.   (251)

Aconite is the deadly poisonous plant known as wolfsbane or monkshood; thus it symbolizes the death lurking within the deceptive innocence of spring's first signs of life.

In Harry's next verse, Eliot reveals his deep knowledge of the meaning of spring in the ancient world — not a time of joy and celebration, but of fear and placation:

Harry

Spring is an issue of blood
A season of sacrifice
And the wail of the new full tide
Returning the ghosts of the dead
Those whom the winter drowned
Do not the ghosts of the drowned
Return to land in the spring?
Do the dead want to return?   (251)

Contrary to our usual associations of spring with new life, the Greek month *Anthesterion* and the equivalent Roman February were both "unlucky and given over to the service of the dead" according to Jane Harrison: "February was the month of the dead, and it was the month of purification" (*PSGR* 49–50). Purification requires sacrifice of a ritual victim, so Harry's words do not signify merely an obsession with morbidity, but rather a knowledge of spring in the ancient world as "a season of sacrifice": "The animal sacrificed, be it sheep or goat or dog, is itself a placation to ghosts or underworld powers ... the primary gist of the sacrifice is to appease and hence keep off evil spirits; it is these evil spirits that impair fertility: in a word *purification is the placation of ghosts*" (53). The dead do "want to return" in spring — the "wail of the new full tide" of life brings "ghosts of the dead" rising up, demanding vengeance for their death: "The ghost demands blood, not to satisfy a physical, but so to speak a spiritual thirst, the thirst for vengeance" (Harrison, *PSGR* 61).

Harry chants, "Spring is an issue of blood" because the suppliant can only be purified by washing in blood, just as Orestes ritually cleansed himself of "the bloody hand" of murder by washing in "blood from a young victim" mixed with clear "running waters" (Lattimore 151). According to Harrison, "the ghost below demands the blood of the victim washed of from the polluted suppliant: when the ghost has drunk of this, then, and not till then, there is placation and purification" (*PSGR* 60). Such Hellenic rituals have obvious parallels with Christian symbolism: the Christian can be purified of sin by washing in the blood of the lamb of Christ, and Harry feels a sense of "defilement" that perhaps suggests original sin, particularly since it is associated with his mother's sexuality. However, Harrison makes it clear that purification to the ancients contained no notion of sin in a Christian sense: "Purity was not *spiritual* purity in our sense — that is foreign to any primitive habit of thought. ... But the purity of which the ancients knew *was*, though in a widely different sense, *spiritual* purity, i.e. freedom from bad spirits and their maleficent influence" (53). Orestes washes, not because he is guilty of the sin of murder, but because he will be harrassed by vengeful ghosts if he does not rid himself of "the smell of human blood," as the Erinyes cry: "like hounds after a bleeding fawn, we trail/our quarry by the splash and drip of blood" (Lattimore 144).

In the next verse Mary reminds Harry that the ultimate purpose of all this bloody sacrifice is fertility, that "pain" and "joy" are inextricably bound. Again she is reminiscent of Persephone:

Mary

Pain is the opposite of joy
But joy is a kind of pain
I believe the moment of birth
Is when we have knowledge of death
I believe the season of birth
Is the season of sacrifice   (251)

Persephone experiences death and sexuality simultaneously during her sojourn in the underworld where she eats pomegranate seeds symbolic of insemination, then returns from the underworld to her mother, Demeter, bringing life out of death and assuring humanity of eternity. For Mary as a Kore, the eternal physical cycle of life out of death and death out of life is sufficient, and she wants to draw Harry back into the "hollow tree" of the natural world that they shared as children. However, her imagery in the final seven lines of their "lyrical duet" suggests a birth out of this teeming natural world that is monstrous:

Mary

For the tree and the beast, and the fish
Thrashing itself upstream:
And what of the terrified spirit
Compelled to be reborn
To rise toward the violent sun
Wet wings into the rain cloud
Harefoot over the moon?   (252)

These lines are reminiscent of Yeats' "Second Coming," and Eliot seems to be comparing Mary's vision to Yeats' pagan "*Spiritus Mundi*," the vast Sphinx rising out of the desert to replace Christianity after "twenty centuries of stony sleep" (Yeats, *CP* 185). But she asks a question, and her words imply doubt: "what of the terrified spirit" of nature? It seems helplessly "compelled to be reborn" over and over again, a pointless cycle for Eliot without Christ to give life meaning beyond death. However confidently Mary urges Harry to share the maternal world of physical rebirth that she desires, she herself doubts its ultimate meaning. The beast with its "wet wings" and "harefoot" suggests an apocalyptic vision of the taloned, winged bird-woman, condemned to, and "terrified" of, an eternity of "identical circles," meaningless cyclical rebirth around and around the natural world. Mary's reunion with Harry brings her the strength finally to break away from Wishwood, but it has come "much too late/Then, for anything to come for me:" Harry did not come "for" her and it is "too late" for her to fulfill the fecund promise of the Kore (285).

Mary's promise of regeneration brings Harry a brief moment of light, "news/Of a door that opens at the end of the corridor,/Sunlight and singing" (252). He is tempted to join her in "singing and light," but he is prevented by the sudden appearance of the Eumenides:

Harry

That apprehension deeper than all sense,
Deeper than the sense of smell, but like a smell
In that it is indescribable, a sweet and bitter smell
From another world. I know it, I know it!
More potent than ever before, a vapour dissolving
All other worlds, and me into it.   (252)

The Eumenides seem to be described here through the metaphor of incense in Catholic and Anglican worship, "a sweet and bitter smell/ From another world" of Christian eternity, bringing an "apprehension deeper than all sense" that dissolves "all other worlds" of the senses. Indeed, Eliot emphasized in a letter to his director, E. Martin Browne, that "the Furies are *divine* instruments, not simple hell-hounds" (Browne 107). The dual pagan/Christian role of the Eumenides here does seem most contradictory, as critics have attested. How can these representatives of ancient matriarchal religion be turning Harry away from Persephone to Christ? But it must be remembered that they lead Harry first to his mother, then to Mary, and finally to Agatha in a series of progressive steps in his spiritual quest. Eliot describes them as Erinyes, "sleepless hunters ... their claws distended," because they drive Harry toward the female archetypes he must confront, just as Orestes must be tried for matricide in order to be purged and liberated. In the same speech, Eliot describes them using the Christian imagery quoted above because they are also beneficient Eumenides, leading Harry toward Agatha/Athene and beyond, to the patriarchal god she represents.

After the Erinyes appear, Harry rejects Mary in terms that seem unnecessarily cruel, but stem from his own terror of the physical world she offers:

Harry

... If I had realized
That you were so obtuse, I would not have listened
To your nonsense. Can't you help me?
You're of no use to me. I must face them.   (253)

Mary is too earth-bound to help Harry further on his spiritual quest. She is doomed to sterility, a sad ending for a Kore, but as Agatha reminds her, "You and I, Mary,/Are only watchers and waiters: not the easiest role" (246). Both these female archetypes remain "wander[ers]" in the "neutral territory/Between two worlds" — the bifurcated worlds of body and spirit according to the patriarchal faith Harry seeks (285). Contrary to Smith's conclusions that Harry is identified with "the spirit of the new year struggling for rebirth" in this scene with Mary, in which "he uses the imagery of the ritual sacrifice of rejuvenation," Harry explicitly rejects the physical renewal offered by Mary through the spring fertility imagery of their duet (Smith 137). Like the Hyacinth girl's spurned offer in Part I of *The Waste Land*, this is another example, according to Eliot, of the inefficacy of fertility ritual to renew in the modern world.[2]

The next step in Harry's pilgrimage occurs in his confrontation with Dr. Warburton, the first scene of Part II. The old doctor, who "looked after all the boys/When they were children," has been called in by Harry's family, who are worried about his erratic behavior and his "dangerous fancies" that he has killed his wife (235–237). In Carol Smith's view, Warburton fulfills Cornford's "ritual role of the cook-doctor" who assists in the painful "conversion of the old into the new," since he "spends the entire interview trying to impress Harry with the seriousness of Amy's illness and imminent death, symbolically expressing the ritual fate of the impure old god," while Harry "assists the cook-doctor's purposes by moving one step closer to his victory over the old god" (139, 143). But Smith overlooks the bristling antagonism of this scene: Warburton is not a "spiritual assistant" but rather an opponent. Harry does not "assist" the doctor's purposes, since Warburton in no way wants to see Harry attain victory over Amy. Rather, they repeatedly conflict because Warburton's purpose is to defend Harry's mother and to urge Harry "To make her happy for the time she has to live" (261).

As a servant of the mother's will in opposition to the son, Warburton is analogous to Aegisthus, Clytemnestra's lover. While there is no explicit evidence that Warburton was Amy's lover, Eliot repeatedly stresses his long intimacy as "an old friend of the family" (237). Amy seems to mark him as her own when she insists on telephoning him: "If anyone speaks to Dr. Warburton/It should be myself. ... I will ring up the doctor myself" (237–8). She chides Harry for not immediately noticing him when they enter the room, in an attempt to promote a paternal-filial relationship between them, since "he's known you longer than anybody, Harry" (255). She then asks the doctor to escort her to dinner:

Amy

Will you take me in, Doctor?
I think we are very much the oldest present —
In fact we are the oldest inhabitants,
As we came first, we shall go first, in to dinner.

Warburton

With pleasure, Lady Monchensey,
And I hope that next year will bring me the same
honour.   (256)

It is understandable that this passage, with its emphasis on age, would suggest to Smith "the ritual procession and feast in celebration of the renewal and conversion of the old into the new" as the "cook-doctor" leads the old god to "sacrificial boiling or stewing". However, Warburton is not leading Amy to her death, as he clearly expresses the "hope" that she will go on living so that they can celebrate together in future years. Rather, their elaborate courtesy here suggests a familiar flirtation between them that has endured from their youth in the age of Victorian chivalry. Warburton's love for Amy, while hardly the incestuous sexual passion between Aegisthus and Clytemnestra, still glimmers in his longing comment, "It's only when I get an invitation to dinner/That I ever see your mother" (256).

When Amy finds out that her second son, John, has been in a minor car accident, Warburton "forbids" her to leave the house because of her ill health. Instead he will "report back" to her. Reluctantly she agrees, but asks, "Can I trust you?"

Warburton

You have trusted me a good many years, Lady Monchensey;
This is not the time to begin to doubt me.   (265)

Just as Amy has trusted Warburton "a good many years," Aegisthus is Clytemnestra's most trusted ally: "my good friend, now as always, who shall be for us/the shield of our defiance" (Lattimore 82).

While Aegisthus is "no weak thing" in Clytemnestra's eyes, Orestes sees him as dominated by his mother, a coward since he let a woman do his killing for him. The angry son expresses nothing but contempt for "this brace of women; since his heart/is female" (104). Harry is similarly contemptuous of Warburton, whose heart is also dominated by his care and concern for female interests, as he tries to impress Harry with the urgency of his mother's ill health and imminent death:

Warburton

I wanted a private conversation with you
On a confidential matter.

Harry

I can imagine —
Though I think it is probably going to be useless. ...

Warburton

It's about your mother ...

Harry

What about my mother?
Everything has always been referred back to my mother ...

(259)

Harry's responses show his irritation with Warburton. He knows the doctor wants to talk about Amy, refuses to listen, and instead asserts himself: "You must let me explain, and then you can talk." Indeed, as each insists on talking and refuses to listen, their dialogue expresses the thrust and parry of a swordfight. Far from assisting the "cook-doctor's purposes" as Smith believes, Harry is in fact defying him. He will not be forced into compliance with his mother's will; rather he will impose his own will on his mother's spokesman, just as Orestes triumphs over Aegisthus. Like Orestes, Harry insists on representing his father. To each effort Warburton makes to bend him to his mother's "happiness," he parries by asserting the memory of his father: "But if you want to talk, at least you can tell me/Something useful. Do you remember my father?" Discouragingly, his adversary responds: "I really don't see/ What that has to do with the present occasion/Or with what I have to tell you" (260). Again Harry returns his thrust, repelling news of his mother as "either something that I know already/Or unimportant, or else untrue. But I want to know more about my father."

Amy, like Clytemnestra, has deprived her children of their father. Harry is an Orestes, the "orphaned child of the eagle-father," as he describes the pathos of "children whose father is lost" through the machinations of their mother and her "whispering" sisters:

Harry

I hardly remember him, and I know very well
That I was kept apart from him, till he went away.
We never heard him mentioned, but in some way or another
We felt that he was always here.
But when we would have grasped for him, there was only
                          a vacuum
Surrounded by whispering aunts: Ivy and Violet —
Agatha never came then. Where was my father?   (260)

Harry's plea, "Where was my father?" echos Orestes' helpless yearning to reach his father beyond the grave:

Orestes

Father, o my dread father, what thing
can I say, can I accomplish
from this far place where I stand, to mark
and reach you there in your chamber
with light that will match your dark?   (104)

If Harry can evoke even a single memory of his father from the clearly reluctant Warburton, he will have one more precious piece of the past his mother deprived him of and he will be one step closer to victory over the familial "ghosts" that have haunted his life. Again Warburton tries to discourage him: "Harry, there's no good probing for misery," but he finally admits, in the lines already quoted, that Harry's parents "separated by mutual consent/And he went to live abroad. You were only a boy/When he died. You would not remember." Harry responds in triumph: "But now I do remember" (260). In

spite of Warburton's resistance, Harry has extracted enough informa-
tion about his father to spur an important memory. By systematically
refusing to acknowledge his mother and forcing Warburton instead to
answer his need for memories of his father, Harry has defeated his
mother's lackey as effectively as Orestes' sword cut down Aegisthus.

His memory stimulated by Warburton's clue, Harry now recalls the
day his father died:

Harry

I remember the silence and the hushed excitement
And the low conversation of triumphant aunts.
It is the conversations not overheard,
Not intended to be heard, with the sidewise looks,
That bring death into the heart of a child.
That was the day he died. Of course.
I mean, I suppose, the day on which the news arrived.

Warburton

You overinterpret.
I am sure that your mother always loved him;
There was never the slightest suspicion of scandal.   (260)

Warburton's response here is curious. Indeed, the undercurrents of
this conversation are complex and significant. By confusing the day of
his father's death with the day "on which the news arrived," Harry is
in effect accusing his mother of killing his father, and through that
murder of blighting his own manhood, just as Clytemnestra murdered
Agamemnon and deprived Orestes of his kingship, his inheritance
from his father. The "whispering aunts" are merely his mother's pawns,
bringing "death into the heart of a child," although Harry is always
careful to except one aunt from league with his mother: "Agatha never
came then." For Agatha loved his father and will become Harry's
patroness, just as Athene adjudicates her father's will and saves Orestes
in the final play of Aeschylus' trilogy.

His mother sealed her triumph over his father with a kiss of death:
"That night, when she kissed me,/I felt the trap close." Warburton's
response, quoted above, is a weak attempt to defend Amy against
Harry's accusation and reveals his own sense of guilt. Understandably
confused by it, Harry replies, "Scandal? who said scandal? I did not"

(261). What scandal could Warburton be referring to? It would appear to be Amy's lack of love for her husband, and perhaps his own complicity as her lover in that betrayal. But just as Orestes dismisses Aegisthus with contempt, "of Aegisthus' death I take no count:/he has his seducer's punishment, no more than law" (128), Harry is not the least bit interested in Warburton's role in these events. He has gained one essential memory of his father, which has given him the strength to continue reaching beyond the grave that separates them: "If you won't tell me,/I must ask Agatha. I never dared before" (261).

The doctor concludes that Amy "has only lived for your return to Wishwood" and tells Harry, "Your mother's hopes are all centred on you" (262). But the son again rebuffs his mother's domination, merely responding: "Hopes? ... Tell me/Did you know my father at about my present age?/ ... What did he look like then? Did he look at all like me?" The victory is complete. Having rediscovered his father, Harry wants to identify with him and in so doing achieve his own initiation into manhood through that identification, just as Theseus becomes a man by finding his father's sword and Orestes begs his father's aid in regaining his inheritance. For only the father can give "the gift of lordship": "Father, o king who died no kingly death, I ask/the gift of lordship at your hands, to rule your house" (110).

Indeed, if this play has any ritual parallel, it is the common tribal initiation rite for adolescent boys that is commemorated, according to Harrison's interpretation, in Dionysus' "dithyrambos," the youthful god's "second birth" or initiation into his father's realm:

> The Father-god "cries aloud" ... This loud, clear, emphatic utterance makes us expect some weighty ritual pronouncement, and such a pronouncement immediately follows: "*Come, O Dithyrambos, enter this my male womb.*" The child is to be born anew, not of his mother Semele, but of his father Zeus.   (*T* 35)

Dionysus' second birth from Zeus' thigh represents a purely spiritual rebirth, a mythical expression of his incarnation into the heaven of the Olympian gods and a severing of his tie to the Earth-mother. For Harrison, this "New Birth of the Dithyramb" reflects a universal "tribal rite of initiation": separation from the mother at adolescence, rituals testing strength and endurance, and finally acceptance into the "Man's House" where the youth will live from then on among his fathers and fellow men:

The birth from the male womb is to rid the child from the
infection of his mother — to turn him from a woman-thing
into a man-thing. Woman to primitive man is a thing at once
weak and magical, to be oppressed, yet feared. She is charged
with powers of child-bearing denied to man, powers only half
understood, forces of attraction, but also of danger and repulsion, forces that all over the world seem to fill him with dim
terror. ... Man cannot escape being born of woman, but he can,
and, if he is wise, will, as soon as he comes to manhood, perform ceremonies of riddance and purgation. (36)

Woman "charged with powers of child-bearing" is a force of both
"danger and repulsion" to Eliot and to his young hero. Indeed, *The
Family Reunion* may be considered one long "ceremony of riddance and
purgation" of the mother's physical ties, so that Harry may be spiritually reborn: first his rejection of Mary's offer of sexual renewal, then
identification with his father and defeat of his mother, and finally "entering the male womb" of Zeus or, in Christian terms, accepting the
spiritual calling of God the father.

That Harry has gained new power over his mother through his
defeat of Warburton and identification with his father is indicated in
the scene of comic relief that follows. Adopting Shakespeare's method,
Eliot uses comedy to alleviate the intensity of Harry's confrontation
with the doctor.[3] Like Hamlet, Harry puts on an "antic disposition" in
his bantering repartee with Winchell, a Dogberrian "country sergeant,"
who comes to report his brother's car accident. And also similar to
Hamlet, there is method in Harry's madness. When Winchell is announced by the maid, Denman, Harry questions his reality:

Harry

Nothing can have happened
To either of my brothers. Nothing can happen —
If Sergeant Winchell is real. But Denman saw him.
But what if Denman saw him, and yet he was not real?
That would be worse than anything that has happened. (262)

Throughout this scene two levels of reality are contrasted: physical
reality that is seen empirically and an inner reality of the spirit,
symbolized by the Erinyes, that is invisible to all but Harry. This confusion, a source of Harry's pain elsewhere in the play, here provides

comedy. From his first entrance Harry has shown contempt for the members of his family who are blind to spiritual reality and live totally in the realm of the senses: "You are all people/To whom nothing has happened, at most a continual impact/Of external events" (234). "Nothing has happened" to their internal, spiritual selves because they have lived in "a continual impact/Of external events."

Harry may condemn his aunts and uncles for living in a world "that you call normal. What you call the normal/Is merely the unreal and the unimportant" (268), but at the same time he suffers a terrible isolation: "the awful privacy/Of the insane mind." "Wounded in a war of phantoms" he cannot communicate to anyone living in the world of empirical reality (276). The Eumenides are constant reminders to Harry of the spiritual reality that will ultimately lead him to God, but in the meantime they isolate him in a "private world":

Harry

If I tried to explain, you could never understand: ...
Explaining would only set me farther away from you.
There is only one way for you to understand
And that is by seeing. They are much too clever
To admit you into *our* world.   (250)

Winchell is the classic Greek messenger and Harry perceives him as a messenger from "*our* world," the "unreal" world of invisible spiritual truth, primarily because Winchell mistakenly begins to wish him many happy returns, "thinking it was your birthday, not her Ladyship's." There are multiple ironies here: it is really the day of Amy's death, and it is in one sense Harry's birthday, his "dithyrambos" or second birth into divine grace. In irritation Warburton urges the Sergeant to get to the point, since "his Lordship isn't very well this evening":

Winchell

I understand, Sir.
It'd be the same if it was my birthday —
I beg pardon, I'm forgetting.
If it was my mother's. God rest her soul,
She's been dead these ten years. How is her Ladyship,
If I may ask, my Lord?

Harry

Why do you keep asking
About her Ladyship? Do you know or don't you?
I'm not afraid of you.

Winchell presages Harry's growing liberation from his mother
through the comparison with himself and his own dead mother. He
misinterprets Warburton's hint that Harry is ill to mean that Harry is
drunk with celebrating his birthday. Again he is right ironically, for
Harry's "delusions" are really signs of his road to spiritual health. Indeed, he is beginning to celebrate his victory over his mother in this
scene, as he offers the Sergeant a glass of port and encourages him to
join in the conversation about his father. Harry perceives Winchell as
a messenger from the Eumenides representing "her Ladyship" — a
term that could signify either his mother or his wife, and to Harry it
signifies both. When he says, "Why do you keep asking/About her
Ladyship? Do you know or don't you?" he seems to be asking whether
Winchell knows that he has killed his wife. At the same time he is
asking the Eumenides' messenger, "Do you know or don't you" know
that I have begun to defeat my mother? Thus he can assert rather
jauntily, "I'm not afraid of you." That Harry has confused his imagined murder of his wife with his much more important psychic "murdering" of his mother's choking domination, is evident when he continues to press Winchell:

Harry

Well, do you want me to produce her for you?

Winchell

Oh, no, indeed, my Lord, I'd much rather not ...

Harry

You mean you think I can't. But I might surprise you;
I think I might be able to give you a shock.

The "shock" he is soon going to give everyone, is that he is "liberated
from the human wheel." He can "produce" his mother or not, for she no
longer poses a threat to him. Winchell's response shows humorously

how little the dowager's presence is enjoyed by the locals. No one has yet attempted to interpret this enigmatic scene, and I do not see how it can be explained other than as a sign that a successful psychological matricide has taken place and Harry's power has begun to ascend over his mother. That Harry has defeated his mother through identification with his father is further indicated when one of his aunts chides him for "callousness" towards his brother. He replies that he has "all of the rightminded feeling" about his brother, "Only that's not the language/ That I choose to be talking. I will not talk yours." When Amy remarks significantly in response to this, "You looked like your father/ When you said that," Harry continues: "I think, mother,/I shall make you lie down. You must be very tired." His new-found identification with his father gives him the strength to make his mother lie down, for she is now the weaker. Harry's victory, expressed with sympathy now that Amy's threat is gone, and her powerlessness, filled with the pathos of aging, are finalized in his words when he returns:

Harry

Mother is asleep, I think: it's strange how the old
Can drop off to sleep in the middle of calamity
Like children, or like hardened campaigners. She looked
Very much as she must have looked when she was a child. (267)

A number of ritual relics can be glimpsed beneath the surface of *The Family Reunion*, not those identified by Cornford as the structural elements of comedy, but those identified by Murray as the components of tragedy, first in his "Excursis" to Jane Harrison's *Themis*, then repeated in his 1927 *Classical Tradition in Poetry*. Amy's imminent death represents the victory of "Light against Darkness, Summer against Winter," but not as it is celebrated in the comic *komos* and feast; rather, Harry's words above describe a tragic "*Pathos* of the Year-Daimon" (*T* 343). In addition Murray points out that the "Pathos seems seldom or never to be actually performed under the eyes of the audience" but "it is announced by a messenger," and in Winchell we have the messenger heralding Amy's death through telling of his own mother "dead these ten years." There is an anagnorisis — a scene of discovery of recognition — as Harry and Mary relive the memories of their shared childhood, and an agon between the forces of fertility and spirituality in Harry's struggle against Mary's offer of physical rebirth. Harry's final scene with Agatha contains another anagnorisis that leads to a peripeteia or extreme change of feeling from grief to joy. It is his final "Resurrection or Apotheosis or, in some sense, his Epiphany in glory" to use Murray's words (*T* 344). Such ritual forms may communicate "the vital flame, that impersonal and ... inhuman force" Eliot tried to define in his early criticism, but Eliot's drama is primarily Aeschylean: despite the "vessels of a very ancient religion," his allegiance is to "the new wine of reasoning and rebellious humanity." *The Family Reunion*, like the *Oresteia*, tells of individual heroism and the triumph of the heavenly father.

Harry has broken the bondage of the physical mother but he has yet to complete "expiation" and "expurgation." As Agatha says, "knowledge ... must precede the expiation," and her role is to complete Harry's self-knowledge. The final step in Harry's liberation occurs under the guidance of this spiritual mother, just as Apollo sends Orestes to Athena's citadel for "words ... that will have magic in their figures" to resolve his "afflictions, once for all" (137). Maud Bodkin and Grover Smith suggest that Agatha may be equated with Athene, but neither analyze the parallels in any detail and both thus conclude that her "transformation" of the Eumenides is unconvincing (Bodkin 35–8; Smith 207–10). Eliot's letter to his director, E. Martin Browne, gives an important key to interpreting Agatha:

> Now, this attraction towards Mary has stirred him up, but, owing to his mental state, is incapable of developing: therefore he finds a refuge in an ambiguous relation — the attraction, half of a son and half of a lover, to Agatha, who reciprocates in somewhat the same way. And this gives the cue for the second appearance of the Furies, more patently in their role of divine messengers, to let him know clearly that the only way out is the way of purgation and holiness. ... Agatha understands this clearly, though Harry only understands it yet in flashes.
>
> (Browne 107)

"The attraction, half of a son and half of a lover," acknowledges the oedipal origins of Harry's conflict. C.L. Barber is right in describing Agatha and Amy as "figures of the mother at different times or on different levels of consciousness" in order to "licence a normally submerged wish" of childhood sexual desire for the mother (435). But he is wrong in calling Harry's relationship with Agatha a "perverse" "reenact[ment] ... of the childhood moment" of oedipal desire "in the adult present"

(441–2). As Eliot remarks, Harry is "incapable of developing" a sexual relationship of any kind; he finds love and guidance with Agatha precisely because she has been entirely purged of sexuality, indeed, of physicality. Amy, the mother of physical bonds, has been killed and in Agatha Harry finds the kind of spiritual "high companionship" Harrison describes in the "early matriarchal, husbandless goddesses, whether Mother or Maid, to the male figures that accompany them" (*PSGR* 273).

Athene has just such a relationship to her young heroes Theseus and Perseus, as do most of the female goddesses portrayed in Homer. But according to Harrison, Athene is a "sexless thing," a Kore recreated by "the rising democracy" of Athens and entirely stripped of any connection to earth, to the mother, to physicality: "Nowhere is this artificiality, this unreality of Athene ... so keenly felt as in the famous myth of her birth from the brain of Zeus ... a desperate theological expedient to rid an earth-born Kore of her matriarchal conditions" (*PSGR* 303). Athene herself renounces her tie to the mother in the *Eumenides*, in a speech Harrison calls a "shameful denial":

Athene

This is a ballot for Orestes I shall cast.
There is no mother anywhere who gave me birth,
and, but for marriage, I am always for the male
with all my heart, and strongly on my father's side.
So, in a case where the wife has killed her husband,
                                                              lord
of the house, her death shall not mean most to me.
                                                    And if
the other votes are even, then Orestes wins.   (161)

The Erinyes cry out at this betrayal, "Darkness of night, our mother, are you here to watch?" But Athene is born from the mind of the father and she embodies patriarchal values as the *Homeric Hymn to Athene* attests, in which "she is manifestly ... Reason, Light and Liberty; she is born at the rising of the Sun" (*PSGR* 303). In the *Eumenides* she establishes the Areopagus, justice through trial by jury instead of blood revenge, and then she frees the matricide. Harrison's feminism is obvious when she writes, "we cannot love a goddess who on principle forgets the Earth from which she sprang," but the opposite is true for

Eliot's young hero — he can only love the asexual "abstraction" that is Athene/Agatha.

Harry comes to Agatha seeking truth as the final step in his pilgrimage: "What I want to know is something I need to know,/And only you can tell me. ... I have thought of you as the completely strong,/The liberated from the human wheel. /So I looked to you for strength" (273). So too Orestes arrives, "a clean and innocent supplicant," looking to Athene for strength (151):

> *Orestes*
>
> I call upon Athene, queen of this land, to come
> and rescue me. She, without work of her spear, shall win
> myself and all my land and all the Argive host
> to stand her staunch companion for the rest of time.
> Whether now ranging somewhere in the Libyan land
> beside her father's crossing ... or {on} enshrouded foot
> rescuing there her friends, or on the Phlegraean flat
> like some bold man of armies sweeps with his eyes the
>   scene,
> let her come! She is a god and hears me far away.
> So may she set me free from what is at my back.   (145)

This speech provides a vivid picture of Athene and her role in the pantheon. She is clearly identified with men as Orestes describes her "beside her father's crossing," and as a warrior "like some bold man of armies," but it is significant that she will "rescue" him "without work of her spear." Athene represents the will of the father, but tempered by mercy. Only Athene can moderate between Apollo and the Erinyes for she is at once woman, yet "all for the father." She casts her deciding ballot for Orestes, and in so doing, decrees with Apollo that ties of blood no longer reign supreme over ties of law: "So, in a case where the wife has killed her husband, lord/of the house, her death shall not mean most to me" (161).

If murder could have resolved the situation, Orestes would have no need of Athene, since he already has the aid of Apollo, whose hatred of the Erinyes is virulent. They are in Apollo's eyes,

>   lewd creatures,
> repulsive maidens ... with whom no mortal man,
> no god, nor even any beast, will have to do.

It was because of evil they were born, because
they hold the evil darkness of the Pit below
Earth, loathed alike by men and by the heavenly gods.   (137)

Apollo considers the Erinyes "evil" because they represent the
physicality of the Earth-mother, the vaginal "evil darkness of the Pit
below" that lures men to a physical death unalleviated by a paternal
heavenly eternity. Apollo urged Orestes to matricide, declaring "it was
I who made you strike your mother down." He embodies the
misogynistic disgust and fear that we have seen expressed in Eliot's
Sweeney poems as he tries to drive the Erinyes from his sanctuary:
"The whole cast of your shape is guide/to what you are, the like of
whom should hole in the cave/of the blood-reeking lion, not in oracu-
lar/interiors, like mine, wipe off your filth" (141). However violent
Apollo's hatred may be of matriarchal rituals "where mutilation lives,"
matriarchal blood-law where "by judgment given, heads are lopped
and eyes gouged out," and matriarchal sexuality where "by the spoil
of sex the glory of young boys is defeated" (141), it is not sufficient to
protect Orestes nor to defy the Erinyes' "age-old distributions of power."
They cry in answer: "Shame, son of Zeus! Robber is all you are. /A
young god, you have ridden down powers gray with age" (140). Matriarchal principles cannot be eradicated for they have a powerful claim in
human existence.

But Athene knows that the Erinyes "too, have their work, govern-
ing physical life, fertility and sterility. If they are "brush[ed] aside"
they will "sicken all my land to death" (152). Just as Demeter Erinys
blighted the land in her rage over the loss of Persephone, the Erinyes
"shall let loose on the land/the vindictive poison" of sterility, for they
"have borne what can not/be borne" (163). So Athene converts them
through the "sweet beguilement" of her "persuasion," promising them
"a place of your own, deep hidden under ground that is yours by
right" where they will "win first fruits/offerings for children and the
marriage rite for always," ensuring continuity of the "human seed"
(164, 7). She converts the Erinyes, "Angry Ones," to Eumenides,
"Kindly Ones," who give life. The Earth-mother's representatives
have been restored as part of the Olympian hierarchy, reaffirming
"the luminous evidence of Zeus" (163). In Harrison's words, "Aeschylus has given us the peaceful evolution" instead of the "fight
between the two poles" of matriarchal and patriarchal religion and
social structure (*T* 393).

Agatha is parallel to Aeschylus' Athene, in that she is contemptuous of women and dissociates herself from them, just as Athene declared herself "always for the male." Agatha considers her thirty years of teaching women at Oxford nothing more than "solitude": "Alone, among women, in a women's college,/Trying not to dislike women" (282). Mary, who studied under Agatha, suffered as much from her dominance as from Amy's: "I know I wasn't one of your favorite students:/I only saw you as the principal/Who knew the way of dominating timid girls" (245). Agatha is certainly, like Athene, "all for the father": she loved Harry's father and she gives Harry the final understanding of his father that liberates him, just as she liberated his father from Amy, and just as Athene's vote for Orestes frees him from the Erinyes. She was invited to Wishwood long ago to alleviate Amy's "loneliness" in her cold "childless" marriage, yet characteristically Agatha united with the man, instead of her sister.

Agatha

There are hours when there seems to be no past or future,
Only a present moment of pointed light
When you want to burn. When you stretch out your hand
To the flames.   (274).

Agatha describes her love for Harry's father in images of heat and light to signify that such asexual love partakes of eternity, "when there seems to be no past or future," and divinity in its "pointed light." That their love was a purely spiritual "flame" is apparent since Amy became pregnant, not Agatha: Amy bore the physical seed, Agatha the spiritual soul. Her role as Athenian Kore — the maiden who spurns physical motherhood, as opposed to Persephonean Kore, the maiden who becomes mother — is preserved, as she says to Harry: "I felt that you were in some way mine!/And that in any case I should have no other child" (275). So it is fitting that Harry's dithyramb or second, spiritual birth should take place through this anagnorisis with Agatha as she reveals the long-hidden secret that his father, although "not suited to the role of murderer," had plotted in desperation "how to get rid of your mother":

Harry

In what way did he wish to murder her?

Agatha

Oh, a dozen foolish ways, each one abandoned
For something more ingenious. You were due in three months
time;
You would not have been born in that event: I stopped him. ...
I did not want to kill *you*!
You to be killed! What were you then? only a thing called
'life' — (274)

Here Agatha is exactly analogous to Athene: she "casts her ballot"
for Harry by preserving his life; she averts violence and prevails through
mercy; she is "all for the father" yet she knows that "only a thing called
'life' " — physical life, the realm of the Erinyes — must also be honored.
Harry responds to her cry, "But I wanted you!" by acknowledging union, "And have me"; thus he is in a sense given a second birth through
her love. Agatha's revelation has taught him, just as Athene teaches,
that "everything tends towards reconciliation." Harry must accept his
humanity, accept that he is "still befouled, /But I know there is only
one way out of defilement — /Which leads in the end to reconciliation"
(279). Only Agatha was capable of leading Harry to "reconciliation,"
just as only Athene can liberate Orestes from the Erinyes, through
conciliation, mercy, and persuasion. Thus Agatha convincingly converts the Furies into Eumenides, instruments of divine grace. When
they appear for the final time, Harry is no longer afraid and under-
stands their significance:

Harry

And you shall not think I am afraid to see you.
This time, you are real, this time, you are outside me.
And just endurable. I know that you are ready,
Ready to leave Wishwood, and I am going with you. (278)

Not only does Agatha in effect give Harry his earthly father, but
also, like Athene, she simultaneously opens the way to his heavenly
father: "You may learn hereafter,/Moving alone through flames of ice,
chosen/To resolve the enchantment under which we suffer" (275). Like
Orestes, Harry has expiated familial suffering; but unlike Orestes, he is
to go on seeking, "moving alone" through a kind of dual baptism in
"flames of ice." As Harrison explains, "in fire is a great strength" and

"water too is full of sanctity, of force, of *mana*." The "child is weak and helpless" and "the baptism of water and the baptism of fire are to the same end, the magical acquisition of ghostly strength." Even "in ancient Christian ritual before the candidate was immersed a blazing torch was thrust down into the font" (*T* 34).

Harry accepts the path to God that Agatha holds open for him in imagery that is consistent throughout Eliot's work: he will "worship in the desert" at "a stony sanctuary and a primitive altar,/The heat of the sun and the icy vigil" (281). His vow expresses the strength he will find in divine love through the fire/sun and water/ice imagery of primitive baptism (281). And, in the moment Agatha reveals to him this sun-drenched spiritual path, Harry experiences peripeteia: "I feel happy for a moment, as if I had come home." He has found that happiness consists of "a different vision" (275).

The play's "lyrical duet" between Harry and Agatha balances the early duet between Harry and Mary, but this one is efficacious. Both sing of the past, each blighted in their separate ways by Amy, the rapacious harpy, "until the chain broke" and each finds God, symbolized by the sun and the "unwinking eye." Agatha "only looked through the little door/When the sun was shining on the rose-garden," but "then a black raven flew over" (276). David E. Jones, among others, has pointed out that "the moment in the 'rose garden' " is "a central symbol in Eliot's work" that "seems to represent the moment of illumination which human love can give" (98). Agatha's glimpse of sunlight "through the little door" symbolizes her relationship with Harry's father. Harry too experienced a prior glimpse of love when he heard Mary's words like "sunlight and singing" through "a door that opens at the end of the corridor" (252–3). Obviously, the "black raven" in Agatha's lyric refers to Amy, whose dark wings of domination blotted out the sunlight. Agatha continues:

> And then I was only my own feet walking
> Away, down a concrete corridor
> In a dead air. Only feet walking
> And sharp heels scraping. Over and under
> Echo and noise of feet.
> I was only the feet, and the eye
> Seeing the feet: the unwinking eye
> Fixing the movement. Over and under.   (277)

Here the imagery attests to the painful solitude of Agatha's thirty years since parting from Harry's father. She walked away from him into a "dead" existence, in which all she could do was to keep walking. Eventually Agatha becomes aware of "the unwinking eye" of God, watching over her feet as if she were no higher in creation than Prufrock's "pair of ragged claws/Scuttling across the floors of silent seas." She envisions an uncompromising God, yet his ever-watchful "eye" provides consolation for the barrenness of her existence. Harry tells of a similar experience when he was haunted by harpies symbolic of his mother, "shrieking forms in a circular desert" that recall the pointless "identical circles" of natural life:

> Weaving with contagion of putrescent embraces
> On dissolving bone. In and out, the movement
> Until the chain broke, and I was left
> Under the single eye above the desert.   (277)

"Putrescent embraces" symbolize his parents' loveless sex, spread to the child like a "contagion," the "defilement" he has had to acknowledge and expiate, while "In and out, the movement" signifies at once the motions of their coition and the pointless circularity of physical existence without God. When the chain to the past, to his mother and the "love of created beings" is broken through communion with Agatha, Harry too finds "the single eye above the desert" which is a "traditional symbol for God" as Grover Smith points out (211). Now Harry and Agatha meet in a holy communion, purified by the "judicial" paternal eye, in the rose-garden of human love sanctified by the divine:

> The chain breaks,
> The wheel stops, and the noise of the machinery,
> And the desert is cleared, under the judicial sun
> Of the final eye, and the awful evacuation
> Cleanses.
> I was not there, you were not there, only our phantasms
> And what did not happen is as true as what did happen,
> O my dear, and you walked through the little door
> And I ran to meet you in the rose-garden.   (277)

Harry is finally "liberated from the human wheel." Now too the "noise of machinery" — mechanized existence without spirituality — stops and Harry finds himself alone in a silent desert symbolic of eternity, "cleared" of the shrieking birds of matriarchal physicality, empty but for God — "the judicial sun/Of the final eye." The loathsome eye of the Gorgon and the plural eyes of the Erinyes with their relentless stare have all been subsumed into the "final eye," wiped away in an "awful evacuation" that cleanses. With Agatha, Harry has for the first time found union and therefore confirmation; so too Orestes declares himself after Athene's intercession, "alive again in the estates of his father, all by the grace of Pallas Athene" (162). However different Eliot's vision of the maternal archetype is from Joyce's — as different as Demeter is from Athene — Harry, like Stephen Dedalus, has been symbolically reborn through union with the female archetype, freed from the crippling bonds of childhood to go forth as man.

7: THEMIS IN *TO THE LIGHTHOUSE*: JANE HARRISON AND VIRGINIA WOOLF

The Olympian gods — that is, the anthropomorphic gods of Homer and Pheidias and the mythographers — seemed to me like a bouquet of cut-flowers whose bloom is brief, because they have been severed from their roots. To find those roots we must burrow deep into a lower stratum of thought, into those chthonic cults which underlay their life and from which sprang all their brilliant blossoming.

— Jane Ellen Harrison, *T* xi

Of all the modernists, Woolf's relationship to Harrison was the closest. She knew Harrison personally from 1904 to her death in 1928, visited her in Cambridge, London, and Paris, and refered to her familiarly in diaries and letters as "Jane" or "dear old Jane." She owned copies of several of Harrison's works, including *Ancient Art and Ritual* "inscribed to her on Christmas 1923 from the author" (Marcus, *LP* 195); the Hogarth Press published Harrison's and her companion, Hope Mirrlees' translations from Russian in 1924, and Harrison's

Reminiscences in 1925. Woolf's intimate knowledge of Harrison's work has been assumed with justice by feminist scholars Jane Marcus and Bonnie Scott Kime, among others. The tribute to Harrison in *A Room of One's Own*, discussed in Chapter 3, as well as Woolf's use of Harrison as an example of the "immense" "advance in intellectual power" among women since the sixteenth century in "The Intellectual Status of Women," her counterattack to Desmond MacCarthy's claims in *The New Statesman* of women's intellectual inferiority, all show the inordinate respect she had for Harrison's scholarship (*DVW* II, 339). Marcus calls Harrison "Woolf's great role model and mentor" (*LP* 139), and analyzes in detail her influence on *A Room of One's Own*, *The Years* and *The Pargiters*, while Patricia Maika has discussed parallels with Harrison's work in *Between the Acts*.

The picture of Harrison that emerges from Woolf's diaries and letters is somewhat clouded by Woolf's ambivalent envy/distaste for Hope Mirrlees, Harrison's young companion with whom she lived and traveled in her later years, "over-dressed, over elaborate, scented, extravagant, yet with thick nose, thick ankles; a little unrefined" (*DVW* II, 75). Comments about Mirrlees, such as "she knows Greek and Russian better than I do French; is Jane Harrison's favourite pupil" and "do you admire her novels? — I can't get an ounce of joy from them, but we like seeing her and Jane billing and cooing together" indicate perhaps a hint of jealousy that Mirrlees, although vulgar and a poor novelist according to Woolf, won the love of such an admired maternal figure (*LVW* II 384–5; III 164).

For Woolf's respect for "Jane" is consistently evident: in a letter to Jacques Raverat, she describes Harrison as "a gallant old lady, very white, hoary, and sublime in a lace mantilla," and praises her "superb high thinking agnostic ways" (III 58). She records taking "tea with Jane, raised in bed, with her old white head lifted up, on pillows, very aged & rather exalted" a month before Harrison's death in April 1928 (*DVW* III, 176). Shortly thereafter, Woolf recalls this final visit, seeing her, "like a very old person, whom life has tossed up, & left; exalted, satisfied, exhausted," and Woolf returns home "to work & work, as hard as I can," perhaps with that image vivid in her mind of an "exalted" foremother who lived passionately for her work and died justly "satisfied" with her accomplishments (III, 180). In the same letter to Raverat, Woolf describes commiserating with Harrison over the "religious revival" and the "defection" of many of her generation back to the Christian church. Woolf's understanding of Harrison's lifelong antipathy to patriarchal religions is evident also in her description of Harrison's rather depressing Protestant funeral: "Who is 'God' & what the Grace of Christ? & what did they mean to Jane?" (*DVW* III, 181).

The similarities in their thought are striking, and in particular, the way in which their feminist visions reassert the transcendence of the female principle. Both associated merger and sensibility with femaleness, with the mother. Both associated individualism and rationalism with maleness, with the father. Both sought in their work to resurrect the primacy of mother over father, of mysticism over rationalism, of merger over separation, of collectivity over individuality. Although this impulse is apparent in all of Harrison's works, her most aggressive statements of it occur in the book she considered the culmination of all her work on ancient Greek religion, *Themis*.

In *Ancient Art and Ritual*, derived from *Themis*, Harrison wrote, "in the old ritual dance the individual was nothing, the choral band, the group, everything," while "in the heroic *saga* the individual is everything." The epic poet celebrates "*klea andron*, 'glorious deeds of men,' of individual heroes; and what these heroes themselves ardently long and pray for is just this glory, this personal distinction, this deathless fame for their great deeds" (159). So too, the gods of the Homeric period, the Olympians, express individualism and separation: "the highly personalized, individualized god is fashioned on the highly personalized, individualized self, and the essence of the sense of self is separateness, or consciousness of the severance of one self from other selves, and of that self as subject and distinct from objects" (*T* 473). Products of "consciousness," the Olympians represent an exaltation of rationality. "Such deities are not an instinctive expression, but a late and conscious representation, a work of analysis, of reflection and intelligence," unlike the more primitive "mystery-god" or "Year-Daimon" such as Dionysus, who "arises out of those instincts, emotions, desires which attend and express life" and are projections "rather of the group than of individual consciousness" (xii–xiii).

> Broadly speaking, these Olympians represent that tendency in thought which is towards reflection, differentiation, clearness, while the Eniautos-Daimon represents that other tendency in religion towards emotion, union, indivisibility.[1]   (xxi)

Harrison clearly relates the gender binarism of these two contrasting notions of deity to its origins in cultural conceptions of maternity and paternity. "The social structure represented by the Olympians is the same as that of the modern family, it is patrilinear," whereas the "figure of Dionysos, his thiasos, and his relation to his mother and the Maenads, is only to be understood by reference to an early social structure, known as matrilinear" (xxi). The *thiasos* is the group of attendant worshippers, themselves *daimones*, such as Dionysus' satyrs and Maenads, from whom he is never separate. For Harrison, the group marks the matriarchal deity, while the patriarchal god is essentially solitary.

> The divine figures of Mother and Child reflect the social condi-
> tions of a matriarchal group with its rite of adolescent initia-
> tion; its factors are the mother, the child, and the tribe, the
> child as babe and later as Kouros [young man].   (41)

Later, when "chiefly through the accumulation of property, matriar-chy passes and patriarchy takes its place, the relation of mother to child is less prominent; the child is viewed as part of the property of the father." Patriarchal religions reflect this shift by idealizing father and son, and attempting to erase mother (41). Thus the myths of miraculous paternal births, such as Athene from the forehead of Zeus or Dionysus' "second birth" from the thigh of Zeus, express the "super-imposition" of patriarchal cults over matriarchal.

No wonder Harrison was so "delighted" with the fragmentary *Hymn of the Kouretes*, discovered in the "temple of Diktaean Zeus" on Crete, and no wonder it became "the natural and necessary plot" for *Themis*. In it she finally found evidence that even the "Father of Gods and Men," the "archpatriarchal *bourgeois*" Zeus, had derived from matriarchal origins (xiv–xv). She had found a text that "embodied this very group-thinking, or rather group-emotion toward life," in which worshippers "sink their own personality and ... by dancing to a com-mon rhythm, above all by the common excitement, they become emotionally one, a true congregation, not a collection of individuals" (45–6). In the *Hymn of the Kouretes*, the young male dancers invoke Zeus as the "greatest Kouros, who was clearly a projection of the thiasos of his worshippers," i.e., a projection of themselves as a group (xiv–xv). Thus the *Hymn* portrayed, for Harrison, a Zeus prior to the solitary, individualized Olympian:

> Nowhere save in this Hymn do we hear of Zeus with attendant
> *daimones*. He stands always alone, aloof, approached with awe,

utterly delimited from his worshippers. ... The Hymn brings us face to face with the fact that Zeus once had a *thiasos*, once when he was a young man, a Kouros. When he grew up to be the Father, it seems, he lost his *thiasos* and has gone about unattended ever since. (12)

For Harrison, to disconnect from the *thiasos* is death for the god. Olympians are "the last product of rationalism, of individualistic thinking" and "cut off from the very source of their life and being, the emotion of the *thiasos*, they desiccate and die" (48), whereas in matriarchal religions, the "mystery-god" is an expression of emotion and of group unity, "the impulse of life through all things, perennial, indivisible" (476).

Harrison makes some leaps in her theory that are probably insupportable anthropologically, such as her belief in the widespread existence of matrilinear societies and her assumption that initiation rites of the "New Birth" to separate adolescent boys from women are associated only, or even primarily, with matriarchal cultures (36–8). The point is that her imaginative recreation of a female-dominated past, almost a feminist utopia, constituted a daring attack on the patriarchal intellectual establishment and its control of historical and scientific constructs. Indeed, Harrison's "Themis" is an attempt to restore a great mother behind all: "behind Gaia the Mother, and above even Zeus the Father, stands always the figure of Themis" (xxi–xxii). Themis *is* a manifestation of Gaia, but she is also beyond that a concept; she is "behind" and "above" mother and father, able to subsume their gender binarism within a larger all-embracing "female" context, according to Harrison. She is "Doom," but in the public sense, the judgment of the group, that constitutes the laws of civilization, indeed, civilization itself:

> Out of many *themistes* arose Themis. These *themistes*, these fixed conventions, stood to the Greek for all he held civilized. They were the bases alike of his kingship and of his democracy. These *themistes* are the ordinances of what must be done, what society compels; they are also, because what must be will be, the prophecies of what shall be in the future... (483)

Thus Themis is the basis of the *polis*, the "very spirit of the assembly incarnate." She is "the force that brings and binds men together, she is 'herd instinct,' the collective conscience, the social sanction" (485). Again, this "Themis" may be largely Harrison's recreation, but it is a daring one. All those concepts so dear to patriarchy: Athens as the flower of civilization, the *polis*, the *agora*, kingship, democracy, law, organized religion and ethics, *all* originate in the mother, in the female (for Harrison) concept of union and of collectivity.

It is even more interesting when object relations theory and Lacanian theory are applied, like a tissue overlay, to her reconstructions of Themis and of the matriarchal religions that lay behind all. It is apparent then that what her utopia symbolizes is a return to the preoedipal mother/child unity that is prior to any sense of subject as separate from object, prior to the intervention of the "law of the father" as the third term. As she herself wrote, the advent of the patriarchal Olympian gods signifies "consciousness of the severance of one self from other selves, and of that self as subject and distinct from objects" (473). In Lacanian theory, the father, symbolically as the phallus or "third term," breaks apart the preverbal dyad of mother/child. By prohibiting mother, the phallus creates loss and desire, which originates the formulation of symbolizing language, the basis of a first concept of self, and the internalization in the individual of the "law" of patriarchal culture, the "nom du père". For Harrison, as Lacan, the father is separation, individualism, "reflection, differentiation, clearness"; the mother is instinct, desire, "emotion, union, indivisibility" (xxi). The father is "the sense of the self [as] separateness," whereas the mother is the erasure of boundaries, the merger of self into a whole, "dancing to a common rhythm."

Amazingly, Harrison prefigures Julia Kristeva as well in her discussion of a primitive language derived from the mother that predates symbolic verbalization. Harrison's reading, like Woolf's, was remarkably wide-ranging and eclectic. She cites two anthropological sources, a Mr E.J. Payne's *History of the New World*, 1899, and a Mr Crawley's *Idea of the Soul*, 1909, for her discussion of "modern linguistic" (473–4). But the quotations from Mr Crawley and her interpretations of them, indicate that she went entirely her own way with their concepts:

> It used to be thought that language began with nouns, the names of things, to which later were added qualifying adjectives. Still later, it was held, these separate nouns were joined by verbs expressing relations between subject and object. ... Modern linguistic tells quite another and, for psychology and

primitive religion, a very instructive tale. Language, after the purely emotional interjection, began with whole sentences, *holophrases*, utterances of a relation in which subject and object have not yet got their heads above water but are submerged in a situation. ... As civilization advances, the holophrase, over-charged, distintegrates, and, bit by bit, object, subject and verb, and the other 'Parts of Speech' are abstracted from the stream of warm conscious human activity in which they were once submerged. (473–4).

What is Harrison's "holophrase" but Kristeva's "semiotic"? As a "signifying disposition," the semiotic "is not that of meaning or signi-fication: no sign, no predication, no signified object and therefore no consciousness of a transcendental ego" (Kristeva 133), just as Harrison's "holophrase" predates "nouns, the names of things" and their qualifiers, as well as verbs that express "a relation" between distinct or separated "subject and object." Attributes of the semiotic are "heterogeneousness," "rhythm" and "intonations" that express the "archaisms of the semiotic body," the body that is "dependent vis-a-vis the mother" (133, 136). Although semiotic processes "prepare the future speaker for entrance into meaning and signification (the symbolic)," they are "instinctual and maternal" (136).

Like Kristeva's semiotic, Harrison's holophrase does not express ideas but relations, and her water analogy reveals that it is a preoedipal maternal relation that is being expressed, "in which subject and object have not yet got their heads above water." The origins of this lan-guage are womb-like, as subject and object, child and mother, are "submerged" in a "stream of warm conscious human activity." Kristeva echoes Lacan when she writes that "language as symbolic function constitutes itself at the cost of repressing instinctual drive and con-tinuous relation to the mother" (136). So too for Harrison, it is the advance of patriarchal civilization that disintegrates the stream and abstracts the "Parts" from the whole. Gone is the *"holopsychosis*, that *symbiosis* of which the holophrase is the expression;" i.e., the symbiosis of the preoedipal mother/child dyad, which the holophrase expresses, is lost forever, repressed in the unconscious. The holophrase is a lan-guage that regresses to a preoedipal time, before object relations are realized, before the intervention of the paternal third term, and before separation into self and other. Just as Kristeva believes that poetic language can reinstate the "archaic, instinctual, and maternal territory"

(136–7), so Harrison's "savage" can re-experience "holopsychosis," a psychic memory of preoedipal oneness through "dancing to a common rhythm." "If he dances alone he will not dance long; but if his whole tribe dances together he will dance the live-long night and his emotion will mount to passion, to ecstasy," a mystical experience of the "unbounded Whole" in which transcendence of ego boundaries is achieved (43).

Thus Harrison's entire oeuvre, but particularly its culmination in *Themis*, constitutes, in Cixous' words, an "anti-logos weapon." She constructs a gigantic cultural "return to the body" in her recreation of a matriarchal past and her confiscation of spiritual transcendence for chthonic religions based on the mother/child dyad. No wonder she was ostracized and criticized by the academic establishment for being "intemperate" and "unreasonable"; she spoke a different language and told a different history. This, as Jane Marcus has contended, must have been inspirational for Woolf: "Rich in imaginative resourcefulness and eloquent in style, Harrison's work aroused Woolf's own quest for a female past" (*LP* 37). Like Eliot, Woolf shared a deep attraction for the spiritual collectivity Harrison advocated, but unlike Eliot, of course, she did not abandon this vision of spiritual and sociological unity at the door of a patriarchal faith. Woolf's and Harrison's work intersect at so many points, for Woolf, too, attempted to recreate a collective consciousness through her art, to dissolve subject/object separation, to defy ego boundaries, and to deconstruct patriarchal certitudes.

Woolf's antipathy to egotism is well known. Similar to Harrison's "individualism," she associated it with separation, isolation, with the father, and with male intellectual constructs. After describing her father's rages in *Moments of Being*, Woolf concludes: "The fact remains that at the age of sixty-five he was a man in prison, isolated. He had so ignored, or disguised his own feelings that he had no idea of what he was; and no idea of what other people were. ... From it all I gathered one obstinate and enduring conception; that nothing is so much to be dreaded as egotism" (146–7). James Naremore commented long ago that Woolf criticized Joyce's stream-of-consciousness technique in her essay "Modern Fiction" because "she felt that his experiments tended to imprison the reader inside an individual ego." By the time of *To the Lighthouse*, Naremore continues, "she had come more and more to describe a reality which transcends the self" (63). Like Harrison, her method was to try to recreate collective experience in her art, through a "multipersonal subjectivity": "even when she is depicting a kind of inner emotional life, she seems to stress that this life is not confined to individuals. Her books are full of scenes where whole groups of people share thoughts and become like a single organism — [for example] the skywriting airplane sequence in *Mrs. Dalloway*" (Naremore 73).

Jane Marcus, too, has discussed Woolf's view that the "ego is the enemy ... male, aggressive, and domineering." Again, similar to Harrison's derogation of individualism, Woolf's aversion to ego constitutes an "attempt to eliminate the father" from the "psychic triangle of mother, father, child" (*AA* 81–2). Both Marcus and Margaret Homans have commented on the famous passage in *Room of One's Own*, where the narrator becomes disgusted with the "I, I, I" that lays like a "straight dark bar" across a male narrative. She is "bored" with its "dominance" and its "aridity," for "nothing will grow there" (*AROO* 104). For Woolf "virility" is "self-consciousness," just as for Harrison the Olympian god is the culmination of "individualistic thinking." Cut off from collective emotion, "the very source of their life and being," the Olympians "desiccate and die," just as Woolf portrays the "aridity" and infertility of male egotism in art.

According to Marcus, not only do Woolf's "novels advance a collective idea of character," but they challenge the reader as well to give up "his individual relationship to author and text" and become "part of a collective audience" (*AA* 81–2), just as Harrison envisioned the origins of drama in collective rituals where "all are actors, all are doing the thing done, dancing the dance danced" (*AAR* 126). Like Harrison, Woolf attempts to replace the " 'egotistical sublime' of the patriarchy" with a "democratic feminist 'collective sublime' "(Marcus *AA* 81–2). According to Homans, too, Woolf's style "reverses the usual relations between margin and center [and] models an anti-authoritarian world. Woolf typically employs elusive, unlocatable speakers because, among other reasons, she deeply distrusts 'I'" (4–5). Homans cites Toril Moi, who has also defined Woolf as the stylist of "decentered" writing, who "undermine[s] the notion of the unitary self, the central concept of Western male humanism" (Moi 7). Harrison's texts, it is easy to see, also attempt to "reverse the usual relations between margin and center" by finding in matriarchal religions the "*origines*" of Greek civilization. She too "models an anti-authoritarian world" in her deconstruction of Olympian hierarchy and substitution of collective emotional experience as the source of Hellenic spirituality. She "undermines the notion of the unitary self" completely with her consistent emphasis upon "group-emotion."

Jane Marcus' suggestion that "Woolf's vatic charwomen and ancient crones embody Jane Harrison's concept of *Themis*," indeed, that all "Woolf's women are themis incarnate, the voice of civilization," is well worth pursuing in more detail in the case of Mrs. Ramsay (*LP* 17); moreover, Mr. Ramsay is Olympian Zeus as described by Harrison. The parental gender binarism of *To the Lighthouse* is exactly that of Harrison's patriarchal Olympians versus the matriarchal mystery-gods. Mr. Ramsay is isolation, "the last product of rationalism, of individualistic thinking"; Mrs. Ramsay is union, "the impulse of life through all things, perennial, indivisible." Mr. Ramsay is "analysis, reflection and intelligence"; Mrs. Ramsay is the "instincts, emotions, desires which attend and express life." Mr. Ramsay is symbolic logos; Mrs. Ramsay is semiotic holophrase.[2]

The contrast in the Ramsays' ways of thinking is immediately brought out in their disagreement over the weather and the following day's projected journey to the lighthouse. " 'It won't be fine' "; "What he said was true. It was always true. He was incapable of untruth; never tampered with a fact" (Woolf, *TL* 4). Whereas, attuned to her son's terrible disappointment, Mrs. Ramsay counters his "fact" with emotion, " 'But it may be fine — I expect it will be fine,' " (4). Mr. Ramsay is accordingly "enraged" by what he perceives as "the extraordinary irrationality of her remark, the folly of women's minds"; whereas, "to pursue truth with such astonishing lack of consideration for other people's feelings," is to Mrs. Ramsay "an outrage of human decency" (32).

Beating "up and down, up and down" the terrace, reciting Tennyson's "Charge of the Light Brigade," Mr. Ramsay identifies with "*klea andron*, 'glorious deeds of men,' of individual heroes," and he longs for "personal distinction" and "deathless fame for ... great deeds," to use Harrison's words. In Woolf's brilliant parody of his "splendid mind" striving to leap in thought from Q and R into the unknown, he can call upon all the epic heroic ideals to aid him: "Qualities that would have saved a ship's company exposed on the broiling sea ... endurance and justice, foreshight, devotion, skill, came to his help. ... Qualities that in a desolate expedition across the icy solitudes of the Polar region would have made him the leader, the guide ... came to his help again," but to no avail. He is "stuck at Q" (34–5). Woolf has shown the aridity of logos. "Analysis, reflection, intelligence" are inadequate for transcendence, and the longing for personal immortality is a hopeless one. "The very stone one kicks with one's boot will out-last Shakespeare," Mr. Ramsay realizes, and "his own little light would shine, not very brightly, for a year or two, and would then be merged in some bigger light, and that in a bigger still" (35).

Totally preoccupied by his place, or lack thereof, in a competitive world of individual "great men," Mr. Ramsay, like the Olympian Zeus, "stands always alone, aloof, approached with awe, utterly delimited from his worshippers," such as pathetic Charles Tansley. He attempts to console himself by belittling Shakespeare's genius with a skewed version of utilitarianism: "he would argue that the world exists for the average human being; that the arts are merely a decoration imposed on the top of human life; they do not express it. Nor is Shakespeare necessary to it" (43). He doesn't understand "precisely why it was that he wanted to disparage Shakespeare and come to the rescue of the man who stands eternally in the door of the lift," but the reader knows why. He *is* the man standing "eternally in the door of the lift," the "average human being" who cannot accept that he is one of the multitude, and longs for a genius he does not have, that would have enabled him to ascend in the lift to the top, and achieve the "deathless immortality" of a Shakespeare.

It is wonderfully ironic that his books are about " 'subject and object and the nature of reality' " (23), for he is the Lacanian third term, the "law of the father" that breaks apart the preodipal mother/child dyad, just as his presence interrupts the intimacy of James and his mother, claiming her and invoking his son's oedipal hatred. He is, like Harrison's Olympian god, the "consciousness of the severance of one self from other selves, and of that self as subject and distinct from objects." Once isolated from the objective world, how can the subjective mind know reality? " 'Think of the kitchen table,' " Andrew tells Lily, " 'when you're not there' " (23). There is, Lily thinks, a "muscular integrity" about the kitchen table, as there is about Mr. Ramsay, but she pictures it perched in the "silver-bossed" pear tree, and Woolf shows again, in this symbolic image, the limitations of rationalistic thought as compared to the perennial life force of fertility.

Mr. Ramsay realizes that it is "his fate, his peculiarity," to face isolation, "there to stand, like a desolate sea-bird, alone" (43–4). " 'We perished each alone,' " he quotes from Cowper's "The Castaway" in the third section. He stands for the tragedy of personal immolation in a patriarchal world that has renounced the "thiasos" and exalts the individual ego. As Harrison writes,

> All this, all life and that which is life and reality — Change
> and Movement — the Olympian renounces. Instead he chooses
> Deathlessness and Immutability — a seeming Immortality which
> is really the denial of life, for life is change.   (*T* 468)

Because "he had not done the thing he might have done," Mr.
Ramsay has to "deprecate" the "trifles" in which he finds his true "consolation" and his true happiness. " 'The father of eight children has no
choice,' " he sighs, "concealing" the "pleasure" he takes in his family
and his students — in his connections to others. William Bankes and
Lily "wonder why such concealments should be necessary," but to blame
husband- and fatherhood for his failure is a necessary disguise for the
preservation of his ego, "the refuge of a man afraid to own his own
feelings" (Woolf, *TL* 44–5). He longs for some vision of the lost solitude of his single days, where "One could walk all day without meet-
ing a soul. There was not a house scarcely, not a single village for miles
on end. One could worry things out alone" (69). Would he have fulfilled his genius had he not married, had he utterly isolated himself
alone with thought? Obviously not, for Woolf has already shown that
isolated rationality leads to sterility.

But Mr. Ramsay has not totally renounced "that which is life and
reality — Change and Movement." Intellectually sterile, he is also
physically fertile. His mythic avatars are multiple; not only is he Olympian Zeus, but as the father of eight he can also be identified with
Hades or Ploutos, at once the Lord of the Dead and the fertility god
who impregnates Demeter/Persephone, leading to the birth of the
Sacred Child at Eleusis. "The father of eight children — he reminded
himself. ... They would stem the flood a bit. That was a good bit of
work on the whole — his eight children" (69). Once admitting his
link to creation, his participation in the eternal stream of life, Mr.
Ramsay can feel some sense of accomplishment, despite the fact that
the "little island" of his own individual ego "seemed pathetically small,
half swallowed up in the sea" (69). Mrs. Ramsay "knew that he had
nothing whatever to complain of" because in his children, in the group,
lies his true immortality, the same immortality promised by chthonic,
matriarchal faiths such as the Eleusinian Mysteries (70).

Tina Barr has convincingly established that Mrs. Ramsay is a Demeter
figure and that Woolf closely parallels the Eleusinian Mysteries throughout *To the Lighthouse*, particularly in the ritualistic "Boeuf en Daube"
dinner scene. Mrs. Ramsay is an obvious "goddess of fertility" (Barr

132). Her association with fruit during the dinner scene is comparable to the offering of first fruits during the harvest ritual, the candles are associated with the Eleusinian torches, the pig that appears as the skull in the children's bedroom which Mrs. Ramsay wraps in her emblemmatic green shawl indicates the rebirth of fertility and life from death and sacrifice — these are only the most obvious parallels with Eleusis, and Barr cites numerous others in her detailed discussion (132–7).[3] But Mrs. Ramsay is also beyond the "genial Corn-Mother," beyond even Gaia, the Earth-mother. She is Harrison's Themis, "the force that brings and binds men together."

This is obvious in some of the most striking scenes in the novel, such as when Mr. Ramsay's rationalistic isolation has lead to "fatal sterility," and he seeks her out "to be taken within the circle of life" (37). Clearly she is a Demeter here, a fertility goddess with her spray of "delicious fecundity," but beyond that she is also Themis, drawing the isolated ego back into the group, so that she can assure him "that he too lived in the heart of life; was needed; not here only, but all over the world" (Woolf, *TL* 37). Like Harrison's patriarchal Olympians versus matriarchal mystery-gods, there are contrasting versions of immortality here. The intellectuality and individual heroism through which Mr. Ramsay longs to establish his immortality are barren, whereas the group of which he is an integral part through his marriage to her participates in perennial life, "it was real; the house was full; the garden blowing" (38).

Mrs. Ramsay is Themis, "the very spirit of the assembly incarnate," as well as Demeter, during the dinner scene. As it begins, she is distraught because "Nothing seemed to have merged. They all sat separate." She feels that "the whole of the effort of merging and flowing and creating rested on her" (82). By the time the candles are lit the group has begun to cohere, and within their coherence to experience consolation for the inevitable flow of life and death: "they were all conscious of making a party together in a hollow, on an island; had their common cause against that fluidity out there" (97). By the end of the dinner Mrs. Ramsay has fully established her vision of "eternity," as she peers "into the depths of the earthenware pot" like a matriarchal priestess (105). It is identical to Harrison's "group-thinking, or rather group-emotion toward life," in which worshippers "sink their own personality and ... become emotionally one, a true congregation, not a collection of individuals." The individuals around the Ramsays' dinner table are united into such a congregation and, "Of

such moments," Mrs. Ramsay thinks, "the thing is made that en-
dures" (105).

Many writers have commented upon the profound ambivalence in
Woolf's portrayal of the mother here.[4] In order to draw them all together, male and female, Mrs. Ramsay exerts a force of will that is
"irresistible" and truly "frightening" (101). Lily will "be nice" to Charles
Tansley for once, despite her dread of compromising herself, and Minta
will marry Paul, despite the fact that their marriage is a failure in the
end. Lily feels ambivalently that Mrs. Ramsay leads "her victims to
the altar" as well as inspiring "the emotion, the vibration, of love"
that fills their lives with "abundance" (101). This same seeming para-
dox is true of Harrison's Themis, who is at once the force of "social
sanction," "the collective doom, public opinion" that "begins in convention" and ends as "Law and Justice," and also "the stuff of which
religion is made ... the substratum of each and every god." Themis,
"like Doom begins on earth and ends in heaven" (483–4). Mrs. Ramsay
has just such a dual manifestation. She is the mundane Demeter, guardian of hearth and home, who coerces through the force of "social im-
perative," and she is also a conceptual Themis, and in that aspect she
defies the boundaries of subject/object and generates union through
her association with rhythm, just as Harrison's dancers achieve transcendence through dancing to "a common rhythm." She *is* the pulsating
third stroke of the lighthouse; she also feels time as "the old familiar
pulse ... beating," compelling her to draw those around the table together, and her words echo "rhythmically ... more rhythmically and
more nonsensically," lulling Cam to sleep (63, 83, 115)

Harrison's conception of matriarchal religion is based upon the
preoedipal mother/child dyad; likewise the purple triangle that is Lily's
abstract rendition of Mrs. Ramsay and James functions as a symbol of
dyadic union. "A mother and child might be reduced to a shadow
without irreverence" (53). The form represents a reduction, a merger
of boundaries between the "human shape[s]" of mother and child that
indicates Lily's longing for return to preoedipal oneness with or within
the mother's body. "Sitting on the floor with her arms around Mrs.
Ramsay's knees" is as "close as she could get," and she longs to make
her art "a device for becoming, like waters poured into one jar, inextricably the same, one with the object one adored" (50–1). She tries to
express the "holopsychosis" through the "holophrase" of her art. She
seeks, not the parts, but the whole; not logos, but semiotic unity, "for
it was not knowledge but unity that she desired, not inscriptions on

tablets, nothing that could be written in any language known to men, but intimacy itself, which is knowledge" (51).

Mrs. Ramsay is, like Themis, a conceptual manifestation of subject/object merger. As subject herself, she consistently defies ego boundaries and melds with the objective world. "It was odd, she thought, how if one was alone, one leant to inanimate things; trees, streams, flowers; felt they expressed one; felt they became one; felt they knew one, in a sense were one" (63). Her thought processes, which are not even thought but just "sitting and looking," lead to nonverbal transcendence, as opposed to the deadend of Mr. Ramsay's philosophical gropings. Silent and alone, she shrinks "with a sense of solemnity, to being oneself, a wedge-shaped core of darkness," evoking the image of the purple triangle again (62). As she knits, "her horizon seemed to her limitless" because she has escaped the boundaries of self: "This core of darkness could go anywhere, for no one saw it" (62).

> Not as oneself did one find rest ever, in her experience ... but as a wedge of darkness. Losing personality, one lost the fret, the hurry, the stir; and there rose to her lips always some exclamation of triumph over life when things came together in this peace, this rest, this eternity; and pausing there she looked out to meet that stroke of the Lighthouse, the long steady stroke, the last of the three, which was her stroke. ... Often she found herself sitting and looking, sitting and looking, with her work in her hands until she became the thing she looked at — that light, for instance. (63)

In this passage she experiences the same eternity that Harrison's dancers participate in, "losing personality," as they "sink their own personality," coming together in a rhythmic beat, the third stroke, the pulse of blood, the rhythm of the mother's heart above the womb. "This peace, this rest, this eternity" is repeated at the end of the dinner scene — "again tonight she had the feeling she had had once today already" — as she brings this communion, which she can experience alone, to the group (105).

How different is her solitude from Mr. Ramsay's! Her mind is always interacting with the objective world, whereas he is withdrawn "like a person in a dream" (70). Woolf draws out this contrast in their walk together, which is continually punctuated by her subtextual relations with the objective world of greenhouse, bulbs, flowers, molehills, rabbits (66–70). Finally, "looking up, she saw above the thin trees the first pulse of the full-throbbing star, and wanted to make her husband look at it; for the sight gave her such keen pleasure. But she stopped herself. He never looked at things. If he did, all he would say would be, Poor little world, with one of his sighs" (71). He is the denatured product of a patriarchal culture that, like the Olympians when they "mounted from Olympos to the upper air," became "ashamed of their earth-origin and resolved to repudiate their snake-tails" (Harrison, *T* 451). The Olympian "claims to be immortal," but "the real true god, the Eniautos-daimon, lives and works for his people; he does more he dies for them" — as does Mrs. Ramsay (467).

Barr correctly identifies Lily with Persephone. Clearly, she is the maiden Kore who rises from death, so graphically portrayed as the engulfing powers of night, time, and war in the second section "Time Passes," to reaffirm creation and rebirth through her art in the third section of Woolf's novel. Barr also interestingly points out that Lily and Mrs. Ramsay have exchanged roles by the end:

> In "The Lighthouse" section of the novel, Woolf reverses the position of Lily and Mrs. Ramsay. Lily, at the moment of epiphany, will become identified with Demeter, calling back Mrs. Ramsay as Persephone. She will become both mother and daughter, artist and priestess at Eleusis.   (139)

But Barr sees this relationship as adversarial: Mrs. Ramsay has "relinquished her role as Demeter, creator to Lily" and become "subdued to Lily's will" (135, 142). This is not in accord with the Demeter/Persephone archetype as portrayed by either of what were, undoubtedly, Woolf's sources for the myth and the rituals of Eleusis, Frazer and Harrison. Both stress, as we have seen, that Demeter and Persephone are essentially one, as Harrison puts it, "the older and younger form of the same person." For Harrison, they become differentiated only in that the "Mother takes the physical side, the Daughter the spiritual. ... Demeter as Thesmophoros has for her sphere more and more the things of this life, laws and civilized marriage," while, becoming Queen of the Underworld, Persephone "withdraws herself more and more to the kingdom of the spirit, the things below and beyond" (*PSGR* 275–6).

Mrs. Ramsay and Lily are differentiated in exactly this way. Woolf is clear that both are artists, Mrs. Ramsay in the things of this life —

"bringing them together ... making of the moment something permanent"— and Lily "in another sphere" beyond life, her art, also attempting to grasp permanence out of evanescence (161). Although different in form, the act of creation for both is experientially the same. Lily does not "subsume" or "conquer" the mother in order to become creator as Barr insists; rather she invokes her, to experience communion with her (131, 144). Similar to Stephen in *Ulysses* or Harry in *The Family Reunion*, the artist must experience union with the generative mother in order to become fully creative, because she is the life force.

Harrison wrote, "Art in some sense springs out of Religion," and the connecting "bridge" between them "is ritual" (*R* 84). Lily's act of artistic creation is ritualistic, and in that sense, religious. It begins in rhythm, "And so pausing and so flickering, she attained a dancing rhythmical movement, as if the pauses were one part of the rhythm and the strokes another, and all were related" (158). Although the rhythm is interrupted by her thought processes — memories, fears, her "perpetual combat" with the images she is trying to express — as long as "her hand quivered with life, this rhythm was strong enough to bear her along with it on its current." And its current leads to the loss of ego boundaries "as she lost consciousness of outer things, and her name and her personality and her appearance" (159).

The resulting image is a reprisal of the purple triangle, the "wedge of darkness" now recalled as "that woman sitting there writing under the rock [who] resolved everything into simplicity" (160). Lily's physical longing to be reunited with the semiotic body, "that essence which sat by the boat, ... that woman in grey," is excruciating. Logos is utterly inadequate to express "these emotions of the body." "It was one's body feeling, not one's mind" that Lily is trying to portray (the holopsychosis), which is why she must use an abstract art (the holophrase), one that, in Kristeva's words, does not refer "to a signified object for a thetic consciousness" (133).

Stepping "off her strip of board into the waters of annihilation," i.e., with the boundaries of self utterly annihilated, Lily invokes Mrs. Ramsay, who comes, summoned from the dead, as Barr has pointed out, in virginal white and among flowers associating her with Persephone. Lily has had her "vision," and like any transcendent vision, it cannot be maintained in life, but must be "perpetually remade" (181). However, it is not the work of art that is eternal, "It would be hung in the attics, ... it would be destroyed"; rather, through her "vision" Lily participates, briefly, in an eternal life force (208).

Unlike Mr. Ramsay, she doesn't agonize over the transience of her work. It is through the act, the *dromenon*, to use Harrison's term, that eternity is experienced. *To the Lighthouse* is as much about religious transcendence as it is about artistic creation.

We have seen that in the first section Lily longs for a return to preoedipal union with the mother. In the third section she achieves it. In addition to Mrs. Ramsay's mythic manifestation as Demeter/ Persephone, she is Themis, a "vision" of reunion with the m/Other. Harrison believed that god is born in moments of "group-emotion" when ego boundaries are erased, and when, primarily through rhythm, the many become one (*T* 45–6). She identified these moments of transcendence only in relation to matriarchal mystery religions based upon the mother/child dyad. Woolf's portrayal of Lily's creative act reveals that she believed art is born in the same way, through escaping the boundaries of self and through union with a larger creative, maternal force. For both, the semiotic body is the origin of creativity. As Lily thinks, "She owed it all to her" (161).

ENDNOTES

Chapter 2

1. Thus Tylor and Harrison join a battery of modernists, most notoriously Conrad and Lawrence, who project a primitive "Other" as antidote to a degenerate West. While nostalgically exalting primitives, their narratives still paradoxically reinforce Western imperialist binarisms, as postcolonial critics such as Edward Said and Marianna Torgovnick have established: "The West's image of Africa allows Westerners to play out their sense of the *West's* degenerate condition and to use 'Africa' or other sites of 'the primitive' as fantasized locales for transcendence and renewal" (Torgovnick 275). See Marianna Torgovnick, *Gone Primitive: Savage Intellects, Modern Lives,* Chicago and London: U of Chicago P, 1990. Also Edward Said, *Culture and Imperialism,* New York, Vintage/Random, 1993.

Chapter 3

1. The best general appraisal of Harrison remains Robert Allen Ackerman's several articles from the early 1970s. See "Some Letters of the Cambridge Ritualists," *Greek, Roman and Byzantine Studies* 12 (Spring 1971): 113–136; "Jane Ellen Harrison: The Early Work," *Greek, Roman and Byzantine Studies* 13 (Summer 1972): 209–230; "Frazer on Myth and Ritual," *Journal of the History of Ideas* 36, 1975: 115–134. See also Harry C. Payne, "Modernizing the Ancients: The Reconstruction of Ritual Drama 1870–1920," *Proceedings of the American Philosophical Society* 122 (June 1978): 182–192. It is regrettable that Ackerman chose to write a biography of Frazer instead of Harrison, since Sandra J. Peacock's 1988 biography, *Jane Ellen Harrison: The Mask and the Self* (New Haven: Yale UP) is disappointing. It adds no new material to Harrison studies and reduces her considerable scholarly achievement to a simplistic "Freudian" analysis of her "rage" at "Cornford, her father, and a host of men who betrayed her" and her "inability to separate individual, personal hurt from the general notion of masculine power" (198). Peacock undermines the gynocritical enterprise of reevaluating the work of a marginalized woman writer by focusing on Harrison's love life, and never discussing her work either in the light of feminist theory or classical studies.

Chapter 4

1. See Marilyn French, *The Book as World: James Joyce's "Ulysses,"* Cambridge: Harvard UP, 1976, pp. 243–61; William Walcott, "Notes by a Jungian Analyst on the Dreams in *Ulysses,*" *JJQ,* 9 (Fall 1971), 41; S.L. Goldberg, *The*

Classical Temper: A Study of James Joyce's "Ulysses," London: Chatto and Windus, 1961, p. 293.

2. Because many different editions of Joyce's *Ulysses* are used, I have followed the *James Joyce Quarterly's* system of annotation, citing chapter and line numbers, instead of page numbers, for quotations from *Ulysses*.

3. Contemporary sources for the Eleusinian Mysteries include: Karoli Kerenyi, *Eleusis: Archetypal Image of Mother and Daughter*, Trans. Ralph Manheim, NY: Schocken Books, 1977 (orig. pub. Bollingen Foundation, 1967); George E. Mylonas, *Eleusis and the Eleusinian Mysteries*, Princeton: Princeton UP, 1961; R. Gordon Wasson, Albert Hofmann, and Carl A.P. Ruck, *The Road to Eleusis: Unveiling the Secret of the Mysteries*, NY: HBJ, 1978. Wasson and Ruck's account is delightfully Timothy Leary-esque; they claim to have discovered the barley-based psychotropic drug used in the *kykeon* and so conclude that all the initiates were hallucinating. Mylonas' version seems to be the most thorough, but he has definite views as to what was or was not included in the rituals at Eleusis and rules out other interpretations rather too categorically. Kerenyi's discussion seems the most spiritually oriented.

4. While much attention has been focused on Stephen's dream, relatively little has been said about Bloom's, beyond the fact that it obviously echoes Stephen's. William Walcott, a Jungian psychologist, finds that "there is not enough of Bloom's dream to have any confidence about the meaning" (45), but we can understand Bloom's dream fragment if we see that he envisions himself playing a hierophantic role toward Stephen. When he recalls "Come in. All is prepared. I dreamt. What?" his prophetic dream suggests that the hierophant's ritual objects — torch, communal chalice, *sacra*, and *kykeon* — are prepared as he invites the initiate into the *telesterion* where the climactic visions are experienced (*U* 13.878).

5. See Joseph Allen Boone, "A New Approach to Bloom as 'Womanly Man': The Mixed Middlings in *Ulysses*," *JJQ*, 20 (Fall 1982): 67–85; Suzette A. Henke, "Speculum of the Other Molly: A Feminist/ Psychoanalytic Inquiry into James Joyce's Politics of Desire." *Mosaic*, Spring 21 (2–3): 149–164; Cheryl Herr, " 'One Good Turn Deserves Another': Theatrical Cross-Dressing in Joyce's 'Circe' Episode," *Journal of Modern Literature* VII(2) (July 1984): 263–276; Carol Siegel, "'Venus Metempsychosis' and Venus in Furs: Masochism and Fertility in *Ulysses*." *Twentieth Century Literature*, Summer 33 (1987): 179–195.

Chapter 5

1. The essay is unavailable. Peter Ackroyd discovered Eliot's reference to it in a letter of 11 March 1935 to Rayner Heppenstall, evidence of how enduring Eliot found his early research in anthropology (48). The letter belongs to the

Harry Ransom Humanities Research Center at The University of Texas at Austin, from whom I have received a summary. In his Harvard essay, "Eliot says he argued against the tendency, in studies of primitive tribes, to explain belief or practices only as rationalizations of ritual. Eliot felt that ritual and belief were more interrelated and interactive, but hesitated to assign primacy of cause to either ritual or belief."

2. See Nancy Chodorow, *The Reproduction of Mothering*, Berkeley: U of Ca P, 1978 and Dorothy Dinnerstein, *The Mermaid and the Minotaur*, NY: Harper Collins, 1976.

Chapter 6

1. All future references to these texts will be to these editions.

2. E. Martin Browne, Eliot's director, called *The Family Reunion* "the most diffi-cult to apprehend of Eliot's plays" (90). The long letter Eliot wrote to Browne adds much to an understanding, particularly, of Mary. According to Browne, Mary was "the one who was least clearly conceived at first ... yet she is one of the most important people in the pattern of Harry's redemption," and much of her final richness of character is due to Browne's gentle prodding (112). In the letter Eliot responds to Browne and his wife Henzie's opinion that perhaps "to marry her may have been Harry's right way of nullifying the curse: there might have been real love between them" (103). Eliot was so opposed to the idea of Mary as an endpoint for Harry, that he misunderstood their suggestion that marriage with Mary "might have been" an answer in Harry's past, as Browne points out (116), and read it instead as a proposal that it ought to be Harry's future:

> Now, as to Harry's marrying Mary as a right way of ending the 'curse', here I feel on surer ground. The point of Mary, in relation to Harry, was meant to be this. The effect of his married life upon him was one of such horror as to leave him for the time at least in a state that may be called one of being psychologically partially desexed: or rather, it has given him a horror of women as of unclean creatures. The scene with Mary is meant to bring out, as I am aware it fails to, the conflict inside him between this repulsion for Mary as a woman, and the at-traction which the *normal* part of him that is still left, feels towards her personally *for the first time*. This is the first time since his marriage ('there was no ecstasy') that he has been attracted towards any woman. This attraction glimmers for a moment in his mind, half-consciously as a possible 'way of escape'; and the Furies (for the Furies are *divine* instruments, not simple hell-hounds) come in the nick of time to warn him away from this evasion — though at that moment he misunder-stands their function. (107)

In this letter we can see shades of the marriage that brought Eliot "near to nervous collapse," and his description of the marital "horror" that leaves Harry "psychologically partially desexed" again may explain the castration imagery of the Sweeney poems. As Peter Ackroyd reveals in his biography, Vivien's mental and physical illnesses and her unquenchable demands for his attention drove Eliot to a state of "aggression and brooding on female sexuality" (150) in which he too saw women as "unclean creatures." Mary represents a fictional indication of returning health, a recovery from "repulsion" to "attraction," but Eliot insists that she remain only a first step in Harry's development. Union with her would be an "evasion" of his purely spiritual vocation, and the Furies remind him that his quest must be for "a world" beyond "*this* world," beyond Mary's world of physical creation.

3. Parallels between Harry and Hamlet have been suggested, but unfortunately not fully explored thus far. Matthiesen notes that there are "some echoes of *Hamlet* in Harry's situation," particularly in the "disease" imagery of his conversation with Warburton before dinner, in which Harry compares cancer and murder (168; see also Carol Smith 140). Since Warburton has been summoned to "spy out the cause of Harry's neurosis," Matthiesen equates him with Polonius, but he and Barber both point out that Eliot's criticism of Shakespeare's inability to find an adequate "objective equivalent" for Hamlet's feelings, might equally be applied to his own creation (169; 427).

Chapter 7

1. Harrison coined the phrase "Eniautos-Daimon" to name the amorphous deity invoked almost universally in ancient fertility rituals. It really parallels Frazer's concept of the "Dying God" or king, ritually slaughtered and resurrected to mimic nature's seasonal cycles and to stimulate fertility, but once again, while acknowledging her "immeasurable ... debt" to Frazer, Harrison finds his" 'Vegetation Spirit' ... inadequate." She wanted "a word that should include not only vegetation, but the whole world-process of decay, death, renewal," and she found it in "Eniautos," meaning "a cycle of waxing and waning. ... a cardinal factor in Greek religion" (*T* xvii).

2. Bonnie Kime Scott briefly mentions the applicability of Harrison's "holophrases" to Woolf's expression of "wholeness" through her use of language, but she does not elaborate. See *Refiguring Modernism* II, Bloomington: Indiana UP, 1995, p. 6.

3. My only quibble with Barr's excellent discussion is that most of her sources for the Eleusinian Mysteries are contemporary ones that Woolf could not possibly have read. Where these sources agree as to the content of the Mysteries with what were Woolf's sources — Frazer's *Golden Bough* and Harrison's *Prolegomena* — Barr's argument is convincing. But there is no way Woolf could have paralleled, for instance, Mr. Ramsay's boots with the " 'fancy boots' " worn by the hierophant, since this

detail, to my knowledge, appears only in the 1965 source cited by Barr (141). Had Barr known of Harrison's and Frazer's repeated emphasis upon the essential unity of Demeter and Persephone as one goddess, she would not have had to resort to "modernist irony" as a way to explain Lily's transformation from Persephone into Demeter and Mrs. Ramsay's from Demeter to Persephone, nor seen their relationship as a struggle for dominance (141). Likewise, had she known of the sacred marriage and birth that Frazer and Harrison both theorize occured during the Mysteries, instead of relying upon Mylonas' 1961 view that we can never know what took place, she might have carried her fascinating analogies even further (138). As a reaffirmation of creative power, for instance, perhaps Lily's painting is the sacred child born to both mother and daughter at Eleusis.

4. See, for example, Jane Lilienfeld, "The Deceptiveness of Beauty: Mother Love and Mother Hate in *To the Lighthouse*," *Twentieth Century Literature* 23 (October 1977): pp. 345–76; Maria DiBattista, *Virginia Woolf's Major Novels*, New Haven: Yale UP, 1980, pp. 75–84; Jane Marcus, *Art and Anger*, Columbus: Ohio State UP, 1988, p. 93.

WORKS CITED

Ackroyd, Peter. *T.S. Eliot, A Life*. New York: Simon and Schuster, 1984.

Arrowsmith, William. "The Poem as Palimpsest: A Dialogue on Eliot's 'Sweeney Erect.' " *The Southern Review* 17 (January 1981): 17–68.

Baldridge, Marie. "Some Psychological Patterns in the Poetry of T.S. Eliot." *Critical Essays on T.S. Eliot: The Sweeney Motif*. Ed. Kinley E. Roby. Boston: G.K. Hall & Co., 1985, 48.

Barber, C.L. "Strange Gods at T.S. Eliot's 'The Family Reunion' " (1940). *T.S. Eliot: A Selected Critique*. Ed. Leonard Unger. New York: Rinehart & Co., Inc., 1948, 415–443.

Barr, Tina. "Divine Politics: Virginia Woolf's Journey toward Eleusis in *To the Light-house*." *boundary 2* 20:1, 1993, 125–145.

Block, Haskell, M. "Cultural Anthropology and Contemporary Literary Criticism." *Myth and Literature: Contemporary Theory and Practice*. Ed. John B. Vickery. Lincoln: U of Nebraska P, 1966, 129–138.

Bodkin, Maud. "The Eumenides and Present-Day Consciousness." *Adelphi*, xv, (May 1939) 411–13. Rep. in *T.S.Eliot: The Critical Heritage*. Ed. Michael Grant. Vol. 2. London: Routledge & Kegan Paul, 1976, 384–7.

—— *The Quest for Salvation in an Ancient and a Modern Play*. London: Oxford UP, 1941.

Boone, Joseph Allen. "A New Approach to Bloom as 'Womanly Man': The Mixed Middlings Progess in *Ulysses*." *James Joyce Quarterly*, 20 (Fall 1982), 67–85.

Brivic, Sheldon. *Joyce Between Freud and Jung*. Port Washington NY: Kennikat Press, 1980.

Brown, Ivor. "Review." *Observer*, 26 March 1939, 15. Rep. in *T.S. Eliot: The Critical Heritage*. Ed. Michael Grant. Vol. 2. London: Routledge & Kegan Paul, 1976, 375–7.

Browne, Martin, E. *The Making of T.S. Eliot's Plays*. Cambridge: At the University Press, 1969.

Cixous, Hélène. "Castration or Decapitation?" Trans. Annette Kuhn. *Signs: Journal of Women in Culture and Society* 7:1, 1981, 36–55.

Connolly, Thomas. *The Personal Library of James Joyce: A Descriptive Bibliography*. University of Buffalo Studies. Vol. 22, No. 1. Buffalo: U of Buffalo P, 1955.

Cook, Arthur Bernard. *Zeus*. Cambridge: At the University Press, 1915.

Cornford, F. M. *Thucydides Mythistoricus* (1907). New York: Greenwood Press, 1969.

— *The Origin of Attic Comedy* (1914). 2nd ed. Cambridge: At the University Press, 1934.

Crawley, Ernest. *The Mystic Rose: A Study of Primitive Marriage.* London: Macmillan and Co., 1902.

Darwin, Charles. *The Descent of Man, And Selection in Relation to Sex* (1871). Eds. Bonner and May. Princeton: Princeton UP, 1981.

Deleuze, Gilles. "Coldness and Cruelty." *Masochism.* New York: Zone Books, 1991, 15–138.

Eliot, T.S. "*Ulysses*, Order, and Myth." "Marie Lloyd." "The Use of Poetry and the Use of Criticism." "Poetry and Drama." *Selected Prose of T.S. Eliot.* Ed. Frank Kermode. New York: Harcourt Brace Jovanovich, 1975.

— "The Beating of a Drum." *Nation and Athenaeum*, 6 Oct. 1923.

— *The Complete Poems and Plays.* New York: Harcourt Brace and World Inc., 1971.

— "Euripides and Gilbert Murray." *Art and Letters*, III (Spring 1920): 38. Rep. in *The Sacred Wood.* New York: Alfred A. Knopf Inc., 1930.

— "Four Elizabethan Dramatists." "The Ballet." *The Criterion.* II, 6 (February 1924): 115; III, 2 (April 1925): 441.

— "A Prediction in Regard to Three English Authors." *Vanity Fair.* XXI, 6 (February 1924): 29.

— "War–Paint and Feathers." *The Athenaeum.* October 17, 1919: 1036.

Ellmann, Richard. *James Joyce.* New York: Oxford UP, 1959.

Feldman, Thalia. "Gorgo and the Origins of Fear." *Arion* IV (1965): 484–494.

Freud, Sigmund. "Medusa's Head" (1922). *Collected Papers* V. Ed. James Strachey. New York: Basic Books, Inc., 1953.

Fitzgerald, Robert, Trans. *Sophocles I: Oedipus at Colonus.* The Complete Greek Tragedies. Eds. David Grene and Richmond Lattimore. Chicago: U of Chicago. P, 1954, 77–155.

Frazer, Sir James George. *The Golden Bough.* 3rd edition. Part I, vol. 1; Part IV, vol. 1; Part V, vols. 1 & 2. London: Macmillan and Co. Ltd., 1911.

Fontenrose, Joseph. *The Ritual Theory of Myth.* Folklore Studies: 18. Berkeley: U of California P, 1966.

Forster, E.M. *Howards End.* New York: Vintage, 1958.

Gilbert, Sandra M. and Susan Gubar. *No Man's Land: The Place of the Woman Writer in the Twentieth Century.* Vol. 1, *The War of the Words.* New Haven: Yale UP, 1988.

Gilbert, Stuart. *James Joyce's Ulysses: A Study*. New York: Vintage, 1956.

Hargrove, Nancy D. "The Symbolism of Sweeney in the Works of T. S. Eliot." *Critical Essays on T.S. Eliot: The Sweeney Motif*. Ed. Kinley E. Roby. Boston: G.K. Hall and Co., 1985, 147–169.

Harrison, Jane Ellen. *Ancient Art and Ritual*. "The Home University Library." London: Williams & Norgate, 1913.

— *Alpha and Omega*. London: Sidgwick & Jackson Ltd., 1915.

— *Mythology*. Boston: Marshall Jones Co., 1924.

— *Prolegomena to the Study of Greek Religion*. Cambridge: At the University Press, 1903.

— *Reminiscences of a Student's Life*. London: Hogarth Press, 1925.

— *Themis*. Cleveland and New York: The World Publishing Co., 1912, 1927.

— "Zeus and Dionysos" (review of A.B. Cook's *Zeus*). *The Spectator*. February 27, 1915: 303–304.

Herring, Philip. Ed. *Joyce's Ulysses Notesheets in the British Museum*. Charlottesville: UP of Virginia, 1972.

— *Joyce's Notes and Early Drafts for Ulysses: Selections from the Buffalo Collection*. Charlottesville: UP of Virginia, 1977.

Homans, Margaret. Ed. and Introduction. *Virginia Woolf: A Collection of Critical Essays*. Englewood Cliffs, N.J.: Prentice Hall, 1993.

Horney, Karen. "The Dread of Woman." *International Journal of Psycho-Analysis* XIII 1932: 348–360.

Hyman, Stanley Edgar. "The Ritual View of Myth and the Mythic." *Myth and Literature: Contemporary Theory and Practice*. Ed. John B. Vickery. Lincoln: U of Nebraska P, 1966, 47–58.

Irving, John A. "The Comparative Method and the Nature of Human Nature." *Philosophy and Phenomenological Research,* Vol. 9 (March 1949): 545–556.

Jones, David E. *The Plays of T.S. Eliot*. Toronto: U of Toronto. P, 1960.

Jones, Ernest. *Hamlet and Oedipus*. New York: W.W. Norton, 1976.

Joyce, James. *Ulysses*. Ed. Hans Walter Gabler. New York: Random House, 1986.

Kerenyi, Karoli. "Kore." *Essays on a Science of Mythology: The Myth of the Divine Child and the Mysteries of Eleusis.* Bollingen Series #22. Princeton: Princeton UP, 1969, 101–155.

Kluckhohn, Clyde. "Myths and Rituals: A General Theory." *Myth and Literature: Contemporary Theory and Practice.* Ed. John B. Vickery. Lincoln: U of Nebraska P, 1966, 33–44.

Kristeva, Julia. *Desire in Language: A Semiotic Approach to Literature and Art.* Ed. Leon S. Roudiez. New York: Columbia UP, 1980.

Lacan, Jacques. "The signification of the phallus." *Ecrits.* Trans. Alan Sheridan. New York: W.W. Norton, 1977, 281–291.

Lang, Andrew. *Custom and Myth* 1884. New York: AMS Press, 1968.

— "The Golden Bough." *Fortnightly Review.* Vol. LXIX New Series (LXXV Old Series). Jan to June 1901: 235–248.

— *The Homeric Hymns, A New Prose Translation and Essays, Literary and Mythological* (1899). Freeport, NY: Books for the Librairies Press, 1972.

— *Modern Mythology* (1897). New York: AMS Press, 1968.

— *Myth, Ritual and Religion* (1887). New York: AMS Press, 1968.

Lattimore, Richmond, Trans. *The Odyssey of Homer.* New York: Harper and Row, 1965.

— *Aeschylus I: Oresteia.* The Complete Greek Tragedies. Eds. David Grene and Richmond Lattimore. Chicago: U of Chicago P, 1953.

Lawrence, D. H. "The Novel and the Feelings." *Phoenix* I. Ed. Edward McDonald. New York: Viking, 1964, 755–760.

Lévy-Bruhl, Lucien. *How Natives Think.* Trans. Lilian A. Clare. London: George Allen and Unwin Ltd., 1926.

MacCarthy, Desmond. "Some Notes on Mr. Eliot's New Play." *New Statesman*, xvii. (25 March 1939). Rep. in *T.S. Eliot: The Critical Heritage.* Ed. Michael Grant. Vol. 2. London: Routledge & Kegan Paul, 1976, 371–5.

Madtes, Richard E. "Joyce and the Building of Ithaca." *ELH*, XXXI (Dec. 1964): 443–459.

Maika, Patricia. *Virginia Woolf's Between the Acts and Jane Harrison's Conspiracy.* Ann Arbor: UMI Research Press, 1984.

Marcus, Jane. *Art & Anger.* Columbus: Ohio UP, 1988.

— *Virginia Woolf and the Languages of Patriarchy.* Bloomington: Indiana UP, 1987.

Marett, R.R., Ed. *Anthropology and the Classics*. Oxford: Clarendon Press, 1908.

Matthiessen, F.O. *The Achievement of T.S. Eliot*. New York: Oxford UP, 1947.

McCarroll, David. L. "Stephen's Dream — and Bloom's." *James Joyce Quarterly*, 6 (1969): 174–76.

Moi, Toril. *Sexual Textual Politics: Feminist Literary Theory*. London: Routledge, 1985.

Murray, Gilbert. *Aeschylus, The Creator of Tragedy*. Oxford: At the Clarendon Press, 1940.

— *Five Stages of Greek Religion*. 3rd edition of *Four Stages of Greek Religion* (1912). New York: Doubleday and Co. Inc. 1951.

— *Jane Ellen Harrison, An Address Delivered at Newnham College*. Cambridge: W. Heffer & Sons Ltd., 1928.

— *The Rise of the Greek Epic* (1907). New York: Oxford UP, 1960.

Mylonas, George E. *Eleusis and the Eleusinian Mysteries*. Princeton: Princeton UP, 1961.

Naremore, James. *The World Without a Self: Virginia Woolf and the Novel*. New Haven: Yale UP, 1973.

Nietzsche, Friedrich. *The Birth of Tragedy* (1871). Trans. Walter Kaufmann. New York: Vintage Books, 1967.

Peake, Charles. "Sweeney Erect' and the Emersonian Hero." *Critical Essays on T.S. Eliot: The Sweeney Motif*. Ed. Kinley E. Roby. Boston: G.K. Hall and Co., 1985, 49–56.

Restuccia, Frances L. "Molly in Furs: Deleuzean/Masochian Masochism in the Writing of James Joyce." *Novel: A Forum on Fiction* 18, (Winter 1985): 101–116.

Roby, Kinley. E. Ed. and Introduction. *Critical Essays on T. S. Eliot: The Sweeney Motif*. Boston: G.K. Hall & Co., 1985.

Ruck, C.A.P. "Documentation." *The Wasson Road to Eleusis: Unveiling the Secret of the Mysteries*. R. Gordon Wasson *et al*. New York: Harcourt Brace Jovanovich, Inc., 1978, 75–126.

Rude, Donald. W. "Mr. Eliot Looks Into Chapman's Homer: A Possible Source for 'Sweeney Erect'." *Classical and Modern Literature* 2 (Fall 1990): 55–58.

Ruse, Michael. *The Darwinian Revolution*. Chicago: The U of Chicago P, 1979.

Shechner, Mark. *Joyce in Nighttown: A Psychoanalytic Inquiry into Ulysses*. Berkeley: U of California P, 1974.

Slater, Philip. E. *The Glory of Hera*. Boston: Beacon Press, 1968.

Smith, Carol H. *T.S. Eliot's Dramatic Theory and Practice*. Princeton: Princeton UP, 1963.

— "Sweeney and the Jazz Age." *T.S. Eliot: The Sweeney Motif*. Ed. Kinley E. Roby. Boston: G.K. Hall and Co., 1984, 87–100.

Smith, Grover. *T.S. Eliot's Poetry and Plays: A Study in Sources and Meaning*. Second ed. Chicago: U of Chicago P, 1956.

Stewart, Jessie. *Jane Ellen Harrison, A Portrait from Letters*. London: The Merlin Press, 1959.

Tylor, Edward Burnett. *Primitive Culture*. 2 vols: Vol I, *The Origins of Culture*; Vol II, *Religion in Primitive Culture*. London, 1871. New York: Harper Torchbooks, 1958.

Verrall, A.W. *The 'Choephori' of Aeschylus*. London: Macmillan and Co., 1893.

Vickery, John B. *The Literary Impact of the Golden Bough*. Princeton: Princeton UP, 1973.

Walcott, William. "Notes by a Jungian Analyst on the Dreams in *Ulysses*." *James Joyce Quarterly*, 9: (1971): 37–47.

Walkley, R. Barrie. "The Bloom of Motherhood: Couvade as a Structural Device in *Ulysses*." *James Joyce Quarterly*, 18 (Fall 1980): 55–67.

Warner, John M. "Myth and History in Joyce's 'Nausicaa' Episode." *James Joyce Quarterly* 24 (Fall 1986): 20–34.

Whiteside, George. "A Freudian Dream Analysis of 'Sweeney Among the Nightingales.'" *T.S. Eliot: The Sweeney Motif*. Ed. Kinley E. Roby. Boston: G.K. Hall & Co. 1984, 63–7.

Witt, Karl. *Myths of Hellas; or, Greek Tales*. Trans. Francis Younghusband. London: Longmans, Green, 1883.

Woolf, Virginia. *A Room of One's Own*. New York: Harcourt Brace Jovanovich, Inc.1929.

— "Mr. Bennett and Mrs. Brown" (1924). *The Captain's Death Bed and Other Essays*. New York: Harcourt Brace, 1950, 94–119.

— *The Diary of Virginia Woolf*. Vols. II & III. Eds. Anne Olivier Bell and Andrew McNeillie. New York: Harcourt Brace Jovanovich 1978 & 1980.

— *The Letters of Virginia Woolf*. Vols. II & III. Eds. Nigel Nicolson and Joanne Trautmann. New York: Harcourt Brace Jovanovich 1976 and 1977.

— "The Narrow Bridge of Art." *Granite and Rainbow*. New York: Harcourt Brace & World, 1958.

—— *Moments of Being*. 2nd ed. Ed. Jeanne Schulkind. New York: Harcourt Brace Jovanovich, 1985.

—— *To the Lighthouse*. New York: Harcourt Brace Jovanovich, 1927.

Yeats, W. B. "The Trembling of the Veil." *Autobiographies*. New York: Macmillan, 1927, 133–431.

—— "Among Schoolchildren." "The Second Coming." *The Collected Poems of W.B. Yeats*. New York: Macmillan 1956, 212, 184.

INDEX